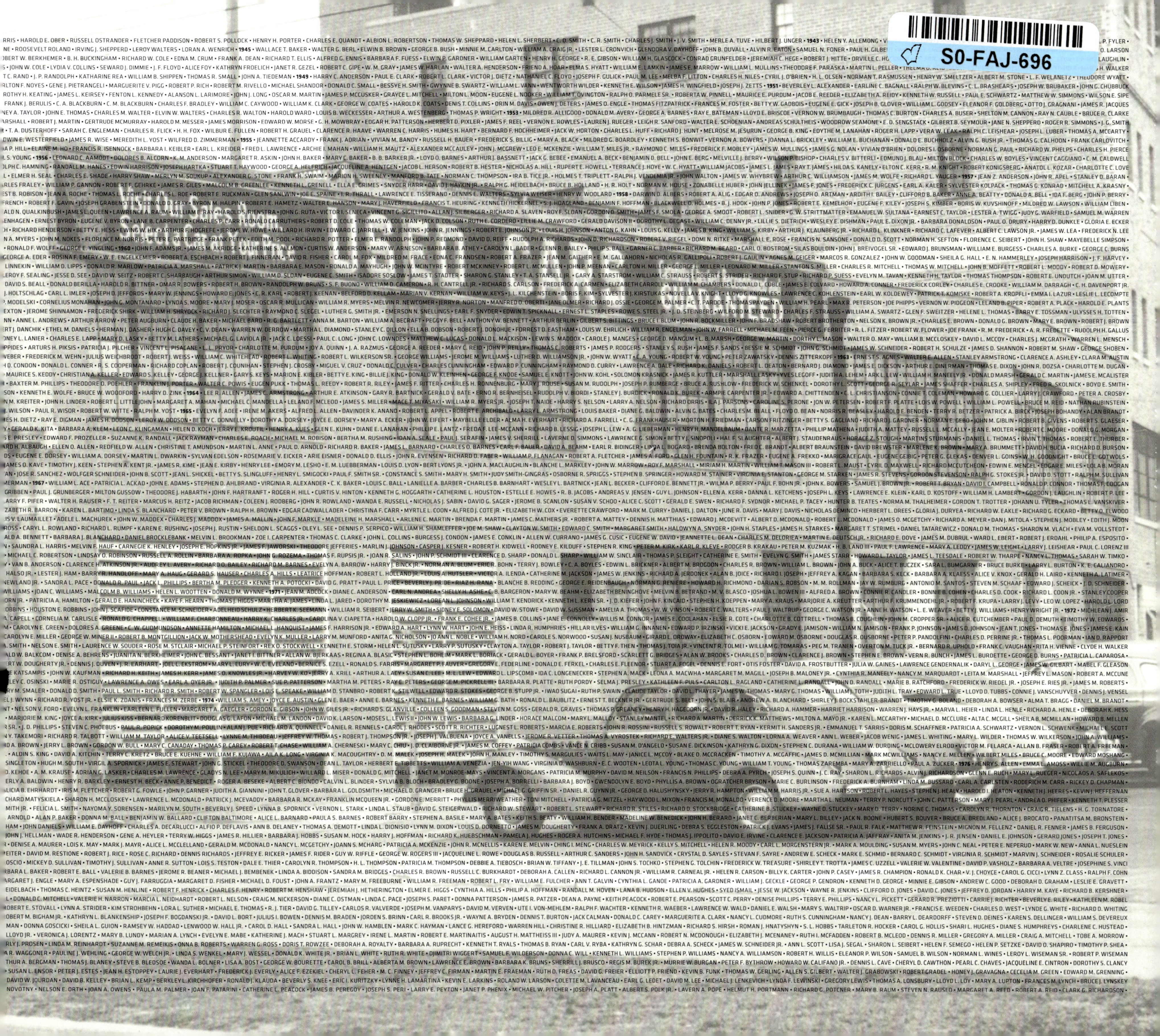

VINCENT E. RICHARDSON • JAN L. RIGHTSELL • CATHERINE C. ROBERTS • JOHN C. RODGERS • CHARLENE E. ROELECKE • JEFFREY C. ROHRBECK • KEITH W. ROPER • STEVEN R. ROSENSWEIG • THELMA A. SALUS • RICHARD A. SCHULMAN • WILLIAM A. SELLERS • MARK E. SIMPSON • PATRICE M. SLERT • NANCY L. SMITH • GLENDA J. SNAVELY • MARGARET D. SPITLER • JODY A. STEPP • RICHARD H. STERNAGLE • THOMAS E. STRIKWERDA • BARBARA L. SUESS • JANET M. SULLINS • SID TACKETT • CARYLON J. TALLMAN • JOANNE E. TART • LLOYD W. TAYLOR • EMMA E. TEWEY • TERRY L. TOMCSIK • C. M. TRENT • CHARLES A. TWIGG • DAVID C. TYSON • JAMES M. UNTERREINER • O. M. UY • ROLAND G. VRANKIN • PAULA WAGNER • MARY L. WARD • CARL A. WATERS • MARY D. WATKINSON • CAROL S. WATSON • STEPHEN G. WEISENBORNE • JOAN Y. WENTLING • MICHAEL E. WHITE • STUART J. WIGHTMAN • HELEN W. WILL • JEFFREY T. WILL • RICKY A. WILLIAMS • ELRIDGE L. WISE SR. • JOY D. WOOD • PAUL D. WORLEY • MICHAEL D. YELVERTON • WILLIE M. YUILLE • **1982** • STEVEN ACHHAMMER • DAVID K. ALLEN • DONALD W. AMANN • WILLIAM M. ANTOSEK • BETTE R. ARING • DALE J. AXENFELD • LAWRENCE R. BACHMAN • PAUL R. BADE • A. T. BAIR • MICHAEL S. BALDWIN • JAMES F. BANDY JR. • DOUGLAS H. BERRY • ROBERT S. BOKULIC • JOHN D. BOLDT • CARL R. BOLES SR. • KATHLEEN BOLLAND • ROGER C. BOWERS • DEBORAH L. BOWLEY • MARY J. BOWMAN • RICHARD D. BRANTLEY • SHEILA T. BROADUS • NED A. BROKLOFF • JEAN A. BRUCE • RITA J. BUCKINGHAM • RICHARD T. BURK • MARLENE E. BURKHARDT • BONNIE M. CAMPBELL • SHIRLEY A. CAMPBELL • KENNETH E. CARBERRY • ERNEST R. CARBONE • DAVID A. CARPENTER • JOSEPH R. CARPINTIERI • ALBERT A. CHACOS • JAMES L. CHEAK • DAVID K. CHEN • ARTHUR D. CHRAPKOWSKI • GUY V. CLATTERBAUGH • DEBRA E. COFFROAD • SARA S. COLLISON • GLENDA P. COMBS • ELIZABETH S. COMISH • NANCY L. COPPERTHITE • MARCIA J. CRAIG • SHARON L. CRAMER • WILLIAM T. CRAWFORD • FRED R. CRUMBAUGH • PAUL P. CURRY • DON E. DAVIS • AMY M. DEBROWER • RONALD A. DENISSEN • MICHAEL S. DENNIS • JAY R. DETTMER • ANNE E. DIETRICH • BRYAN E. DUCK • GENEVA M. EALY • SUSAN M. EARP • E. L. EBBERT • JOHN E. EICHSTEDT • PETER EISENREICH • CHARLES B. ELINE JR. • STEPHEN M. FALATKO • ELIZABETH A. FELLENZ • THOMAS O. FIELD • ANNA S. FONES • MERRITT E. FORD • KIM R. FOWLER • LAURENCE J. FRANK • DOROTHY L. FRANKLIN • DAVID I. FURST • RICHARD M. GIANNOLA • DIANE E. GILES • JAMES J. GILLIGAN • DAVID P. GLOCK • HOWARD S. GOLDBERG • JOHN O. GOLDSTEN • DAVID B. GORMAN • LEONARD P. GROVER • P. M. GUBA • JANA L. HANLIN • TERRY J. HARRIS • IVY M. HARRISON • KATHLEEN D. HARRISON • THERESA J. HASTINGS • JOHN R. HAYES • VIRGINIA N. HEISS • GREGG A. HERBERT • MARK J. HIRSCH • ERIC D. HOLM • JAMES E. HUBBS • JANE E. HUNEYCUTT JR. • JOHN W. HUNT JR. • CHRISTOPHER M. HURLEY • RUSSELL J. IANNUZZELLI • INGA E. INGLES • BRENDA E. JACKSON • BRENDA J. JACKSON • G. C. JARRELL • CHARLOTTEE JOHNSON • EDWARD H. KIDERA • THOMAS J. KISTENMACHER • DAVID C. KNILL • RUSSELL K. KOEHLER • KAREN KOHRI • WILLIAM J. KOHRI • KENNETH W. KOONTZ • SAUL A. KRAVITZ • WILLA M. KRIDER • PHYLLIS R. KROGER • D. R. KUHN • ROBERT L. KULP • BELINDA J. KUNDIN • KENNETH A. LABEL • STUART D. LANDERSMAN • EDWARD P. LEE • FLOSSIE M. LEWIS • KEVIN D. LINDSAY • RICHARD G. LORANGER • BRIAN H. LOUKS • JAMES W. LOWE • TIMOTHY M. LYNCH • KAZUO MAKITA • ANTHONY W. MATTESON SR. • BARRY H. MAUK • DONALD E. MAURER • JACK E. MCCLEAF • DONNA L. MCDONALD • STEVEN A. MCKENZIE • B. C. MCKINNEY • KAREN B. MCMAKIN • PAUL R. MCMULLIN • RACHEL E. MERCER • VINCENT C. MESSER • MICHAEL J. MEYER • GENE J. MILLER • ROBERT D. MILLER • BARBARA C. MITCHELL • JEAN M. MOODY • MARION D. MOORE • WANDA C. MURPHY • BARBARA J. MURR • H. D. NELSON • DAVID W. NESBITT • ARNOLD L. NEWMAN • RONALD G. NIEMANN • DEBORAH A. NORSWORTHY • DAVID J. O'CONNOR • THOMAS J. OLSON • MARK A. OURSLER • KENNETH W. PADGETT • PAUL E. PANNETON • TASOS G. PAPAPETROU • ARTHUR W. PATTEE • CRAIG R. PATTERSON • PATRICIA A. PERCICH • ROBERT E. PHELPS JR. • SUSAN A. PHIPPS • RANDALL C. POE • LEONARD W. POJUNAS JR. • PHYLLIS J. POTTER • ALAN G. PROSSER • JOHN F. REDISKE • DORIS J. REYNOLDS • MICHAEL H. ROBINSON III • JOHN C. ROBINSON • JUDITH A. ROCKEY • ELLIOT H. RODBERG • DANIEL E. RODRIGUEZ • ROBIN G. RUDE • ROBERT A. SALTZBERG • RONALD A. SAXON • LINDA M. SCHWEITZER • VALERIE A. SIMON • HOWARD A. SKAIST • SUZETTE SOMMERER • CHRISTINE A. STARSTROM • KEVIN C. STEIGER • RAYMOND E. STERNER II • DUANE F. STEVENS • GARY A. SULLINS • DANIEL P. SYED • BERT H. TANAKA • KENNETH E. TAPP SR. • MICHAEL A. TAYLOR • ROBERT J. TAYLOR • ERIC R. THEWS • MORGAN J. THOMA • G. E. THOMANN • TERENCE D. THOMAS • GLENDA J. THOMPSON • KACY E. THORNTON • KELLY A. THORNTON • DAVID S. TILLMAN • JEFFREY W. TRAVIS • JOSEPH J. TRAVISANO II • RICHARD A. TRIPLETT • JONATHAN A. TUCHOW • ANDREW N. VAVRECK • RAYMOND F. VERNON • FRANCIS H. WALKER • JUDITH H. WALL • STEPHEN G. WALTERS • JOEL A. WEINER • GEORGE E. WENDAL JR. • PETER C. WHITMAN • CHRISTOPHER E. WILLIAMS • KENNETH E. WILLIAMS • ROBERT L. WILLIAMS • SUSAN M. WILLIAMS • RICK R. YORK • CHARLES B. YUNGKURTH • **1983** • DAVID W. AFFENS • WILLIAM M. ALBRECHT • SPYRIDON M. ALIFRANGIS • L. D. ANDERSON • ANNE ANIKIS • BESS C. ARCHIBALD • STEVEN M. BABIN • KENNETH D. BARBER • LORI A. BARNARD • CAROLYN B. BEINSTEIN • DOROTHY M. BELLOMO • S. G. BHAT • PAUL E. BIEGEL • JEFFREY J. BLANCHETTE • MARY A. BOEHM • MICHAEL E. BOHSE • FLORENCE K. BOLLS • MICHAEL L. BRIERS • JAMES A. BRUZEK • CARL W. BRYSON • ROBERT M. BUCHA • CHARLES A. BUDMAN • ELIZABETH A. BUNDA-LEE • ROBERT M. BURCH • LAWRENCE M. BURNS • LAUREN K. BUSCH • KEITH E. BUSH • LYNNE D. BYRD • ANDREA M. CAMPBELL-WISE • PATRICIA L. CARBONE • PATRICIA A. CAREY • BLISS G. CARKHUFF • HOLLY L. CARTER • BONNIE P. CASHELL • ANDREW F. CHENG • CAROL A. CHILLEMI • ANDREAS K. CHRYSOSTOMOU • LAWRENCE E. CLIFFORD • JAMES M. CLOEREN • BARRET N. COLE • DORIS M. COLEMAN • MARY J. COLSON • JOHN F. COMMANDER • JACQUELINE A. CONCIA • KENNETH G. COYLE • ROBERT M. CRAMBLITT • PAUL J. CRICKARD JR. • MICHAEL Z. CROFT • JAMES P. DARLING • ELAINE C. DAVID • ROBERT E. DAYHOFF • STEVEN E. DEGGENDORF • JOAN B. DEMPSAY • STEVEN D. DIAMOND • G. D. DOCKERY • DONALD D. DUNCAN • JOHN A. ECKER • FLORENDO S. ENCARNADO • GREGORY A. FABELLA • JEANINE M. FALISE • IAN E. FELDBERG • JEFFREY G. FISKE • DAVID K. FLINT • ELINOR FONG • ORMOND L. FORTIER • CATHERINE R. FOSTER • VICTORIA J. FRANKE • CONNIE F. FRAZIER • DAVID E. FREUND • DAVID G. FREYMANN • DOROTHY G. FUCHSMAN • SHIRLEY A. FULLER • BARBARA J. FURST • DORIS T. GARMIZE • SCOTT A. GEARHART • JOY A. GILBERT • STUART A. GOEMMER • ROOT B. GORELICK • MARIAN E. GREENSPAN • RICHARD J. GREGSON • O. H. GRIFFIN JR. • THEODORE C. GUO • WENDY W. GUO • BRUCE N. HAASE • ROBYN L. HALESKI • ROBERT T. HALL • DAVID A. HAMILTON • MARK A. HAMILTON • JOE P. HARRISON • STEPHEN J. HARTMAN • EDWARD A. HASER • GAIL J. HAULTON • MARTIN J. HERMES • BONNY M. HILDITCH • STACY D. HILL • ERNEST M. HINTON • ROBERT G. HOLLAND • ROSALIND L. HOM • JAMES J. HOMER • ETHEL D. HOUSTON • ALBERT J. HOWARD • JONATHAN C. HOWLAND • BARBARA P. HUDGINS • RICHARD L. HUDSON • SHELBY J. HUMBERSON • JEFFREY A. HUMPHREYS • BEVERLY A. HUSMAN • CHARLES A. ILARI • DAVID L. JAMES • EDITH W. JOHNSON • MARK C. KELLER • PAUL A. KELLY • LAWRENCE R. KENNEDY • ANNA M. KIMMELL • DANIEL T. KING • MARGIE S. KLINE • WILLIAM P. KNOPF • MATTHEW I. KOCH • PAUL KORTESOJA • ELINOR F. KRONMILLER • JOHN J. KUJAWA • SUE A. KUNCL • DAVID Y. KUSNIERKIEWICZ • REID A. LACLAIR • RONALD R. LAMBERT • ELLEN M. LEE • CARLTON D. LEIZEAR • THERESA D. LENNON • JEFFREY S. LIN • M. D. LINE • LLOYD A. LINSTROM • JOHN R. LONGO • ROSS LOUNSBURY • DALE T. LUKAS • JAN M. LUSE • JAMES K. LUTZ • JAMES D. MACDONALD • PATRICIA A. MACDONALD • MARY H. MAGEZ • LINDA L. MAIER-TYLER • MEREDITH M. MANCINI • DAVID L. MARABLE • FRANK J. MARCOTTE • BARRY A. MARCUS • JOHN A. MARINO • JANET K. MARKHAM • KATHLEEN E. MARSDEN • J. A. MARTIN • MELVIN A. MARTIN • WILLIAM R. MARTIN • LAURIE A. MATHIAS • KAREN L. MCADAMS • MARIE L. MCCARTHY • LAWRENCE F. MCGOLDRICK • CRAIG W. MCHENRY • DOUGLAS D. MCLENNAN • THOMAS M. MCNAMARA JR. • TIMOTHY M. MCVAUGH • DOUGLAS S. MEHOKE • WILLIAM A. MENNER • JOSEPH E. MERSON • PEGGY L. MERSON • JOHN R. MEYER • OREN B. MILGROME • JAY T. MILLER • KAREN M. MILLER • SHARYN E. MITCHELL • JAMES D. MOONEY • CHARMAINE P. MRAZEK • PATSY F. MURK • ALYCE T. MYERS • CRAIG L. MYERS • JAMES M. NAPIER • MICHAEL NEMESURE • MARVIN L. NICHOLS • GREGORY A. NISWONGER • KEITH A. NORWOOD • GREGORY L. OGLESBY • ROY A. PANTING • MARK T. PAONESSA • SHARON E. PARK • JULIE W. PATTISON • S. J. PATTON • JOHN C. PEDEN • DAVID F. PERSONS • DUANE M. PICKETT • ANGELA D. PORRINO • ANNA M. PORTER • ALLAN S. POSNER • RICHARD POWERS • JOHN M. PRIESTLEY JR. • GEORGE J. QUART • T. Y. RAMBEAU • DEANNA R. RAVENSCRAFT • JAMES M. REESE • KURT A. RICE • JOHN D. RICHARDS • HILDA N. RIVERA • JORGE J. RIVERA • NANCY H. RIVERS • EVERETT E. ROBERTS III • MARGARET M. ROBINSON • NEIL S. ROTHMAN • JAY F. ROULETTE • STEPHEN C. RUSSIAL • DAVID M. RUST • MICHAEL J. RUTH • ROSALIE B. RYAN • CHRISTINE O. SALAMACHA • ANDREW G. SANTO • STEVEN R. SCHACHTNER • ROBERT C. SCHAEFFLER • ARCHIE SCHEUFELE • ANDREW L. SCHLAFLY • MARIANNE F. SCHMIDT • JANE R. SCOTT • STEVEN L. SHADEL • FRANCIS D. SHAUGHNEY • LINDA J. SHIELDS • GARY D. SHIFLETT • PAMELA D. SMALLS • G. L. SMELTZER • CECELIA A. SMITH • MARTIN L. SOLOMON • JAMES C. SPALL • SHARON L. SQUIRES • MICHAEL B. STANTON • JANE F. STERSHIC • CHRISTOPHER J. STIER • MARY L. STULL • SYLVIA STUMPFF • ROGER A. SUMEY • BARBARA SUMMONS • JOSEPH J. SUTER • CAROL L. SWINNEY • LINDA W. TAYLOR • JACQUELINE K. TELFORD • PHILIP H. TEMKIN • DIANE L. THELEN • ANN J. THOMPSON • D. J. THOMPSON • LINDA S. THOMPSON • BRADLEY A. THOMSON • JOHN P. TOWNSEND JR. • TYSON A. TRECANNELLI • CAROL J. TRIMPER • JOSEPH J. TRIOLO • DANIEL W. TURNER • WILLIAM E. TYLER • VAN D. UNDERWOOD • PETER VANDYKE • DAVID M. VANWIE • CHARLES E. VEST • KATHRYN K. VOGEL • WILLIAM R. WALDECK • RO-BURMA W. WARE • LOIS F. WAULDRON • WILLIAM G. WENDELL • PAMELA J. WENTZ • JOHN R. WHILE • RONALD L. WHITE SR. • PEARL I. WISEMAN • THOMAS E. WISNIEWSKI • LUCILLE L. WITHERSPOON • LOUIS J. WOLODZKO • SUSAN M. YINGLING • PATRICE H. ZURVALEC • **1984** • MICHAEL L. ABRAMS • WILLIAM L. ALLEN JR. • DALE J. ALLEN • JOHN M. ANDERSON • LINDA G. BARRY-BOND • DAVID A. BATCHELOR • JAMES R. BELLEFEUIL • RICHARD S. BELLIVEAU • DAVID A. BEMENT • MARK T. BOIES • KENNETH D. BROCKMAN • WARREN D. BROWN • GRACE M. BRUSH • JOAN B. BULHAROWSKI • LINDA M. BURKE • LINDA S. BUTLER • PAUL BUTLER • PAMELA A. CALDER • AMY H. CHANG • MARC A. CLAYTON • BRENDA A. CLYDE • JOHN C. COMPHER • MICHELE H. CONNER • WILLIAM H. COON • WESLEY B. COVELL • TERRENCE E. CRANE • SHARON L. CROOKS • EDWARD G. CUSHMAN • ANDRES E. DAN • LEONARD S. D'COSTA • LEONARD J. DEAN • JOSEPH L. DEVEAUX • MICHAEL H. DIAMANT • NAOMI G. DIBACCO • MAUREEN A. DRAGONE • ROBERT E. ELWELL JR. • LINWOOD E. ENOS III • JOSEPH P. FONTE • BOBBY R. FULCHER • STEPHEN V. GELHAUS • JEFFREY M. GILBERT • RUSSELL A. GIORDANO • KAREN M. GOSNELL • DONNETTA L. GRADY • ELEANOR O. GRAHAM • PERRY E. GREENFIELD • DONNA M. GREGG • TOM D. GROSS • MICHAEL L. HAGLER • JOHN P. HALPIN • MARTIN J. HAMBURG • HOLLY H. HAMILTON • CAROLYN H. HARRINGTON • DAVID A. HARVEY • LOIS D. HENDERSON • RICHARD J. HILDEBRAND • MADELEINE E. HUNTER • PRISCILLA D. HUTCHINSON • WILLIAM A. HUTING • EDGAR G. JACQUES • RUSSELL D. JAMISON • KIRSCH M. JONES • FLOYD JOYNER II • MICHAEL T. KANE • STEVEN R. KERNS • DONALD P. KLINE • FRANK J. KUTCHKO • PATRICIA A. KUYKENDALL • BERNARD J. MACK JR. • THOMAS C. MAGEE • MARIAN H. MAURER • LISA F. MAY • JOYCE N. MAYHUGH • PATRICK J. MCGUINNESS • MAY E. MCMILLAN • PAUL N. MCWHORTER III • WENDY A. MILLER • SANNU MOLDER • ANTOINE S. MONROE • DWAYNE M. MYERS • JUANITA M. NAUDE • LINDA M. NAVEDO • CLAIRE L. NEGAS • JOYCE A. NEHMSMANN • LARRY W. NEMSICK • PAUL D. NORTH • NANCY A. NOVAK • KENNETH W. O'HAVER • EVERETT H. OLIVER II • DANIEL A. OSSING • COLEEN M. PERRY • DONALD R. PETTY SR. • JOHN E. PRITCHETT • JOHN R. REEDER • JOSEPH A. SACCO • THOMAS R. SANDERSON • DARLENE E. SCHNEEBERGER • KENNETH M. SCHNEIDER • JAMES R. SCHUH • STEVEN J. SEVERSON • WILLIAM E. SHAW • EMILY J. SHRIVER • MARTIN J. SINICKI • PATRICK E. SKARP • KATHLEEN S. SKULLNEY • SHARON R. SMITH • MARY P. SOUDER • EDGAR W. SPILMAN • ALBERT A. TOMKO • RICHARD D. TSCHIEGG • MARSHALL E. TYLER • MICHAEL E. VARNEY • STEVEN R. VERNON • CHRISTOPHER J. VOGT • JANICE A. WALKER • JEFFERY W. WARREN • MARY A. WASHINGTON • KATHERINE W. WEEDEN • JACQUELINE N. WEITZEL • JEFFREY J. WELLEN • ROSE G. WILSON • DUANE T. WINTERS • MAUREEN M. WYNNE • SIMONE M. YOUNGBLOOD • PAUL ZAKEL J • NANCY L. ZEPP • CANDY R. ZULICK • **1985** • JOHN L. ABEDOR • JOAN ABRAMS • MARY I. ABRAMS • SUE A. ARMBRUSTER • RAYMOND P. AYLOR III • LINDA K. AYRES • MARK A. BAKER • MARK E. BALDWIN • BRUCE L. BALLARD • JONATHAN C. BARNETT • EDWARD A. BEASLEY • MICHAEL K. BEASLEY • PAUL J. BEDNARZ-KIRSCH • JOHN R. BENEDICT JR. • DOUGLAS G. BENNETT • JOHN R. BERLING JR. • NORMAND A. BERNACHE • STEVEN M. BIEMER • ROBERT S. BLACKMORE • ANNIE S. BLACKWELL • WILLIE D. BLALOCK • JANICE M. BOGASH • RAYNARD T. BOLLING • NANCY M. BOONE • JAMES D. BOWMAN • LORETTA J. BOYCE • SANDRA B. BOYS • SUSAN L. BREACH • JAMES L. BROOKS • KEVIN E. BROWN • SHERRY M. BROWN • CARL L. BRUNDIDGE • MELISSA F. BUCKINGHAM • ALBERT A. BURK JR. • EDWARD J. BURNHAM • JAMES G. BYRD • JIMMY F. CARPENTER • GEORGE J. CARTER • JOSEPH V. CESAITIS • CHRIS C. CHAN • ROBERT L. CHESTER • DANIEL C. CHIN • ELEANOR B. CHLAN • EVELYN R. CLOUGH • JAMES E. COCCHIARO • JOHN R. COLEMAN • JAMES R. CONNELLY • KIM T. CONSTANTIKES • RANDALL W. COOK • KELLEY A. CROVO • KATHLEEN L. CUDMORE • ROBERT L. CULPEPPER • STEPHEN A. CUNDIFF • KEVIN R. CURTISS • DEBORAH L. DAVIDSON • ROGER L. DAVIS • FRANKLIN DELLON • AGNES H. DEWOLFE • DEBORAH K. DILBON • BRYAN S. DOERR • DAVID V. DORE • ROSABELLE R. DRAPKIN • MARY A. DUBBEL • RODNEY G. DULEY JR. • MICHAEL D. DYKTON • HARRY A. EATON • RUSSELL C. EBERHART • LINDA O. EVANS • JAMES T. EVERETT • MICHAEL R. FAITH • MICHAEL A. FALLAVOLLITA • DONALD B. FALTYNSKI • HOWARD S. FELDMESSER • KEITH W. FITCH • JOHN FLORENCE • DARRYL L. FOSTER • KAREN S. FOURNIER • EDNA J. FOWLER • LISA B. FRANCISCO • MURRAY A. FRIEDMAN • ELWOOD A. FRINK • JOSEPH P. GAGLIANO • FELIPE N. GAJATE • KEVIN T. GARDNER • KEVIN J. GARTZ • ALICE A. GENEGA • SHEILA GOLDMAN • TERI L. GOLDSTEIN • WILLIAM P. GRAHAM • ROBERT B. GRAY • WILLIAM J. GREEN • STEPHEN GREIF • TODD W. GRIMES • RAY W. GROSE • SHIRAS E. GUION • GERALD J. GUREVICH • WILLIAM S. GUTMAN • STEVEN A. HAASER • JEFFREY L. HANSON • LORENZ J. HAPPEL JR. • FELECIA A. HARTLEY • ROSS R. HATCH • JAMES B. HEMLER SR. • JAMES T. HEMMINGS • HENRY F. HENLINE • ROBERT R. HENLINE • HARRY E. HICKEY • ALAN S. HODES • THOMAS W. HORMBY • LYNNE HUDSON • DAVID G. HUMES • JAMES D. HUNTER • PAMELA E. HUNTER • JACQUELINE V. IRVIN • JON M. IRWIN • JULIANNE K. IWASKIW • ETTARE M. JACKSON • DAVID S. JACOBS • CARROLL E. JAMES • LYNDA T. JANET • RUSSELL N. JENKINS SR. • EDITH P. JONES • TOMMY J. JONES • MARSHALL J. JOSE • TODD M. KAPITULA • LINDA E. KARNER • ELEANOR C. KENNEDY • SUSAN B. KENNEDY • JOYCE L. KERR • STEVEN Y. KIM • GREGORY A. KIRK • ELIZABETH A. KISSER • WILLIAM R. KOHLER • GERALD C. KONSTANZER • DAVID M. KRALL • PIERRE LAFRANCE • JAMES R. LAMPING • KRISTA A. LANE • WILLIAM A. LAPLANTE JR. • KATHERINE A. LEE • KATHLEEN LEONARD • JONATHAN W. LEPP • AMBER L. LEVINE • DOUGLAS D. LEWIS • CHRISTOPHER C. LIN • SUSAN R. LIVINGSTONE • JEFFREY T. LOVE • RAY J. LUNNEN JR. • STEVEN A. LUTZ • RICHARD E. MALTAGLIATI • CHARLES G. MARKON • ROGER G. MARSHALL • ELIZABETH A. MARTIN • RANDALL J. MAYROVITZ • PETER A. MCCOY • DAVID R. MCDANIEL • CRAIG E. MCDONALD • HOPE R. MCELWAIN • THOMAS R. MCKNIGHT JR. • JAMES M. MCLEAN • MICHAEL P. MCLOUGHLIN • GLENN L. MEYERS • TIMOTHY M. MILLS • MATTHEW MONTOYA • JOHN S. MORGAN • DAVID E. MOSHER • SUSAN V. MUIR • DAVID E. MUSSMANN • JOE V. MYERS • PATRICIA D. NACCI • TRISTAN NEFZGER • PATRICK T. NEWELL • ALICE L. NOTICH • JAMES E. OGILVIE • ELIZABETH A. PAPER • WILFREDO V. PEREZ • ELLWOOD L. PINES • JOHN A. PIORKOWSKI • THOMAS J. POTYRAJ • DANIEL T. PRENDERGAST • ROBIN F. PUCKETT • MARY J. QUINTER • JEFFREY J. RAHENKAMP • DORSEY L. REASER • JOSIAH REED JR. • CHERYL L. REED • OLIVIA M. REINECKE • CONRAD J. REISINGER SR. • EDWARD L. REYNOLDS • CONRAD J. RORIE • BRUCE A. RUSHLOW JR. • SCOTT SALVESEN • DAVID A. SANDACZ • CASSIE L. SCHNEEBERGER • STEVEN H. SHAPERO • BERNARD J. SHAUGHNEY • WOODROW R. SHIELDS • LOUIS W. SHROYER • DAVID G. SIBECK • JEFFREY H. SINSKY • KATHARINE E. SIZEMORE • KEVIN M. SMITH • LORI A. SMITH • MARY M. SMITH • WILLIAM F. SMITH • SCOTT D. SPARROW • RICHARD A. STEINBERG • SHARON M. STERNBERGER • TRACIE R. STEVENS • BASIL J. STOYANOV • KATHLEEN S. STROMBERG • MARY W. STUART • TRISTAN J. TAYAG • LINDA S. TEAL • MARGARET A. TEETERS • ROGER M. THOMAS JR. • HOWARD M. TILLISON • JOHN M. TREVATHAN • ROOSEVELT C. TUCKER • GREGORY B. TURETZKY • ARTHUR E. TURRIFF • KYLE M. UPTON • PERRY L. VESSELS • CARLA A. VIANOS • DAVID D. WAGNER • STEPHEN D. WAJER • MARY B. WALCEK • BRENDA L. WALTERMEYER • KEITH E. WIEBKING JR. • CHARLENE V. WILLIAMS • GARY R. WILLIAMS • JAMES E. WILLIAMS • KAREN L. WILLIAMS • BARBARA J. WILLIAMSON • JEFFREY WONG • CYNTHIA R. WOOFTER • ROBERT A. WRIGHT • DENISE E. YAREMA • RAYMOND L. YUAN • KEVIN P. ZEMEJDA • PAUL J. ZOHORSKY III • DAVID J. ZOTIAN • **1986** • TERRI A. ALBERT • BURTON J. ALEXANDER • SYED W. ALI • WILLIAM H. ALLEN • AGNES E. ANDERSON • ANDREAS G. ANDREOU • AL C. ANSORGE • LOIS A. ARCHIBALD • ROBIN M. ARMSTRONG • GEORGE ATWATER JR. • MARY L. AULT • MARY R. AXENFELD • BARBARA L. BANKERT • ROSE C. BANTA • THOMAS L. BARBAGALLO • LORETTA A. BARTZ • KIRK L. BATEMAN • DANIEL E. BEEDER • CRAIG E. BENNETT • ROBIN J. BETHANY • JOSEPH C. BETTINGER • PAUL J. BIERMANN • GORDAN A. BOLTZ • WARREN J. BOORD • SUE E. BORCHARDT • PAUL K. BOSSERMAN SR. • JESSE L. BRATCHET • ROBERT L. BROWN SR. • DARRIN R. BROWN • RICHARD K. BUTCHER • ELIZABETH J. BUTER • ANGELA M. BUTLER • ESTHER C. CARROLL • ROXANEH CHAMLOU • KEDONG CHAO • JASON J. CHOI • STEPHEN P. CHRISTON • LINDA A. CIMBALJEVICH • DARRYL F. CLAGGETT SR. • JILL J. CLEVENGER • DAVID E. CODDINGTON • MARY L. COE • ERIC S. CONN • KELLY COON • TERRANCE J. CORBETT • FRANCIS D. COURTNEY II • STEPHEN S. CRASS • JOHN A. CRISTION • NORAM D. CROUCH • FRANCIS W. CULLISON • PROTAGORAS N. CUTCHIS • GERALD H. DAUGHERTY • DOUGLAS J. DAWSON • KIRK S. DECKER • CLAGGETT W. DELAUDER • DOROTHY E. DELBRUGGE • MICHAEL T. DENNEHY • KEITH J. DEVOS • JONATHAN D. DOUGLAS • CARA D. DRENNEN • RUDOLPH A. DROBNICK JR. • PAMELA J. DUDECK • JAMES F. DUFFY • MARCENE E. EDELMAN • BERNARD L. EDWARDS • RICHARD L. EDWARDS • JACOB ELBAZ • TIMOTHY J. ENDRES • THOMAS S. ENGLAR JR. • ROBERT E. ERLANDSON • DAVID K. ERMER • DAVID M. FADELEY • ROBERT C. FERGUSON • JOAN P. FISCUS • H. L. FISHER • PATRICIA W. FISHER • TYRONE D. FLORYANZIA • ARLEEN V. FORBES • BARBARA M. FOURNEY • GORDON M. FRANK • LAVERNE R. FRANKLIN • LINDA J. FRIZZELL-MAKOWSKI • PETER C. GALLATI • STEVEN A. GARAND • DEAN S. GARLICK • DAVID G. GAWRON • GREGORY J. GILLETTE • FILENE L. GIORDANO • DELMA M. GORDON • CAROLYN R. GREGORY • ROBERT S. GRESEHOVER • RONALD M. GRIESMAR • JOANNE E. GRIESSER • DALE GRIFFITH • MARK C. GRUBELICH • VIRGINIA L. HAFELE • GREGORY S. HALL • MARY G. HAMILL • KAREN S. HARDEN • SHIRLEY L. HARDY • PAUL D. HARTMAN • THERESA M. HAWKINS • JANE HEAP • DONNA M. HELLMAN • ROBIN J. HERBISON • TRACY C. HERRIOTTS • HOWARD S. HEUBERGER • MICHELE M. HINES • JOANNE HIRSH • DIANA L. HOBLET • JOAN M. HOWARD • HENRY S. HU • PAULA R. ICHNIOWSKI • MICHIHISHIMOTO • ALLAN R. JABLON • ARTHUR T. JACKSON JR. • CHARLES E. JACKSON SR. • JULIUS J. JASKOT • ANN L. JENKINS • MICHAEL J. JENKINS • PAULINE Q. JENSEN • ARTHUR F. JEYES • KERRY JOHNSON • JERALD J. JOHNSTON • CHARLES L. JONES • RICHARD S. JONES • JEFF W. JURVIS • NATALIE R. JURVIS • MERLE W. KEEL • HUGH R. KERN • GREGORY J. KLEIN • DOUGLAS A. KLOTTER • WILLIAM A. KONOPACKI • ROBERT J. KRAFT • BRENDA R. KRAMER • TERRY L. KUES • SZE-PING KUO • BUDDY H. LANE • CHRISTIAN K. LATIMER • DOROTHY A. LEE • ROBERT E. LEE • DAVID S. LEHNUS • JEFFERY C. LESHO • HERBERT L. LESSER • KENNETH S. LEW • DAVID M. LIEBSHAL • JON S. LINDBERG • PETER R. LIVOLSI • JAMES F. LOESCH • FRANCIS J. LOGAN • PAUL C. MARCOTTE • LISA L. MASON • PETER G. MASON • SONDRA L. MCKEON • GARY V. MCPHERSON • RANDALL W. MCQUEEN • STEPHEN J. MEYER • THOMAS D. MILNES • BARRY L. MITCHELL • STEVEN J. MOCHTAK • WALTER J. MORAWSKI JR. • KENNETH R. MOSCATI • THOMAS M. MURDOCK • PATRICIA K. MURPHY • KEITH L. MUSSER • JEFFREY G. NANIS • GUY T. NASH • FRED C. NEWMAN • PATRICIA T. NORLANDER • NEIL H. OH • LAUREN L. PAGE • JAE Y. PARK • KEVIN E. PARKER • THEODIUS PARKER • PATRICIA J. PARTRIDGE • THOMAS J. PERRAULT SR. • JAMES J. PETER • TRI L. PHAM • JOSEPH R. PICK • FERNANDO J. PINEDA • BONNIE F. PORFILIO • GLORIA H. POWELL • WILLIAM J. POWELL • WILLIAM R. PROBECK • CARLEEN M. PULLEN • LINDA M. RAINES • APRA C. RAJPAL • AMY S. RATCLIFFE • JANICE RENNELS • CRAIG W. RICE • JANET L. RICHARDS • JAVIER RIVERA • EVELYN M. ROANE • DOLORES L. ROBERTS • RITA MARIE M. ROBERTS • JOHN R. ROTTIER • J. M. RUDHONIEMI • JEANNE M. SANDRUCK-FAHEY • ANTHONY J. SCARPATI • DAWN B. SCHEPLENG • RANDALL L. SCHRICKEL • LAGERALD SEDGWICK • RALPH D. SEMMEL • JOSEPHINE R. SHINHOLT • DAVID J. SIDES • PAK MAN H. SIU • MARK A. SMALLEY • CAROL F. SMALLWOOD • CONSTANCE M. SMITH • JOAN M. SMITH • PAUL R. SNOW • RAYMOND M. SOVA • BRENDA M. SPAUR • CHARLES W. SPEAR • JANE M. SPICER • ANITA L. SPRICK • JOHN C. STAPLETON • CAROLE E. STEED • MELISSA A. STEVENS • MARVIN B. SUTHER • MARK A. SWANA • LISA A. SZYPERSKI • KAZUE TAKAHASHI • MICHAEL W. THOMPSON • MICHAEL T. TILGHMAN • ROBERT L. TOMKIEWICZ SR. • KHA Q. TRAN • JOYCE A. TUCKER • DANIEL URBINA • CRAIG P. VANDERVEST • MICHELLE VARGO • TAMMY J. WAIGHT • GWENDOLYN A. WALLER • LINDA J. WELCH • JOHN J. WENGRYNIUK • ROBERT S. WERNEK • TINA M. WERTMAN • LORRAINE W. WESTROPE • HANS P. WIDMER • CLIFF E. WILLEY • BRIAN A. WILLIAMSON • TRACY D. WILSON • PATRICIA D. WINTERS • ROSLYN D. WISE • WAYNE L. WISE • LISA C. WITTE JR. • MARY S. WONG • DANIEL E. WOOMER • HELEN E. WORTH • CARL J. YODER JR. • LARRY T. YOUNKINS • BEN P. YUHAS • JOEL F. ZUHARS • **1987** • WANDA L. ADAMS • FARIDA K. AL-HOVERHOLT • E. B. ALVAREZ • MARK S. ASHER • JAMES N. BANKS • JOHN J. BARBAGALLO • TIMOTHY J. BASS • AMY E. BEAHM • JOSEPH S. BECK • KAREN M. BELTON • A. V. L. BIGGIE • KWABENA A. BOAHEN • DONALD W. BOWMAN • MAXINE R. BOWSER • AUDREY H. BROWNLEE • RODGER D. BUCY • KEITH J. BULKIN • MARK D. BULLA • JAMES R. BURNS • NICHOLAS F. BUSCH • MICHAEL H. BUTLER • DENISE F. CABRAL • WESLEY M. CARDONE • DAVID W. CARMAN • MARK L. CHORZEMPA • JANICE M. CLARK • CHRISTINA L. CLINGERMAN • ROBERT V. COFFMAN • STEPHEN G. COLE • JOHN B. COLES • MARGUERITE S. COLGLAZIER • ROSS E. CONKLIN JR. • ALLISON L. CONNERS • YEEVONNE Y. CONNOLLY • KATHLEEN A. COOPER • STEPHAN A. COOPER • GRIFFIN P. CORPENING • JOAN H. CRANMER • SARAH A. CROSMAN • NANCY T. CROWLEY • EDWARD H. DARLINGTON • MICHAEL D. DAVENPORT • D. D. DEARBORN JR. • SHAWN J. DENNIHAN • JEAN-LUC M. DEVIS • ROBERT B. DICKEY JR. • LINDA J. DORSEY • THOMAS E. DOUGHERTY • FRANCES L. DOVE • TERESA M. DUSTIN • WILLIAM R. ECHOLS • REBECCA J. ECKARD • MARK A. ELROD • GERMAINE D. ENDRES • JOAN R. ENGELKEMIER • RAUL FAINCHTEIN • CATHERINE A. FARTHING • SHARON M. FIRLEIN • CRAIG A. FITZPATRICK • KEVIN J. FLEAGLE • DORIS H. FOY • ARTHUR S. FRANCOMACARO • ALFRED FREY • DIANE M. FRIEDEL • ROSALYN R. FURUKAWA • UJJAL K. GHOSHTAGORE • FREDERICK P. GICK III • JEFFREY L. GIRSCH • CHRISTINA M. GLOVER • MARK S. GOETZ • KAREN T. GOLDEE • C. K. GOLDSTEIN • RONNIE M. GOOD • JANICE M. GOUDREAU • LORNA M. GRIFFIN • PAMELA J. HAGLER • ROBIN E. HALEY • GLORIA K. HALL • SHARON L. HASTY • S. EDWARD HAWKINS III • FRANCIS P. HORAN • JAMES D. HUFFAKER • WANDA J. HUTSON • ARCADY P. IWASKIW • LEONARD J. JAKUBOWSKI • JAMES F. JOHNSON JR. • GARY O. KAIN • BEVERLY A. KEANE • EMORY B. KELLY • JO ANNE W. KIERZKOWSKI • JAMES D. KINNISON • SHARON W. KIRKHAM • THOMAS L. KISTLER • ERIC W. KOEHLER • ANNE KOUTSOUTIS • MARY E. KRUEGER • HWAR C. KU • THOMAS L. KUSTERER • MARCELLE E. LADD • KATHLEEN A. LANE • ERIC C. LARSEN • GEORGE K. LEE • JASON E. LEE • HELEN A. LENGEL • SUNG H. LIM • JONATHAN R. LITTLE • KENNETH E. LONG • MARK O. LOPRESTO • MICHELE LOWE • DOROTHY H. MALLERICH • JOHN P. MARPLE • WARREN V. MCCOY • MICHAEL G. MCCULLOUGH • MARK R. MEYER • NATHAN C. MOORE III • CRAIG R. MOORE • KENNETH A. MORNEAULT • JOAN E. MUDGETT • ANNE L. MULVANY • ROBERT W. MURK • MICHAEL A. MUSGROVE • J. B. OAKES • THOMAS E. O'BANNON • DEENA M. PARKER • MARY J. PERINI • MARY E. POE • DARLENE M. POLETO • DAVID L. PORTER • GREGORY J. PORTMANN • BARBARA A. PRUITT • MARY I. PUHL • SALLY A. PUTT • PHILIP H. QUARRIER • ANNA D. RICHARDSON • KIMBERLY A. RODGERS • LEE F. ROGERS • DAVID A. ROSENSTOCK • LAWRENCE G. ROUTHENSTEIN • ALBERTO A. RUSSO • RICHARD J. SAUNDERS JR. • ROBERT P. SAUNDERS • ANDREA L. SAVAGE • DAVID J. SCHEERER • CHARLES E. SCHLEMM II • DAVID SCHLENKER • JOHN E. SCHMIDT • RICHARD J. SCHWINN • AGNES SEDITA • CHRISTINE L. SEIDEL • SURBHI P. SHAH • JAMES D. SHAMBACH • LINDA M. SHELDON • GREGORY R. SHERWIN • JAY SHIM • OODAYE B. SHUKLA • MALCOLM D. SHUSTER • CHRISTINE L. SMITH • WEBSTER F. SMITH • JOHN E. SOBOLESKI • GERALD E. SOMMER • RICHARD F. SPIEGEL • DAVID A. STAUB • KAREN A. STETYICK • ELIZABETH M. STEVENS • LAWRENCE M. STOUT • ELAINE V. STOVER • LESTER R. STRICKLAND • SHARON W. SUMMERS • MONICA A. SWANK • WINFIELD W. TALLEY • DAVID H. TERRY • JO ANN THOMAS • DEMETRIA E. TOLSON • SUSAN A. TURFLE • MARY K. UCHACZ • CLARK A. UPDIKE • DAVID E. VITALOS • DOROTHY C. VOLLMERHAUSEN • ROBIN L. WALTON • NELL WATKINS • JACK W. WERNER • JAMES R. WHALEN JR. • THOMAS B. WHITE III • DENNIS K. WICKENDEN • JOHN G. WILKINSON JR. • LISA A. WILSON • RONALD J. WILTSIE • REINHARDT T. WING • **1988** • DONALD E. ALLISON • BRIAN J. ANDERSON • FRANK G. ARCELLA • MICHAEL B. BENDER • MONTE B. BLACKSBERG • WARREN BOLDEN • WALTER E. BOWEN • STEVEN J. BRUNSON • GREGORY L. BURKS • LISA A. BURRISS • RUSSELL P. CAIN • GLEN E. CAMERON • THEODORE R. CAMPBELL JR. • RICHARD D. CARROLL • ROLAND J. CATALANO • JAMES P. CHRIST • WILLIAM A. CHRISTENS-BARRY • SANDRA P. CLARK • EDWARD J. COLBERT • JOHN L. CONNERY • FRANCIS A. COOCH IV • JEFFREY G. COOLEY • ANDREW C. COON • STEPHEN CORDA • THOMAS M. COTTER • HERMAN L. DANTZLER JR. • STEVEN A. DAVIS • RICHARD T. DAVIS • LOUIS T. DAVIS • ASHRUF S. EL-DINARY • DONALD W. EVANS • ERIC R. EVANS • DAVID G. FISCHER • M. L. FLETCHER • ROBERT J. FOCHT • DAVID M. FOGG • BARBARA L. FRANKLIN • ALEXANDER M. GARDINER • GRANT R. GARRITSON • MICHAEL GINTHER • LAURA T. GOLIASZEWSKI • JAYNE L. GONSALVES • LISA D. GORDON • PHYLLIS M. GORDON • BARRY E. GRABOW • MACHELE A. GRACE • ANGELO F. GRAVAGNA • BETH L. GRAVANDA • THOMAS W. GREENE • ERIC A. GWALTNEY • DAWN A. HALLOCK • STEPHEN G. HAPPEL • THEODORE J. HARTKA • LOIS M. HELLMAN • STEPHEN A. HENDERSON • ROBERT C. HENDRICKS • CAROL A. HERD • JOANNE M. HEREFORD • HOWARD T. HERSCHER • PHILLIP F. HIDER • DAVID M. HOBBS • LEE J. HOBSON • SANDI HOLOWEJ • JEFFREY W. HONCHELL • MARY E. HOWSER • CAMILLE T. HUDSON • BARBARA A. HUETT • TERESA D. HULVEY • JAMES C. HUTCHESON • CHRISTOPHER G. INNANEN • PAUL B. JACKSON • EDNA S. JOHNSTON • ELIZABETH S. JOHNSTONE • JANE A. JONES • THOMAS A. KEHOE • ROBERT L. KELLY II • NANCY C. KING • JAMES J. KINNALLY • JOHN W. KRESSLEIN • ALI E. KUJAWA • RONALD J. LANCASTER • MARVIN J. LANGSTON • KELLEE R. LARKINS • LINDA M. LAVELLE • HEARA LEE • GWEN A. LEWIS • JOHN K. LEWIS • DAVID A. LOHR • ANDERSON O. LYLES • MARLENE E. MACEK • CHERYL A. MANNING • CANDACE B. MARKLE • STEVEN M. MARTIN • TAUNYA A. MCCARTY • CATHERINE M. MCDERMOTT • RICHARD R. MCDONALD • ELLEN S. MCDONNELL • ANN R. MCFARLAND • STEPHANIE J. MCKAY • PATRICIA A. MCLEAN • ROBERT J. MCLEOD • JACQUELINE M. MCLOUGHLIN • PAUL MCNAMEE • REBECCA C. MILES • ROGER D. MOELLER • PAULETTE F. MOORE • DENNIS W. MOY • CATHERINE V. NEWMAN • THU-PHUONG T. NGUYEN • ERNEST W. NORRIS • JOHN W. O'BYRNE • DAVID A. PACKARD • MELISSA J. PAUL • JOHN C. PHILLIPS • ANN F. POLLACK • JUDY K. POOL • RICHARD J. PRENGAMAN JR. • DENISE A. RAKAUSKAS • KATHLEEN M. RASEL • AARON D. REDISH • KAREN D. RENNICH • CHERYL L. RESCH • DAVID W. RICHMOND • STEPHEN L. ROOT • SANDRA N. ROSENBERGER • JOHANNA J. ROWE • MARJORIE L. ROWLETT • JACK T. SANDERS JR. • FRANCIS F. SARGENT • BONITA M. SAYERS-JARVIS • WILLIAM B. SCHAEFER IV • PAUL R. SCHUSTER • DARCY B. SENSENBRENNER • LISA P. SHAMER • DAVID L. SIMMONS • KEITH E. SIMPSON • SUSAN D. SMITH • JEFFREY J. SMOOT • DAVID R. STARK • ORLANDO D. STEVENSON • KATHLEEN A. STOLL • DORA M. TAPP • FAYE C. THOMASON • EDWIN B. TOMPKINS • JENNIE L. TOUCHETTE • STEVEN L. WAHNSIEDLER • FRED D. WATTS • JOHN E. WHITELY JR. • JOSEPH C. WIEBKING • ZINDA L. WIENKE • MARY E. WILLIAMSON • SHIRLEY S. WILLS • BARBARA J. WINKLER • ELFIE WINSTEAD • JAMES R. ZAVODNY JR. • **1989** • ALICE A. ADAMS • ASHOK V. ARDESHNA • TIMOTHY P. BAILER JR. • SHARON M. BAILEY • PHILLIP M. BAKER • SHIRLEY A. BARCASE • MARVIN E. BARKSDALE • JAMES T. BEAL • JON R. BERRY JR. • NICHOLAS D. BESER • TERESA M. BETENBAUGH • JAMES S. BLESSING • WENDY S. BLUM • MICHAEL A. BOST • ELFRIEDE S. BRITTAIN • LAWRENCE M. BROOKS • SAUNDRA D. BROOKS-CARTER • SHARON C. BROWN • HELEN W. BUCKLEY • ROBIN BUNCH • KEVIN P. BURKE • JACQUELINE BUTLER • CHARLES J. CAREY JR. • DAVID G. CASAVAN • PATRICIA A. CHANEL • YALE CHANG • GEORGE CHIU • BEVERLY A. CLEMENTS • PAUL H. COHEN • NORMAN F. COLE • ROBERT A. CONN • MARC R. CONNELLY • CHRISTIAN J. COOKE • CHESTER A. COPPERTHITE JR. • JUDITH P. COUTURIER • WILLIAM C. CRITCHFIELD • CARL A. DAHLSTROM • FLOYD J. DAVIS • RANDY J. DEAN • LORI A. DIONISIO • RICHARD A. DRAGONETTE • MALINDA A. DUVALL • SCOTT A. ECELBERGER • JONATHAN T. ENTNER • LEAH G. EVERHART • RICHARD M. FREAS • WALTER FRISON JR. • LAUREL T. FUNK • WINIFRED J. GALLOWAY • DANTE P. GENTILUCCI JR. • LAURA M. GERHARDT • BEATRICE GILBERT • HELEN C. GILES • DON M. GRUENBACHER • MARK J. HAROLD • LOIS E. HARRIS • JAYNE F. HARVEY • BRIAN K. HEGGESTAD • PAUL J. HEISS • ROBERT E. HICKS • KAREN A. HOLLAND-JOHNSON • JAMES E. HOOPER III • MICHAEL E. HOSTETTER • SHIEW-LUAN Y. HSIEH • LARRIE V. HUTTON • LAWRENCE E. HYATT JR. • BRYAN C. JACOBS • HOWARD L. JAMES • JASON E. JENKINS • ERIN P. JENNINGS • JESSE L. JONES JR. • ANTHONY L. JONES • JERRY W. JORDAN • PHILLIP J. JOYCE • CHARLES J. KARDIAN JR. • DARLENE C. KELLY • PHILLIP H. KIM • FAITH S. KIMBERLING • KELLY A. KRISTEN • KANG H. KWON • MARK A. LANDIS • JOHN A. LANDSHOF • CHARLES H. LANGE • CLAUDETTE E. LAWSON • ROBERT A. LEVENE • DOUGLAS M. LINDSEY • PATRICIA G. LORENZ • ANDREW E. LOVE JR. • MARK H. LUESSE • JOANN M. LUTES • SAMUEL J. MACMULLAN • TAMMY R. MARRAPODI • SHARON A. MAYES • PRISCILLA L. MCKERRACHER • WILLIAM M. MCMILLION JR. • RICHARD C. MEITZLER • GEORGE W. MOE • HIEN D. NGUYEN • TAM M. NGUYEN • ELBERT NHAN • DEBORAH D. NORFORD • DANIEL H. OCKERMAN • CHRISTOPHER P. PARANICAS • MICHELLE T. PARKER • STEVEN F. PARR • DOLORES M. PARRISH • ROBERT A. PATTERSON JR. • MARK A. PAVICH • JAMES H. POLAHA • PHILIPPE O. POULIQUEN • DIANE V. PRATT • SUSAN L. QUINN • ALFRED L. RANDALL • ROBIN RAUL • ALAN D. RAVITZ • MATTHEW J. REINHART • ROBERT S. REINTGES • ANTHONY RIEGER • CHRISTOPHER C. ROGERS • MARILYN I. ROTTIER • LISA G. ROUTHENSTEIN • HARVEY H. RUBIN • HEIDI F. RUBINSTEIN • JOHN SADOWSKY • WALID SALEH • ENNIO R. SANCHEZ • DIANE P. SCHMALL • JANET L. SCZEPANSKI • GEORGE W. SEWELL • ROBERTA J. SHAFFER • SANDRA B. SICINSKI • CLARE M. SIEGMAN • CAROLYN J. SMITH • JOYCE H. SMITH • ROSE M. SMITH • THEODORE R. SMITH • JOANNE M. SMITH-FARRELL • MARY J. SMITHSON • PATRICIA A. SNEAD • LEONARD J. SPILLMAN • RENGASWAMY SRINIVASAN • SHIRLEY F. ST. MARY • PATRICK A. STADTER • CAROL J. STAHL • GARY R. STAMMER • LAWRENCE W. STANTON • FRONA A. STEELMAN • JOYCE M. STEVENS • BRENDA K. STEWART • DAVID C. TARKOW • PETER H. THEUNE • DENISE P. TRAVER • GARY WATSON • DEBORAH A. WHITENER • DEBORAH D. WIGGINS • KIMBERLY L. WILEMAN • MICHAEL P. WILEY • MELISSA T. WINFIELD • SHIRLEY A. WOODS • LAURA L. YEAGER • **1990** • SONDRA H. ALLINGER • WILLIAM M. ASH III • LESIA G. BACON • LESLIE E. BAILEY • JOHN P. BAKER • ISAAC N. BANKMAN • RICHARD W. BELL • BENNIE L. BLAIR • LINDA L. BOWERS • NORMA F. BOYD • WILLIAM L. BRANDENBURG • CHRISTOPHER T. BRITT • CRAIG M. BRODERICK • JAMES R. BROWN • MICHAEL R. BROWN • PATRICIA M. BURKHARDT • KIMBERLY A. BUTLER • MICHAEL Y. CHIANG • ANTHONY COAKLEY • IAN M. COURTNEY • LOIS A. CRAIG • JOSEPH A. CRUNKLETON JR. • CHRISTINE M. CUDMORE • JOANNE A. DAVIS • CHRISTOPHER C. DEBOY • DWIGHT H. DEGROFF III • CORINNE T. DELAYE • ROGER D. DEMAREE • HAROLD D. DEMARSH • ALBERT A. DEMUTH • THOMAS S. DENNEY JR. • STEVEN M. DODGE • CREIGHTON R. DONNALD • JULIE A. DORSEY • SHANA U. DOUGLAS • CYNTHIA G. DOWNS • DAVID V. DURNELL • MARY E. EDGEWORTH • LAURA M. ELLERBRAKE • SUZANNE S. ELLIS • ROBERT W. FARQUHAR • THOMAS A. FEROLI • DINA L. FESMAN • JOAN E. FETTER • RONALD FICO • JOHN T. FOLKERTS • IRA J. FRANCKEL • CATHERINE B. FRITZIUS • M. J. FUNK • PAUL N. GARNER JR. • SHELIA G. GARRIS • LEON R. GARVIN JR. • BERNARD S. GEAGHAN • DAVID P. GIETKA • JENNIFER L. GILMORE • WENDY D. GOODNITE • JULIE A. GOULD • VANESSA M. GREY • STEVEN P. GRIBBEN • PAUL D. GRIMM • JAMES M. GUARNERI • WARREN T. HARDEN • PATRICK M. HARE • DAVID C. HECHT • CAROLE A. HELFERSTAY • JOSEPHINE W. HENDERSON • CHRISTOPHER B. HERSMAN • BRYAN D. HEYDON • KATHLEEN A. HIETT • SARAH E. HIGH • ROBERT G. HOLLINGSWORTH • ERNEST L. HOLMBOE • SHIRLEY B. HOOFNAGLE • MARY M. HOPKINS • MARY M. HORTON • MICHAEL A. HOUSE • GRACE D. HOUSTON • TIFFANY S. JACKSON • EUGENIA T. JACOBS • ANDREW JAHNS • TANYA R. JANSEN • RICHARD F. JENNINGS • BRIAN K. JENNISON • ROBERT C. JERNIGAN • SEAN M. KELLEY • HYUNWOO W. KIM • KENNETH V. KITZMAN • TROY L. KLEIN • GARY L. KLINE • ERIC G. KNOX • ANTHONY R. KOBYLSKI • BRUCE A. KOPP • STEPHEN M. KORESKO • KATHLEEN L. KUMMER • FEI T. KWOK • WILLIAM J. LA CHOLTER • DAVID M. LAZOFF • DEBORAH J. LEOPOLD • RAY Q. LIN • ANN M. LOFTON • MORRIS L. LONDON • JOSEPH LOVCHIK • SHIRLEY R. LOWRY • NAN Q. LU • MELVILLE H. LYMAN • CHARLES J. LYNCH • JOSEPH P. MADDEN JR. • NANCY C. MAGNUSSON • MICHAEL D. MANDELBERG • LAURENCE P. MANZI • KARIN W. MARR • DONNA G. MASON • WILLIAM W. MATTES JR. • SCOTT G. MAURER • CONSTANCE J. MCCLAIN • DOUGLAS D. MCDIARMID • LINDA M. MENGEL • ALAN P. MERGENTHALER • PHILIP W. MILLER • JOSEPH A. MIRAGLIOTTA • JAMES B. MITCHELL • JAMES P. MORAN • DORSEY F. MORGAN • RICHARD C. MORGAN • AMIR-HOMAYOON NAJMI • SHANNON E. NELSON • LINDA H. NEWMAN • RAYMOND J. NOSKO JR. • LAWRENCE I. OFFENBERG • ROBERT J. OGDEN II • KIRSTEN L. O'NEILL • MICHAEL J. PACKARD • KAVITA K. PATEL • EUGENE J. PAWLIKOWSKI • LARRY J. PAXTON • MAURICE C. PERDOMO • FAY A. PERRY • DZUNG L. PHAM • BRIAN S. PICKETT • THERESE F. QUARANTA • SCOTT T. RADCLIFFE • RUBY M. RANDALL • CHARLENE J. RASMUS • TOMMY K. REDMOND • JOHN F. RITTER • JACK C. ROBERTS • GERALD J. ROMICK • ANNIE G. ROSCOE • ALLAN P. ROSENBERG • DANIEL ROUSEFF • WILLIAM M. SANDERS • EDWARD D. SCHAEFER • STEPHEN L. SCHEIREY • HELEN L. SEMKIW • ROBERT D. SHERMAN • KIMBERLY A. SHIFFLETT-SMITH • ELIZABETH A. SHUCK • BENJAMIN E. SIEGRIST • KAREN L. SLEGEL • FREDERICK G. SMITH • MARTHA H. SMITH • ELIZABETH N. SOLURY • JANET A. SPEDDEN • PETER J. STAEHLING • RONALD L. STANFORD • DAVID W. STEPP • JOSEPH P. SULLIVAN • DEBRA A. THOMAS • KARL E. THOMPSON • RICHARD L. TYSOR • CHERYL S. VOLK • ROBERT F. WALSH JR. • PHYLLIS A. WANN • SHARON A. WARNER • BRENT K. WASHINGTON • PAULA K. WEBBER • NINA N. WEST • PAUL D. WHITEHURST • JORDAN T. WILKERSON • MARGARET WILLIAMS • GEOFFREY P. WILSON • SCOTT R. WISOR • RICHARD J. WYANT • TERI L. YANCOSKY • DAVID J. YEMC • JENNIE L. YEP • WARM S. YUAN • ADAM H. ZYSNARSKI • **1991** • ROBERT E. ADAMS • DAVID W. AHA • HANI W. AKHRAS • ANDREW A. ANDREWS • JACQUELINE G. APPLONIE • DAVID A. AULT • LISA G. BAILEY • KATHLEEN A. BAUMAN • JEFFREY A. BECKER • LLOYD A. BEST • KELLY J. BETZER • MATTHEW G. BEVAN • VIPUL BHATNAGAR • DAVID W. BLODGETT • LISA A. BLODGETT • LISA A. BOEHME • CRAIG S. BREITENBACH • KURT T. BRINTZENHOFE • HEATHER L. BULKIN • AUDREY M. BULLOCK • WYLIE R. BURGE • NATHANIEL BUTLER • MARY A. BUZBY • MARC A. CAMACHO • JANIS R. CARACOFE • GLENN M. CAREY • CHRISTOPHER J. CHASE • KEEFER D. CORRICK • DAVID E. COWLES • IAN J. CRAIG • PETER W. CRICKMAN • CHERYL L. DELLER • NICHOLAS W. DEMATT • DELORES J. DOMBROWSKI • STEPHANIE D. DOWELL • WILLIE R. DRUMMOND • CHRISTOPHER J. DUHON • DENNIS D. EDWARDS • MICHAEL J. ELKO • CARL J. ERCOL • TINA M. FENNELL • DAWN K. FINNERTY • JOAN M. FORRESTER • ANTHONY L. FRANKLIN • ELIN H. FRYE • DEBORAH L. GARTRELL-KEMP • BRENDA S. GARVIN • NIKOLAOS A. GATSONIS • LEO R. GAUTHIER JR. • KIMBERLY O. GENOVESE • GEORGE O. GILL • RONALD C. GLASER • ALEX GOFFIN • SAMUEL L. GORDON • ROBIN L. GRASSO • MYRON P. GRAY • ROBERT R. GREEN • KAREN E. GREENE • CHRISTOPHER W. GREGORY • BARBARA H. HAGLER • ROBERT K. HAMILTON • DEENA M. HAMMOND • DENNIS B. HANEY • PATRICK J. HARTMAN • DWAYNE A. HAWBAKER • HELEN M. HEINTZ • PAUL F. HEMLER JR. • CONNIE B. HENNINGS • PETER M. HESSER • RICHARD H. HILLSLEY • CAROLYN L. HOBBS • JONATHAN M. HODAPP • DOUGLAS B. HOLLAND • CRAIG S. HUGHES • RUTHANN L. HUMPHREYS • DANIEL G. JABLONSKI • DOROTHY L. JACKSON • CARRIE J. JOHNSON • JAMES L. JOHNSON • PATRICK L. JOHNSON • TIMOTHY L. JOHNSON • JOCELYN C. JONES • JEFFREY J. JORGENSEN • DENISE E. KALE • JACQUELINE H. KANG • HOWARD T. KAUDERER • JEFFREY S. KENNY • FRANCIS R. KILLELEA • RICHARD C. KOCHANSKI • ANITA P. KOEHLER • DEBRA L. KOPP • HARRY M. KREITZ JR. • JEANNE W. KRUHM • KENNETH D. KUYKENDALL • NICHOLAS J. LANGHAUSER • HOWARD A. LAZOFF • BINH Q. LE • SEPPO J. LEHTONEN • ELIAHU LEV • DUANE L. LINSENBARDT • EVELYN M. LOOMIS • ROBERT C. MACKENZIE • MICKEY O. MARSHALL • JOHN H. MATLICK • TERESSA A. MATTES • JOHN T. MCCORMICK JR. • PHILIP J. MCNALLY • SETH J. MESSING • MICHAEL L. MINER • RONALD W. MITNICK • LEROY S. MOBLEY JR. • JEANNE MONTGOMERY • DEBORAH L. MOORE • KAREN L. MOORE • JOSEPH N. MULE' • CHAD A. MULLINIX • GRAHAM A. MURPHY • MARIA E. NEELY • ANDREAS A. NICHOLAS • SHIN-ICHI OHTANI • BARBARA M. PAROJINOG • KARUNGULAM N. PARTHASARATHY • RAJEN L. PATEL • JOHN R. PENCE • STEPHEN P. REBETSKY III • SAMUEL P. REYNOLDS JR. • GREGORY C. RICE • JUDY E. RIDGLEY • BYRON M. ROGERS JR. • IRIS M. ROSA • CRAIG T. ROWLAND • DIANE M. RUSH • LEROY J. SAMUELS JR. • ROBERT D. SANDERS JR. • RON C. SCHULZE • MARK A. SCOVILLE • JOHN R. SEESHOLTZ • DEBRA S. SEIBERT • DOUGLAS S. SHELTON • GEOFFREY L. SILBERMAN • FRANK J. SLUJTNER • BRIAN E. SMITH • GARRETT A. SMITH • DAVID J. SOISSON • THOMAS S. SPISZ • JAMES F. STAFFORD • MICHAEL E. STONER • MARTHA J. STUM • THEA L. SWAVELY • ARCHANA SZPAK • EUGENE P. THEUS • DARNELL E. TOWNSEND

• MICHAEL S. TRACEY • LAURIE B. TUBBS • THOMAS J. URBAN • LORA S. VANEGAS • PATRICIA A. WADE • COMPTON E. WARD • DOUGLAS S. WENSTRAND • JANINE Y. WHITE • STUART W. WHITING • LILLIAN D. WILDER • JOHN L. WILHELM • BRIDGET S. WILSON • DANIEL S. WILSON • SIMON P. WING • GARY R. WINKLER • DIANA M. WITHERSPOON • SEATON B. WOODY • LUTHER O. YOUNG JR. • REBECCA W. YUAN **1992** • ROBERT T. ALSTON III • MARCIA J. AMOS • DONALD E. ANDERSON • GLORIA J. BALLIET • MATTHEW J. BELLIA • G. S. BITNER • DEBORAH R. BLANCHARD • CAROL E. BOCK • ALLEN J. BRIC • WILLIAM A. BRISTOW • REYNARD N. BURGESS • JAMES B. BURNS • COLLEEN CAMPBELL MILLER • JOHN C. CASPER • MICHAEL W. CHAMBERS • WENDY W. CHIU • DALE E. CLEMONS • RYON K. COLEMAN • JAMES J. COSTABILE • BRUCE G. COURY • KEVIN F. COX • GEOFFREY CROWLEY • ALAN J. CUSACK • JEFFREY A. DAVIS • VITO G. DEL-GUERCIO • ROSE M. DEMPSEY • SHARON K. DUBOIS • DAVID W. DUNHAM • COURTNEY B. ECKLER • ROBERT B. EVANS • FREDRICK R. FACEMIRE • CAROLYN M. FAITH • ERIC M. FIORE • PAMELA J. FOWLER • GINA G. FRASER • PAUL M. FURTH • ANTHONY F. GENOVESE • SHERI GEORGE • JOSEPH GEZELTER • ERNEST J. GOEBEL • PHILIP M. GOLDSTEIN • ARMANDO GONZALEZ • HERMIONE C. GRAHAM • YANPING GUO • STEPHEN J. HANNIGAN • MARGARET A. HARLOW • JOHN C. HARRIS • KENNETH L. HARRISON • RAYMOND J. HARVEY • MELISSA A. HERBERT • HILARY L. HERSHEY • CATHERINE L. HETTINGER • DAVID S. HOHMAN • MARGARET L. HOOKS • ROBERT J. HOUGHTON JR. • JAMES W. HOWARD • SCOTT A. HYER • RUSSELL L. JANUSZ • THERESA A. JOHNSON • JEFFREY E. JOHNSTON • KENNETH E. JONES • STEPHEN M. JONES • MICHAEL J. KENNEDY • SUSAN L. KIRK • DAVID R. KOHLER • DAVID G. KUPPERMAN • ESTHER H. KWON • PAUL M. LAFFERTY • JOHN E. LANSBERRY II • TANYA S. LAU • GERALD A. LEE • DALE C. LINNE VON BERG • ROBERT R. LUTZ • JAY A. MARBLE • THOMAS C. MASON • RALPH L. MCNUTT JR. • ROBERT E. MENTLE • NANCY L. MITCHELL • GLENN T. MOORE • EDWARD J. MOSES • ROBERT A. NICHOLS • RONALD J. NICOLA • JOHN E. O'BRIEN • MEHUL B. PATEL • JAMES M. RISHEL • MICHAEL B. ROOSA • CAMIL F. SAMAHA • DEBORAH A. SCHREIBER • IMAN W. SCHURMAN • SOL SCHWARTZ • ANN C. SETHERLEY • LINDA C. SIMS • KEENAN C. SMITH • ERIKA L. SPENCER • KATHLEEN M. STISTED • KEITH E. STROUD • LINDA Y. SUNG • JOSEPH F. SVEHLA • ORVAL L. SWEENEY • QUYEN L. TRAN • PETER W. TROLL • BRIAN A. TRUCKENBRODT • MEHUL K. UDANI • KAREN P. VAUGHN • JAMES T. VELKY • LUCIANA C. VILLEGAS • JASON L. WELLS • BRUCE D. WILLIAMS • DAVID C. WILLIAMS • KEVIN A. WILMORE • JENG-HWA YEE • STANLEY E. YOUNG • **1993** • VASSILIS ANGELOPOULOS • RHONDA L. BADDOUR • ROBERT J. BAKER • LU A. BELL • GARY K. BELLAMY • CLYDE E. BETHEA III • ROBERT J. BIEGALSKI • ALAN P. BRAUNSTEIN • ALFRED T. CAFFREY • LAURA A. CASTNER • MICHELLE H. CHEN • DOUGLAS A. CORNWALL • RONALD J. COTE' • LINDA R. CRAWFORD • MAX C. CURRENT • BARBARA A. DAGGETT • GEORGE DAKERMANJI • LUCIO DEMEIO • DENIS J. DONOHUE JR. • JEFFREY J. DUMM • OWEN E. FLYNN • CAROLYN B. FREAS • JUDITH FRENCH • LAUREN M. GRAYBEAL • LARRY H. GREEN • DAVID L. GRESHAM • RICHARD S. HALL • PAUL A. HANKE • DAVID O. HARPER • SAYED H. HASSAN • MICHAEL J. HERLIHY • CHARLES L. HIETT • EVA D. HOWARD • TARESA V. HYMAN • JOHN P. JACKSON JR. • CHRISTIAN JACQUEY • JUDITH G. KATZMARK • CHARLES W. KENNEDY • PHAEL C. KOJZAR • MEGAN L. KRATOCHWILL • NATALIE D. LACEY • DALE A. LARUE • DAVID R. LEWIS • STEVEN A. LLOYD • JULIE A. LONG • MICHAEL A. MARSICANO • MICHAEL J. MCGUNIGALE • JOANNA K. METZBOWER • ELEANOR S. MILAN • GALEN B. MILLER • HARRY L. MILLER • MICHAEL E. MINEHART • TANKA T. MURRAY • THERESA G. NESTER • JON C. O'DONNELL • ROBERT OSIANDER • NEIL F. PALUMBO • WILLIAM D. PATOW • PATRICIA L. PURWIN • JENNIFER L. RAU • KELLIE M. RICH • LINDA M. ROGERS • SCOTT E. SCHLEMMER • CAMILLE A. SCHUMACHER • JEAN G. SCHUTT • GEORGE M. SCOTT • LORI A. SHAW • JACK M. SHEPPARD • KENNETH E. SHIPLEY • MICHAEL R. SMITH JR. • KENNETH D. SPARKS • SANDRA K. STEWART • ROBERT L. STRAUCH • PAUL S. TARANTINO • ROBERT M. TAYLOR • CATHY B. TELEKY • KELLY R. TILTON • SUSANNE M. TOROK • LINDA M. TOSSMAN • DENISE B. WELLER • CHARLES R. WESTGATE SR. • JAMES W. WHITE • PAUL D. WIENHOLD • RENEE L. ZABELA • THEODORE J. ZABORA • ALAN D. ZIMM • GREGORY D. ZUDOCK • **1994** • GRAHAM P. ALLYN • TIMOTHY A. AXNESS • TIMOTHY P. BARRETT • BRADLEY O. BATES • EILEEN F. BAUST • LINDA L. BERLING • SCOTT M. BEZICK • GERARD S. BOGNASKI • RICHARD L. BOURGEOIS • TIMOTHY H. BRADLEY • DUNCAN A. BROWN • RODNEY L. BUTLER • SCOTT L. CARPENTER • TAMMI L. R. CARPENTER • SCOTT G. CASPER • ROBERT O. CHINN • JENNIFER S. CLARK • DONALD J. CLOPEIN • LOUIS A. COLANGELO JR. • JUDITH E. COOKSON • KIM A. COOPER • PATRICK B. CUSICK • STEPHEN M. D'ALESSIO • MONIQUE M. DANSBERGER • JANET DAY • ROBERT DEMAJISTRE • JON S. DUBRO • LIEN T. DUONG • CHRISTOPHER L. EDDINS • JAMES J. EICHERT • EMILY C. ELKO • RICHARD D. ELLERY • CLOYD A. ELLIS • KIM G. ENDRES • JOHN L. FARNAN • ADRIANE J. FAUST • ELLEN A. FIELDS • MALCOLM B. FORD • WARREN A. FRANK • CATHERINE H. FRAZIER • MARK K. GAITHER • JAMES C. GARCIA • JAMES B. GARY • LUKE GOEMBEL • EVA L. GREER • DOUGLAS E. GRIFFIN • PAUL GULOTTA • MARTIN R. HALL • RICHARD R. HEISLER • KATHLEEN A. HELBIG • TERRY L. HIPP • KIRK E. HOOBLER • ELISABETH A. IMMER • PAMELA D. JADWICK • EARLEEN U. JAMES • THOMAS W. JOHNSON • LISA J. JOHNSTON • ROBERT L. JORDAN JR. • JULIA K. KAGIWADA • ERIN KALBARCZYK • VLADIMIR KARASIK • CONLEY B. KING • STANLEY F. KOZUCH • JOYCE A. KRAUS • DENISE M. LAFLUER • JAMES L. LAMB III • KENNETH J. LARSEN • THOMAS W. LEFEVERE • ANGELICA D. LILLY • KEVIN M. LYONS • WILLIAM H. MANTHORPE JR. • FRANCIS H. MARLO • BARBARA P. MARROW • ALBERT W. MARSHALL • MAUREEN P. MAYER • JAMES V. MCADAMS • KEVIN M. MCCAFFERTY • DOROTHEA M. MCCALL • RODNEY A. MILLER • JOHN I. MOORE III • DANIEL MORRISON • LARRY E. MOSHER • SIMON MOSKOWITZ • SCOTT L. MURCHIE • TENI E. NARGIZ • BENJAMIN J. NIEPORENT • CHRISTINE M. OAKES • JOHN M. O'MORE • JAMES V. PALMER • NIKOLAOS P. PASCHALIDIS • MICHAEL J. PATE • ROBERT S. PATTAY • WAYNE J. PAVALKO • MICHAEL G. PFARR • SHARON H. POWELL • RUSSELL K. RANEY • LAWRENCE E. RASKIN • MICHAEL C. REICHLE • MARY KATHERINE E. REYNOLDS • CHARLES R. ROBBA • CHRISTOPHER M. ROBBINS • MICHELLE M. ROCKWELL • BRADLEY M. ROSENBAUM • DANA M. SCHLICHTING • FRED D. SETH JR. • CHARLES L. SETTLE • EDWARD J. SHEEHI • THEODORE G. SHOLAR • ROBERT P. SKINDER • BLAKE F. SMITH • CATHERINE M. SMITH • THOMAS P. SPRIESTERBACH • ANGELA P. STANTON • THOMAS N. STEWART • WILLIAM H. SWARTZ • ROBERT S. TEICHMAN • CHARLES R. TEUTON • BEVERLY K. THOMAS • PAUL E. TILSON JR. • RODNEY D. TIMM • ROBIN A. WALKER • RUSSELL H. WALTERS • CHARLES R. WELSH • THOMAS D. WHITAKER • ZORITA L. WHITE • DALE W. WILSON • DIANA L. WINDSOR • CHRISTINE A. WYANT • ELIZABETH M. ZECCARDI • **1995** • DEREK G. ANDERSON • DEBRA M. ANGERMAIER • JOHN F. APPLEBY • JOHN M. BACHKOSKY • GEORGE P. BARDSLEY • VIKKI R. BAZZLE • STEVEN F. BERGMANN • DAVID M. BERSTEIN • ORLANDO M. BETANCOURT • WILLIAM R. BITMAN • MORTREESE K. BLAIR • CARL W. BLAKE • LANCE M. BODNAR • JAMES J. BOGARD • JENNIFER A. BOSTAK • WILLIAM D. BRODERICK • MICHAEL J. BURKE • RICK A. BUTLER • MICHAEL S. CAPRON • CLARK R. CARSON JR. • ROBERT J. CHAFIN • CYNTHIA L. CHASE • DENNIS W. CHILES • ROBERT E. CLAY • ALICIA COMBS • ALLEN E. CRAWFORD • VERONICA M. CROUCH • AUDREY A. CUSTER • MICHELE E. D'ANNA • WAYNE H. DEESE • DIANE L. DORSEY • BERNARD K. ESTABROOK • THOMAS J. EUBANKS • ARTHUR D. FARRINGTON • KATHLEEN G. FARRIS • PATRICK A. FERAT • JOHN H. FEWER JR. • KENNETH M. FISCHER • TERRIE B. FISHER • THOMAS A. FRENCH • PATRICIA L. GALLATI • ISMAEL L. GARCIA • MICHELLE D. GUEVARA • WILMAN J. GUEVARA • MICHAEL A. GURSKI • THOMAS J. HANNIBAL SR. • KENNETH W. HARCLERODE • MICHAEL A. HARRIS • PATRICK J. HIGGINS • NATHAN R. HINES • JOHN A. HULL • BARBARA A. JOHNSON • MICHAEL A. JORDAN • STEPHEN W. KAY • DAVID G. KENNEY • JOHN F. KLAFIN • JAMES W. KNISLEY JR. • ADAM W. KOBULNICKY • JOHN E. KOSKIE • ZACHARY R. KULIS • MARTHA B. KUSTERER • DENNIS J. LANAHAN • DIANE M. LAPIERRE • RUSSELL S. LAYMAN • LUCILLE LINARY • ANNE B. LONG • ELIZABETH M. MACASKILL • WILLIAM H. MAUGER • ERIC O. MCGIFFIN • JAMES C. MCNABOE • MICHAEL D. MCPHERSON • MIGUEL A. MEJIA • ALAN A. MICK • STEPHEN P. MILLER • GENNADIY I. MISHIN • CHARLENE MOON • MILLARD F. MORGAN • EMILY B. MORRIS • THEODORA P. NICHOLAS • RUTH E. NIMMO • IVETTE M. OGDEN • PAULETTE PAYNE • RAYMOND R. PAYNE • JOHN T. POOLE JR. • MARC A. PRICE • MARSHALL S. RADFORD • DEREK L. ROCKETT • JOHN A. ROMANO • ORLANDO SANTIAGO • TERRIE J. SCHAFER • CHERYL K. SEYMOUR • JAMES B. SHARKEY • DAVID M. SHAW • ROBIN L. SHELLMAN • RICHARD A. SHELSBY • DAVID P. SILBERBERG • ROGER L. SIMPSON • DEXTER G. SMITH • SHEILA A. SMITH • THOMAS C. SMITH • EDWARD A. SMYTH • THOMAS S. SOTIRELIS • LAURA P. STRAUSBAUGH • RICHARD A. STRAUSS • IRVING J. SUMMERS JR. • PAZHAYANNUR K. SWAMINATHAN • JEFF C. TAYLOR • RICHARD L. TERRY • GEORGE G. THOMAS • LISA M. THOMPSON • PETER M. TRASK • BERNARD G. TYDINGS • DONALD J. VISLAY • DAVID P. WATSON • EDWARD L. WEEDON JR. • CHERYLL J. WENCHEL • KEVIN B. WENCHEL • BARBARA A. WENSUS • EDWARD D. WILDER JR. • KAREN P. WILEY • DEBRA S. WILHELM • WILLIAM O. WILSON JR. • ANTHONY L. WILSON • MICHAEL L. WISE • EDWARD WRIGHT JR. • WALTER J. WYNN • GLORIA M. YORK • JOHN R. ZABER • **1996** • EDWARD B. ALLEN JR. • WILLIAM M. ANTOSZEWSKI • TIMOTHY M. AQUILINO • JUAN I. ARVELO JR. • JOHN A. BANTA • KARL D. BAR-LEV • JOHN H. BARRETT III • ANGELA L. BARRIOS • CAROL A. BATES • CHAD W. BATES • WALTER BENDER SR. • WILLIAM J. BLACKERT III • MATTHEW P. BLAIR • BARBARA J. BLOUNT • SAMUEL BOSTON JR. • WILLIAM J. BROCK • SUSAN P. BROWN • HOWARD S. BURKOM • ROGER A. BURNETT • DAWN M. BUTTION • MARLENE T. CAHILL • LORETTA A. CANAN • HARRY M. CAPINO • DENICE M. CAREY • MICAH A. CARLSON • ANTHONY CASASNOVAS • LYNNE M. CHAMPITTO • KATHERINE A. CHRISTIAN • ROBERT B. CHRISTIANSEN SR. • DANIEL J. CHRISTINE • DAVID E. COLBERT • CHRISTOPHER M. COLLOUGH • THERESA M. COOLAHAN • GEOFFREY J. COSDEN • TARA L. COWGILL • GARY L. COYLE • MICHAEL A. CRAMER • GLORIA J. CRITES • CHARLES W. CROSSETT • ARTHUR R. CROUCHER II • DOUGLAS G. CROWE • ERICA T. DAVIS • PATRICIA H. DE BLANDER • AREND W. DEBOLT • PHILIP L. DECOLA • ALLISON S. DENNIS • MICHAEL G. DENNIS • BARRY C. DEROZE • NATALIE N. DICKINS • DONNA J. DINOTO • JOHN P. DOLINISH • WILLIAM C. DOVE • GEORGE R. DRAKE • MARGARET S. DULLNIG • PETER L. EIRICH • GLORIA J. ELGIN • DOUGLAS A. ENG • LARS M. ERICSON • CHARLES R. ETHERIDGE III • JANET S. FANT • JONATHAN S. FARRIS • DARREN K. FEDERROLL • TADD W. FELDT • TERRY C. FINNEY • PAUL D. FISHER • CAROLINE A. FITZGERALD • JENNIFER L. FLERLAGE • JAMES K. FRANKE JR. • DENNIS E. FREEMAN • PATRICIA M. GADDY • TERRY K. GANTENBEIN • JEAN M. GARBER • RUSSELL W. GARRETT • ROBIN F. GARY • STEVEN GELSIE • CULLEN L. GERHART • JANINE C. GETTIER • LINDE A. GHERE • LEE ANNA R. GHOSH • STEPHEN W. GIGUERE • CORNELIA C. GILBERT • ROBERT H. GOLDFARB • ELSIE G. GOODWYN • ANN L. GOSSARD • GREGORY M. GRASON • STEPHEN R. GRAY • DEANNA M. GREEN • KIMBERLY E. GREMPLER • THERESA L. GRISSOM • ALAN W. CRONLUND • PAULA R. GUFFEY • ALFRED E. HALL • SHANNON M. HALL • KAREN S. HALLORAN • HYUNG S. HAN • JON D. HANDIBOE • JAY T. HARRELL • NATHAN S. HARRIS • MARK A. HEIM • VICTORIA L. HELLER • TERRI D. HENSHAW • LUCIA M. HILL • MARK L. HILL • CHARLENE M. HINES • LUCINDA P. HOLLINGSWORTH • STEPHEN S. HOLLOMAN • GREGORY M. HORSTKAMP • JEFFREY P. HUBERT • ESTHER D. HUDDLE • NICOLE M. HUGHES • SHANE F. HUTTON • TODD D. JACKSON • VOYLE E. JAMES • VIMLA JASHNANI • AMANDA L. JENKINS • RUTH J. JOHNSON • ROBERT W. JORDAN • TED A. KEDZIERSKI • MICHAEL J. KELLEY • WILLIAM C. KENWORTHY JR. • DANIEL W. KERCHNER • ARAM E. KHALILI • MIN S. KIM • ERIC M. KLATT • BRENDA B. KNIGHT • DONNA L. KOCZAJA • EDWARD D. KOSKIE • WILLIAM E. KOZAK • JAMES A. KRUG • SCOTT K. KUCZMA • WILLIAM L. LAIN • JUAN R. LANDER • ROBERT J. LANDLE • CHRISTOPHER B. LANGHAGE • PETER M. LEPOER • DENNIS L. LESTER • DANIEL J. LEVINE • KAN LIOU • BETH S. LIVINGSTON • KRISTEN M. LLOYD • MICHELE B. LOHR • GLEN A. LONG • STEVEN P. LUNDFELT • RUSSELL M. LYONS • TIMOTHY P. MAGNANI • MANI S. MAHJOURI • PATRICK C. MALONE • DOUGLAS W. MANNING • KRISTI D. MARREN • LESLIE D. MARSTEINER • PATRICIA A. MARTIN • RAMONA M. MARTIN • STEPHEN E. MASON • JAMES C. MAYFIELD • JOSEPH M. MAZZAFRO JR. • BRIAN E. MCGRATH • KAREN R. MCMANNIS • JOSEPH F. MCNALLY • ROBERT D. MCTEER • JOHN A. MICHAEL • HARRY J. MILLER • RICHARD L. MILLER • WALTER L. MITNICK • KATHLEEN C. MITTRICK • ANDREW F. MOOR • PATRICK N. MORGAN • MARGARET K. MORRIS • TIMOTHY J. MORRIS • SEIBERT L. MURPHY • GEORGE M. MURRAY • ANTHONY R. NARDO JR. • TODD M. NEIGHOFF • MICHAEL H. NEWKIRK • LAMONT A. NOBLE • ANDREW C. OAK • AMY M. O'CONNOR • WILLIAM D. OLYHA • ROGER S. OSGOOD • SUSAN C. OWENS • RAYMOND C. PARKS JR. • RAJ I. PATEL • DAVID M. PATRONE • LARRY F. PAUL • GEORGE S. PEACOCK • PATRICIA A. PECK • LINDA M. PECO-DEHOFF • MICHAEL J. PEKALA • WENDE C. PETERS • BRYAN J. PFISTER • CHRISTOPHER J. PHELPS • CYNTHIA M. PIPKINS • TODD B. PITTMAN • JAMES R. PONTIOUS • VALERIE F. PORTNER • TINA L. POWELL • ROSA W. ROBERTS • MICHAEL ROONEY • CHRISTOPHER A. ROSS • LARRY ROYSTER SR. • DANIEL H. RYDER • MARJORIE S. SATTLER • FREDERIC J. SCHANTZ • JEFFREY J. SCHEROCK • JOHN R. SCHNEIDER • CHRISTOPHER P. SEXTON • KENNETH E. SHAFER • BERNADETTE J. SHANK • BRUCE W. SHANK • CORY C. SHEFFER • MARIA Y. SHEN • SUSAN L. SHIPLEY • ROBERT M. SHUFORD • OMA L. SIEGFRIED • RACHAEL D. SIMMONS-CANGELOSI • CAROL A. SKEENS • JOHN K. SMITH • STERLING T. SMOOT • CAROL A. SNIEGOSKI • MARTIN G. SOMMERVILLE • EDGAR H. SOUDER • NIQUIA C. SPENCER • MERLE C. SPIVEY • HARRY E. STELLO III • VALERIE I. STETSER • CHRISTINE H. SUH • KEVIN E. SUTTON • MARK D. SWITLICK • PATRICIA A. TAYLOR • JOHN C. TIGHE • EVERETT TOM • STEVEN M. TOWNSEND • THOMAS T. TRAN • CARRIE L. TUCCI • MARNAY H. TURNER • THOMAS W. TURNER • GEORGE C. UECKER • MERRICK J. VAN DONGEN • MARGARET F. VAN VLIET • THOMAS J. VELLANI • ADAVIKOLANU R. VENKAT • SHON D. VICK • KIMBERLY A. VONTOBEL • KARL F. WAGNER • BILL WALKER • SHEILA M. WASHINGTON • ZANA W. WATSON • THOMAS P. WEIDEMANN • DONNA J. WELTNER • LARRY H. WHITE • MICHAEL J. WHITE • STEPHEN E. WIEPRECHT • SAMUEL K. WILLIAMS • LORI H. WILLIAMSON • DAWN M. WILSON • TIMOTHY S. WOLTERS • KAINAM T. WONG • GEOFFREY S. WRIGHT • DAVID C. WU • PAMELA J. YOUNG • GRICELIS ZAYAS • ADAM J. ZECCARDI • **1997** • GERALD S. ADAMS • TYRONE ADAMS • RIA N. ALEXANDER • WILLIAM R. ALLMON • SUSAN A. ANDERSON • GARY I. APPELBAUM • SHAHANA B. AZIZ • SURJIT S. BADESHA • PATRICIA L. BARDSLEY • CHRISTOPHER R. BARKER • ROBIN J. BARNES • OLIVIER S. BARNOUIN • DAVID W. BENNETT • PIETRO N. BERNASCONI • JUDY BITMAN • EVA M. BLACK • RALPH K. BODENNER IV • AARON L. BODOH-CREED • ALICE F. BOWMAN • JANET L. BOYCE • WILLIAM B. BRINCKERHOFF • ANNE G. BROKLOFF • LAUREN A. BROWN • LISA M. BROWN • CAROL S. BRUEGGEMEIER • TIMOTHY P. BUSH • SUSAN M. BYRD • UNO P. CARLSSON • PAUL D. CARR • GREGORY E. CARSWELL • LINDSEY L. CARTER • FREDERIC T. CASE • CARLOS M. CASTILLO • CHI CHEN • DAVID N. CHEN • SHENG CHENG • KANAYA R. CHEVLI • MARTHA I. CHU • DEBORAH A. CLANCY • MARK E. CLARK • MATTHEW J. CLAUSSEN • WILLIAM M. CLEM • VONDELL L. COLEMAN • BERNARD F. COLLINS • GORDON A. COLLINS • MICHAEL R. CONNELLY • CYNTHIA A. CRAIG • EMILY E. CRANE • KEVIN M. CROPPER • JARRETT H. CROWLEY II • ERIN N. DASTE • ROBERT W. DAVIS II • JENNIFER A. DAVIS • WAYNE F. DELLINGER • KENNETH L. DEMERY • PATRICIA K. DETWILER • DEBORAH L. DOMINGUE LORIN • ED B. DORAN • JULIEANN B. DOW • ANDREW S. DRIESMAN • KEVIN D. D'SOUZA • FRANCIS C. DUMONT • MAWULI DZIRASA • SHANA O. ELEY • KAREN ELSBREE • DAVID F. EMMONS • JAMES F. ENGLER SR. • DAVID G. ERICKSON • JOANNE L. ERICKSON • JOYCE E. FARRARE • TACY L. FELICIANO • DAVID W. FENNELL • KARL B. FIELHAUER • GEORGE T. FORBES • MARK A. FORSMAN • DENEEN B. FOX • JEREMY T. FREUND • DAVID A. FRITZ • DAVID A. FROMMER • RUBEN E. GALARZA • HUGH A. GALLAGHER JR. • ROBERT G. GAY • BRIAN L. GEESAMAN • VISHAL GIARE • RENEE A. GIORDANO • JONATHAN A. GITELMAN • SCOTT B. GOLDBLATT • CHRISTOPHER GRAHAM • BRENDA L. GREEN • BEVERLY E. GREENWALD • JOSEPH A. GREGOR • DAVID R. GRIGGS • KENNETH R. GROSSMAN • ANDREW J. GUENTHER • GABRIEL GUNDERSEN • ELIZABETH J. HABERT • DENNIS K. HAGGERTY • MARY E. HALL • RONALD E. HALL • ELMER J. HALLEY JR. • PAUL D. HARDY • CHARLES G. HARE II • RHONDA S. HARMISON • JUANITA L. HARPER • MARY P. HARRISON • GAIL L. HELM • ANDREW M. HELTEN • MARILYN C. HENDERSON • KELLY A. HENORA • MARTHA S. HEWITT • TINA M. HIGGINS • JAMES L. HILLMAN • SUSAN E. HINDLE • JOHN V. HITE • MARK E. HOLDRIDGE • ROBERT F. HOLSOPPLE • SHARON K. HRIN • DAVID C. HUMM • MARY JANE S. HUNEYCUTT • DEBRA S. HURT • STEPHEN R. HUTCHINSON • BRIAN J. IRWIN • NOAM R. IZENBERG • CHAD A. JACKSON • MARCIA M. JACKSON • MARGARET M. JACKSON • KATHRYN C. JACOBS • CRAIG H. JOHNSON • BEVERLY A. KAHRL • MATTHEW J. KAZANAS • JOHN F. KEANE • MICHAEL F. KENNEDY • ERIC M. KESSLER • JAMES C. KIRK • DANIEL J. KIRSHBAUM • LISA L. KLEIN • BERNARD E. KLUGA • MARK L. KOEHLER • KAMINI R. KOTHARI • KEVIN A. KOTLARSKI • MARCIA K. KOURY • GREGORY B. KRAMP • THOMAS A. KREITZBERG • ANTHONY P. KRENZER • CARLA M. KRIVAK • WILLIAM M. KROSHL • KIN-CHUN K. KWONG • MARISA A. LALEKOS • DAVID B. LAVALLEE • JAMES C. LEARY • MICHELLE LEE • CRYSTAL D. LEMLEY • MICHAEL P. LENZI • ROSEMARY E. LEROUX • TRENA C. LILLY • SHARON X. LING • SHAWN P. LONDO • JOSEPH M. LUSTIG • HOPE A. MACKENZIE • VERNELLE A. MADISON • JOAN C. MANILI • SHIRA M. MARKOWITZ • JOHN A. MARKS • KAREN S. MARSICO • MICHAEL J. MASSARELLI • KATHERINE P. MATTHEWS • BARBARA A. MCBRIEN • CHRISTOPHER S. MCDONALD • ERIN M. MCDONALD • JEFFREY M. MCDOUGALL • CHRISTINE M. MCLEAN • DANIEL J. MCMORROW • CHARLES B. MCVEY • WILLIAM W. MENTZER • TIMOTHY A. MEUSHAW • JAMES F. MILLER • CHARLES D. MILLIGAN • SANDRA A. MISCH • MICHELE E. MITCHELL • MICHAEL F. MONIUS • MICHAEL G. MOORE • ZHIJING G. MOU • TERRENCE L. MUCHA • ELIZABETH A. MURPHY • KEVIN E. MURPHY • MAUREEN MUSTAPICH • STEPHEN E. MYERS • WANDA L. NELSON • MICHAEL J. NEUENHOFF • MICHAEL S. NEWELL • MICHAEL A. NICEWICZ • JOSEPH E. NICKERSON • JEFFREY H. NIEPORENT • JOHN M. NOLEN • STANLEY J. NOVINSKY III • STEVEN J. OFFENBACHER • CYNTHIA C. O'KEEFE • JOHN M. O'NEIL • RYAN P. O'NEIL • MARJORIE V. O'RIORDAN • DOUGLAS A. OURSLER • LEE M. OZBUN • BRANT D. PALMQUIST • THOMAS P. PARKS • ALAN D. PATRICK • EDWARD K. PATRICK • DENNIS S. PATRONE • CHARLES M. PATZELT • KEVIN B. PETTEE • CHRISTINE D. PIATKO • DENTE D. POLAND • GEORGE W. POLLITT • GREGORY E. PRIEUR • JOSEPH H. PROSSER • LOUIS A. RANDALL • CLIFFORD L. RATLIFF • TIMOTHY D. REARDON • STEPHEN P. REED • JARRETT F. REID • JOHN D. REID • SARAH E. RENNIE • ROGER R. RHUDY • THAREN RICE • IOLA M. RICHARDSON • REGINALD S. RICHARDSON • JAMES W. RIDGLEY • THOMAS K. RITTERHOFF • BRIAN P. RITTERMANN • JAN M. RIZZUTO • MICHAEL D. ROBINSON • ROBERT P. ROGER • GABE D. ROGERS • DAVID R. ROTH • KURT A. RUCKELSHAUS • JAMES R. RUTH • CRAIG R. RUTHERFORD • ANSHU SAKSENA • MARK A. SALADA • COLLIN W. SCHAFFER • PETER F. SCHOLL • DAVID L. SCHOLLER • STEVEN J. SCHWAN • CRAIG J. SCOTT • WILEY L. SCRIVNER • MARTHA A. SHAFER • JANINE L. SHAFFER-BRILL • HONGXING S. SHAPIRO • BARBARA A. SHAPTER • WEN-JONG SHYONG • RAJEEV S. SIGAMONEY • GENE P. SIGGINS JR. • MICHAEL J. SILBERGLITT • STEPHEN H. SILVIOUS SR. • MARK M. SKRAKOWSKI • CARL O. SMITH JR. • PAMELA A. SMITH • PETER L. SMITH • JILL C. SNAVELY • LAURENCE J. SOUDER • DEBRA L. SPANGLER • REBECCA V. ST. CLAIR • ABRIAN E. STEVENS • JACQUELINE A. STOCK • DINA TADY • JOHN J. TAMER • ROBERT M. TAYLOR JR. • DEANNA K. TEMKIN • JANICE A. TERRY • JASON O. THORPE • HALA J. TOMEY • DONALD R. TRACEY • MARIANNE C. TROSSBACH • TAMARA L. TUCKER • SABIHA UMAR • NAUMAN UPPAL • RONALD J. VAUK • RONALD J. VERVACK JR. • PAUL A. VICHOT • KEVIN E. WADDELL • DAVID A. WALLACE • WILLIAM C. WALTON • I-JENG WANG • WINNIE E. WEEKS • EDWARD F. WEITZNER • HAROLD R. WHITE JR. • JOSEPH WIELGOSZ • PHILLIP G. WILKINS • KERRY WILLIAMS • ARTHUR N. WILLOUGHBY • BARBARA A. WILSON • FRANK H. WINTERLING • HELENE L. WINTERS • GARY C. WORRELL • JAMES C. WRIGHT • ARDEN E. YOUNG • MINDYU • XUN ZHU • DIETER ZOELLNER • **1998** • MICHAEL A. ALLEN • RICHARD C. ANDERSON • MIQUEL D. ANTOINE • ROGER B. ARROWOOD • KOJO ASAFO-AGYEI • RA'ID S. AWADALLAH • DENNIS W. BAILEY • KEVIN C. BALDWIN • JEFFREY D. BARTON • JUERNENE F. BASS • ANDREW N. BEACH III • ROBERT C. BEAN • MICHAEL R. BEHR • JAMES S. BELLE • ANDREW W. BENNETT JR. • KEVIN M. BETTS • NINA S. BLACKMON • CHRISTOPHER M. BOSWELL • DAVID J. BOTTO • MICHAEL P. BOYLE • JACK L. BURBANK • STEVEN P. BURNS • ROBERT C. CAPELLINI • ZACHARIAH O. CARLON • KEITH S. CARUSO • CHRISTIAN E. CASILLAS • DEBORAH K. CHEN • DENBY R. CHEW • CHRISTINA T. CHOMEL • JUSTIN A. CHOMEL • STANLEY L. CHRISTIAN • ANTHONY L. CLINTON • SHERRELL L. COMPTON • JEFFREY E. CONTE • TIMOTHY J. CORNISH • MARY E. CUMOR • HEATHER L. CURRAN • M. T. DANDASHI • MARGARET ANN G. DARRIN • DAWN G. DAVIS • OCTAVIA L. DAVIS • ANTHONY F. DEBELLA • RICHARD J. DEBOLT • DANIEL J. DECICCO • ANGELO DIAZ • EVELYN R. DIXON • VIRENDRA K. DOGRA • JOHN H. EARLE • ROBERT T. EDWARDS • ROBERT H. FEWSTER • RANDALL F. FISCHBACH • KOK S. FONG • NICOLA J. FOX • KEITH L. FRANCIS • TERRY L. FRANK • TIMOTHY M. FREY • GWENDOLYN L. FURR • ROBERT B. GAITHER JR. • RAYMOND D. GANT • GREGORY L. GERSHMAN • DONALD L. GEYER • CRISTINA L. GILLASPIE • RAYMOND J. GILLIN • TIMOTHY C. GION • ELI J. GLASER • ELVA A. GRAY • MATTHEW W. GREEN • WILLIAM K. HALL • DAVID K. HAN • MARY E. HARRIS • DAVID V. HEINBUCH • JOSHUA M. HENLY • WILLIE E. HIRES • GEORGE C. HO • RAYMOND P. HOGAN • NATHAN J. HORNBURG • ANNE HORNER • JEAN C. HORTON • DOUGLAS B. HUDSON • EDWARD E. HUME JR. • LINDA A. HUNT • JAMES J. JACKSON • PETER W. JACOBUS • BARBARA G. JOHNSON • WILLIAM H. JONES JR. • PANKAJ R. KARNIK • PATRICK J. KARVAR • ALLEN C. KEENEY • DANIEL KIM • MICHAEL KLEINBERGER • SANAE D. KUBOTA • ANDREW LEE • ANDREW M. LENNON • PAGE K. LEVENDIS • CYNTHIA L. LEWIS • CAROL B. LEYDIG • KIMBERLY A. LICHTENBERG • WIRAK LIM • REGINA A. LOUIS • LAURA M. LOYNES • PATRICK J. MACDONALD • VALERIE A. MALLDER • KATHERINE A. MALLOY • PERRY M. MALOUF • JODY L. MARCHAND • REBECCA M. MARINER • JANE E. MCDUFFIE • LORA-LEE L. MCHALE • CRAIG A. MELLENDICK • SCOTT C. MILLER • BARRY L. MILLS • DEANNA L. MORROCCO • RESA A. MUHLER • STACY D. MURPHY • ROBERT P. NANCE • MASAHITO NOSE • GARY B. OBENSKI • JAMES M. O'CONNOR • KIMBERLEY A. PALMER • DEVASHISH N. PARIKH • CHAD R. PATTERSON • JOSHUA C. PATTERSON • ADAM V. PETERSON • LINDA A. PHIPPS • SARAH J. PIEKUT • WILBERT F. PIERSON • STEVEN R. PINE • LISA K. PRESTON • RONALD C. PRIETZ JR. • DEBORAH R. PROCTOR • MATTHEW E. ROSENTHAL • KARL F. RUPPERT • RICHARD M. RUZICKA • GURPARTAP S. SANDHOO • RENAE L. SCHEIBER • LYNN P. SCHEIDER • ROBERT W. SCHIRMER • STEPHEN F. SCHREURS • DIANA SCHULIN • JOHN L. SCHULTZ • ROBERT E. SCHULTZ • KIM K. SHAW • DANIEL H. SIMON • ELIZABETH R. SKINNER • TRACIE H. SMART • WILLIAM E. SMITH JR. • ROBERT K. SMITH • TANDIWE B. SMITH • JUSTIN C. SPORER • JANIS E. ST. CLAIR • KIM M. STERRETT • JAMES M. STRATTON • CYNTHIA A. STREAMER • AVAINE STRONG • JEFFREY R. SUAREZ • RANDOLPH T. TATE • SCOTT T. TAYLOR • CAROLYN A. THOMAS • CASSIE M. THOMAS • LISA M. TOPLANSKY • ANNETTE M. UY • FRANCOIS P. VAN REMOORTERE • BETH A. VARNEY • REBECCA F. VERTES • KURT A. WALRAVEN • NADIR H. WASHINGTON • PATRICIA L. WATKINS • AMY S. WELLS • ANNE-MARIE A. WILLIAMS • CHRISTIAN P. WILLIAMS • PAMELA M. WISDOM • NANCY E. WOODS • JOHN D. WYLIE • **1999** • JULIA ABRAHAMS • ASHOK K. AGRAWAL • PRADEEP K. AGRAWAL • KEVIN G. AILINGER • FRANCIS R. ALI IV • STEFAN R. ALLEN • HOLLIS H. AMBROSE • JEFFREY S. ANGELL • DAVID G. ATHMAN JR. • EVAN M. ATKINSON • LEO D. BALK • BENJAMIN H. BARNUM • GEORGE R. BARRETT • JAMES T. BEATTY JR. • KERRI B. BEISSER • ERIC A. BENFER • JACQUELINE A. BERNARDI • PAUL A. BIENHOFF • AMY J. BILLUPS • IRA M. BLATSTEIN • PATRICK S. BLEVINS • ANN B. BONNER • JOHN C. BRISCOE • JOSHUA B. BROADWATER • ROLAND J. BROOKS • JEFFREY C. BROWN • MYRON Z. BROWN • MICHAEL R. BUCKLEY • HASANI R. CARAWAY • REBECCA CASANOVA • MICHAEL W. CASTLE • YAMIL J. CHAAR • ROBERT W. CHALMERS • JOHN L. CHAMPION • MARGIE R. CHAR • JAMES C. CLANCY • CHARLOTTE COLYAR • JONATHAN D. COOPERSMITH • DERYN E. CROCKETT • JAMES M. DANG • BRADLEY J. DAVID • JOHN M. DAVIES • COLLEEN A. DAVIS • ANNE M. DEMAJISTRE • JONATHAN T. DESENA • DONALD J. DOW • ALLEN J. DRIVER • LEE J. DUCHARME • DELALI DZIRASA • JENNIFER L. ECKER • ROBERT C. EIDSON • TANOS M. ELFOUHAILY • VICTOR I. EMELI JR. • ERIC A. ERICSON • WILLIAM P. ERVIN • ERIC R. FARMER • TIMOTHY W. FELDMANN • CLAYTON R. FINK • BARRY L. FLANAGAN • DAVID A. FLANIGAN • PAUL D. FOTHERINGHAM • CONSTANTINE M. FRANGOS • JONATHAN Z. GEHMAN • STEVEN E. GEMENY • ALICE L. GERSH • ANGELA M. GILMOUR • ANTHONY J. GLAZIER • FLORIE A. GODDARD • TODD A. GOLDFINGER • CAROLINE R. GOODMAN • JOSEPH R. GORNATI • ROBERT E. GRACE • ERNEST R. GRAF • KRISTIN M. GRAY • HAL S. GREENWALD • DOUGLAS E. GROSS • DOMINICK GULOTTA • LINDA G. GURRY • PAUL GUSH • JOSEPH W. HABER • TANISHA O. HALL • MARVINE P. HAMNER • BRIAN W. HARRIS • GREGG A. HARRISON • DANIEL J. HEIN • ROBERT L. HENDERSON • JOHN P. HESLIN • ROBERT T. HIDER JR. • BONNIE L. HIGGS • ELIZABETH U. HILL • CHRISTIAN K. HOGE • LETITIA A. HOGUE • GENE G. HOLLAND • BRIAN L. HOLUB • JOHN C. HOOVER • MARIO C. HOWE • WILLIAM K HUDSON • DAVID W. HUTCHISON • LESLIE M. JACOBI • LYNETTE W. JENNINGS • ERIC A. JOHNSON • ERIK W. JOHNSON • LOUIS E. JOHNSON • PREM K. JOHNSON • DAVID H. JONES • AMY K. KARLSON • CRAIG A. KELLY • JOHN F. KINZER • KRISTIN L. KOBLISH • MARC A. KOLODNER • WILLIAM M. LABUDA • ALLISON A. LAPIERRE • CRISTAL D. LAPRADE • CYNTHIA S. LATHE • DARLENE LATTIMER • ROBERT R. LECORCHICK • WILLIAM J. LEES • MICHAEL P. LEVESQUE • LAUREN A. LEVY • WILLIAM M. LEWIS • KENNETH R. LOHR • JAMES LONGO • WAYNE A. LOSCHEN • MICHAEL LUCKS • BARBARA A. MACBRIDE • MARK N. MARTIN • CAROL MAYS • MARK E. MCCREEVY • ANDREW D. MEEKINS • NAIM M. MERHEB • STEPHEN P. MICHAELS • ADAM J. MILLER • BRUCE E. MILLER • MYCHAL R. MILLER • MISTRA MOAZAMI • CHRISTOPHER A. MONACO • CHARLES L. MONJO • KARA L. MOORE • ALBERT B. MUADDI • EDWARD G. MUHLER • MERERTU MULUGETA • SEAN P. MURPHY • PATSY A. MYERS • WILLIAM N. MYERS • TONYA C. NEAL • CARLINA Z. NEUMANN • MANUEL R. NEVES • PAULINE M. O'CONNOR • ERIC A. OLSEN • ANTHONY G. OPEKA • STEPHEN M. ORLOFF • SUSAN T. PAGAN • PETER J. PARASKA • HYON W. PARK • ROBERT M. PATCHAN • DOUGLAS E. PAUNIL • GARY E. PECK • KAREN S. PENNY • RON Y. PEREL • ALEXANDER S. PERRY • RICHARD PITRE • CHARLIE W. PITTMAN JR. • DAVID W. PORTER • MARY M. POWERS • MICHAEL A. PRATSCHER • LOUISE M. PROCKTER • VICKI B. QUALLS • GENE RABER • LINDA R. REESE • LISA C. REULE • JOHN K. RHOADS • JOHN W. RIGGIN III • RICHARD T. ROCA • STEPHEN B. ROGERS • KENNETH W. ROSS • STEPHEN A. ROSS • CHRISTOPHER M. RYDER • JEAN G. SAINT LOUIS • DAVID M. SAPP • DAVID H. SCHEIDT • IRINA T. SCHENERMAN • KENNETH M. SCHMIDT • RICKE O. SHANK • PETER J. SHARER • JOHN L. SHISSLER III • STEVE K. SHOLLENBERGER • JIH-HONG SHUE • ALETHEA SMALLS • BERNARD SMITH • SAMUEL J. SOPLEY • CHRISTOPHER T. SOLLUTTO • MICHAEL P. SPITCAUFSKY • VINCENT R. ST. GEORGE • PETER STANKOVICH • LAURA A. STEACY • ROBERT G. STRADER JR. • LOUIS E. STRIGARI • KATHERINE A. SULLIVAN • RICHARD S. SVOBODA • WAYNE E. SWANN • JAMES J. SYLVESTER • ELSAYED R. TALAAT • JENKA C. TATA • JUDITH G. THEODORI • DIMITRIOS N. THIAKOS • TERENCE F. THOMAS • ANTHONY T. TRIPOLI • RONALD E. VERBOS • KUSHAGRA VERMA • ROBERT E. WALLIS • SUZANNE C. WALTS • DAVID K. WAWRO • JENNI C. WEAN • ELISSA • **2000** • PATRICIA L. ADAMS • RICHARD C. ADAMS • ZACHARY AGATSTEIN • ANTHONY Q. AIKEN • LESLIE G. ALLEN • NORMA J. ALLEN • VICKIE L. ALLEN • GAIL M. ALLENDER • KATHERINE J. ALLENDER • JACK M. ANDERSON JR. • FRANK D. ANDERSON • MICHAEL P. ANDERSON • NICOLE L. ANDERSON • SARA J. ANGARITA • MARC W. APPLEGATE • ADAM K. ARABIAN • MEHRAN ARMAND • ANDREW M. ASHER • MICHAEL A. ATKINSON • TIMOTHY J. ATKINSON • ERIK N. AUGER • RICHARD D. AVILA • JOHN M. BACON II • SHERIDAN R. BAILEY • GRAHAM Z. BAKER • MICHAEL J. BALUCK JR. • ROBERT J. BAMBERGER JR. • AMIT BANERJEE • FREEMAN E. BANKS • JOHN F. BARNES • WILLIAM K. BARTLEY • MARTIN A. BASSIN • MATTHEW D. BAUGHMAN • AMY J. BAYES • CHARLES H. BAZZLE • JOHN E. BEARD • CHRISTOPHER T. BEATTY SR. • PETER D. BEDINI • EDWARD A. BEIGEL • ADAM A. BEKIT • JEAN T. BELL • JOSEPH L. BENDEN • ANDREA J. BENDER • CAROL M. BENDLIN • JOHN BENSON • JUSTUS BENSON • PHILLIP A. BERLINICKE • ARTHUR D. BERNARD • CAROLYN D. BETHEA • BARRY V. BETTS • MARK W. BETTS • RAYMOND S. BIRDSELL • STEPHEN M. BJERKAAS • ROSS A. BLAUWKAMP • PATRICIA M. BOGGS • JENNIFER A. BONNEY-RAY • MELISSA L. BOSSIE • ROSIE V. BOWEN • DAVID C. BOWER • TIMOTHY P. BOYLE • JOHN E. BRADY JR. • STEVEN D. BRAGUE • PONTUS C. BRANDT • JESSICA M. BRAUN • PATRICIA A. BRECH • VINCENT R. BRODERICK • OTIS BROOKS JR. • KEITH D. BROWN • PAMELA R. BROWN • JOHN J. BRUBAKER • JONATHAN R. BRUZZI • ANNE B. BRYANT • ANNETTE E. BUCHAL • CHRISTIAN E. BUCKINGHAM • JASON C. BUNN • PHILLIP O. BUNTS • KATHERINE R. BURNS • LOUIS P. BUTLER • CHRIS J. CALAMARI • RICHIE E. CAMPBELL • KIMBERLY M. CAPERS • CYNTHIA D. CARR • BRADLEY D. CARSON • WAYNE C. CARSON • DON E. CARTER • ANNE-MARIE CASTILLO • JENNIFER L. CHAFFEE • STEPHEN C. CHAN • GLENN A. CHASE • ROGER J. CHEN • KRISHNA R. CHENNAMANENI • DONALD E. CHESLEY • TECK H. CHOO • ROBERT B. CHRISTIANSEN JR. • CLAUDIA CHUNG • CAROL J. CLARK • CHARLES R. CLARK • MARION E. CLARK • DAVID O. CLEVELAND • ALLISON E. CLINE • JOHN S. CLINGERMAN • MARTHA J. COATES • STEVEN L. COLEMAN • DAVID J. COLLIE • JOSEPH M. COMPERIATE • JONATHAN L. COOK • WENDY A. CORRETT • CAROLINE S. COSENTINO • CASH J. COSTELLO • SHARON L. COSTIGAN • JOSEPH N. CRAIG • JAMES C. CROOKSTON • AMELIA M. CUBBAGE-LAIN • LAURA M. CURRY • ROSEMARY A. DALEY • WILLIAM P. D'AMICO • JONATHAN J. DAMMONS • MICHAEL K. DANIEL • CHARLES G. DARRELL • LAUREN B. DAVIS • MARK A. DAVIS • TASHA N. DAVIS • NORA R. DAY • SUSAN L. DEARDEN • DAVID A. DECAMARA • CAROLE B. DERRICK • ROBERT M. DEVERS • JANA L. DEWITT • MARJORIE D. DICKEY • GRACE R. DIPIETRO • LOUIS DISTEFANO • SUSAN C. DOERING • JAMES L. DOUGHTY • MICHELLE D. DOUGLASS • RUSSELL M. DOUTHETT JR. • SHERRY A. DRABEK • MARVIN E. DREWRY • ROBERT P. DRUPP • RAYMOND A. DUDDERAR • MICHELLE R. DUDLEY • TIMOTHY S. DUNLEVY • MARK S. DYESS • STEPHEN J. EAGLES JR. • LANCE E. EARWOOD • DONNA L. EAST • LOU ANN ELINE • DONNA M. ELLIOTT • ANDREW D. ELLIS • DANIEL W. ENGFER • CHARLES L. ENSEY JR. • JAMES J. FALISE JR. • DAWNIELLE FARRAR-GAINES • MICHAEL A. FATEMI • CHRISTINE S. FATZ • ANDREW B. FELDMAN • PATRICK B. FELDMAN • JENNIFER A. FERAT • JOSE M. FERNANDEZ VEGA • WALTER G. FIELDS JR. • CHRISTINE M. FINK • NANCY M. FINTA • FISSEHA B. FIRESENBET • JENNIFER M. FISCHER • JAMES G. FITZGERALD • WILLIAM L. FLEMING • BRIAN K. FLEMMING • ANDREW A. FLERLAGE • GREGORY I. FLOWERS • BRAND I. FORTNER • RICHARD K. FOSTER • PAUL A. FRANK • JOSEPH M. FREEZE • KRISTIN A. FRETZ • JOANNE S. FREY • BARBARA L. FRIEND • THOMAS M. FRITZ • DEREK L. FULK • RAYMOND N. FULTON JR. • LEE ANN D. FULTS • BRIAN K. FUNK • ROBERT M. FURROW • MICHAEL F. GALLAGHER • GUILE R. GAMBHIR • MANJULA GANAPATHI • STANLEY J. GANTZ JR. • JOAN C. GARRETT • ELIZABETH L. GARTLAND • ROBERT E. GAYLOR • TAMMY K. GEORGIANNA • EMMANOUIL K. GEORGOULIS • JOHN H. GESKEY II • ROBIN C. GETTIER • DAVID R. GIBSON JR. • BEATRICE M. GIBSON • AMIKAM J. GILAD • REBECCA J. GLASS • MARTIN L. GOMEZ • SANDRA L. GORDON • SHERI D. GORHAM • KEVIN H. GORMALLY • GEORGE I. GRAHAM SR. • SHINDANA S. GRANDISON • STEPHEN M. GRANT • LAURA A. GREBE • ERIC M. GREENBERG • IRENE GREENBERGER • DANIEL G. GREENSPAN • MICHELLE C. GREINER • RUTH G. GRESSER • MATTHEW P. GREY • DAVID C. GROSH • WAYNE R. GRUNBERG • KATHLEEN C. GUTHRIE • CATHERINE A. GUYER • JULIO E. GUZMAN • ERIN E. HACKETT • ANGELA T. HALL • MONIQUE Y. HAMILTON • ANDREW J. HARRIS • STUART D. HARSHBARGER • GEORGE W. HARVEY JR. • MAUREEN F. HARVEY • MOHAMMAD R. HASHEMIAN • CHRISTOPHER B. HASKINS • SUZANNE HASSELL • PATRICIA A. HAWLEY • DAVID J. HEINE • CHERILYN M. HENDRIX • MELVIN E. HENNESSY JR. • KAREN Y. HICKS • STUART W. HILL • TRACY A. HILL • KEN C. HO • MARSHA A. HODGE • ROBERT H. HOLDER III • CHARLES G. HOLIDAY II • TENISHA R. HOLLOWAY • KARL J. HOLUB • ROBERT H. HOOD • CATHERINE A. HORN • DARYL M. HORREY SR. • RONALD L. HOWE • KEVIN W. HUBER • AARON K. HULL • MICHAEL R. HUNTER • HUGH H. HURT III • TOAN B. HUYNH • ALEXANDER G. IHDE • HARITH A. IKRAM • L. S. INGRAM • JOANY JACKMAN • NYKIA L. JACKSON • MARK S. JACOBS • ELIZABETH A. JARVI • SHAO-CHIANG J. JEN • AMY C. JOHNSON • JONATHAN S. JOHNSON • THOMAS E. JOHNSON • ELIZABETH R. JONES • JOANETTE JONES • SOPHIE A. JONES • VIOLA A. JONES • TROY E. JORDAN • JANENE A. KALB • EFFIE J. KANE • BRIAN L. KANTSIPER • CRAIG J. KAPLAN • WILLIAM T. KASCH • AARON KATZ • JEFFREY A. KEITH • MARY R. KELLER • JEFFREY S. KELLEY • SEAN C. KELLY • CHARLES W. KERECHANIN II • DAVID M. KIICK • HYOSUB KIL • DAVID I. KIM • KATRINA M. KINDLE • TONETTE R. KING • MARK E. KINZIE • GERALD R. KIRWIN • JOHN M. KLIMEK • TAMMY A. KOLARIK • ANUROOP KOTHA • SANDRA L. KOURCE • YANNI A. KOUSKOULAS • STEVEN M. KRAFFT • KARL D. KREATSCHMAN • CHRISTOPHER J. KRUPIARZ • MARY C. KUHNS • MICHAEL C. KULKUSKY • GLENN J. KUSTER • MICHAEL T. LAMAR • ROBERT J. LAMPRON JR. • ALAN H. LANDAY • ROLAND D. LANG JR. • STEVEN E. LANGS • DAVID LARIO LOYO • BRIAN K. LARSON • SCOTT M. LASLEY • SEAN C. LAUGHERY • DAVID S. LAWRENCE • GEOFFREY S. LAWRENCE • BARBARA A. LEARY • BRYAN J. LEAVENS • KIM J. LEE • SHERLEY A. LEE • KENNETH J. LEENSTRA • ESTHER M. LEEPER • RANDY A. LEMIEUX • FREDDIE C. LEWIS JR. • DOUGLAS L. LEWIS • MELANI A. LEWIS • CHERYL L. LIBERTO • KAY K. LIN • TIMOTHY A. LIPPY • EDWARD B. LITTLEFORD • STEFANO A. LIVI • CHRISTINA S. LOPEZ • BRIAN K. LOUGHERY • SARAH B. LUDDY • WILLIAM L. LUEDEMAN • RHONDA D. LYNN • WILLIAM M. MACIEJEWSKI • DAVID D. MAGNELLI • MARTHA B. MALLARDI • LYNDA D. MALLORY • GEOFFREY A. MARCUS • JUDITH H. MARCUS • ROYCE C. MARSINGILL JR. • NORMA J. MARTIG • MICHAEL A. MARTIN • RAE S. MASON • LAWRENCE MATHIS • DWAYNE A. MCCALL • ANDREW A. MCCARTER • CHRISTOPHER B. MCCUBBIN • ROBERT L. MCDONALD • MARGARET A. MCGARRY • LARRY D. MCGEE • GRACE M. MCGONNIGAL • ROBERT C. MCMAHON JR. • ALLAN D. MCQUARRIE • MARILYN J. MEAGHER • LISA G. MERCILLIOTT • MARISSA D. MERCREADY • ANDREW C. MERKLE • NELSON E. MERTZ • THOMAS J. MEYERS • WESLEY P. MILLARD • CRAIG MILLER • JOEL D. MILLER • MICHAEL L. MILLER • ROBERT P. MILLER • KATHERINE F. MILLS • GERRY MON • MICHAEL F. MONTGOMERY • ROBIN L. MONTGOMERY • ADAM T. MOODY • KAMARIA I. MOON • FAHMEENA D. MOORE • TODD F. MOORE • WANDA M. MOORE • RALPH L. MORGAN • MELANIE L. MORRIS • ROBERT S. MORRIS • WILLIAM H. MOSBERG IV • DANIEL P. MUHONEN • JAMES R. MUMAW • BENJAMIN T. MUNION • ERIC C. NABER • PAUL B. NEEB • DIANE C. NEMEC • MELANIE G. NEWBROUGH • BINH T. NGUYEN • WENDY L. NIBECK • NICOLE M. NICHOLSON • STEPHEN M. NICKEY • LOWELL T. NIEMAN • MARY NIEMELA • CAROL A. NOLF • MICHAEL H. NOLL • RUTH N. O'BRIEN • CYNTHIA A. OETTING • HASAN N. OGUZ • TONY ONG • ALEX I. ONYENWE • RASHEED T. ORIDEDI • DAVID J. ORLIN • CONRAD F. ORLOFF • DANIEL J. O'SHAUGHNESSY • SRCAN OSMANAGICH • GAIL K. OXTON • MICHAEL E. PAFFORD • SEUNG H. PAK • SEZIN A. PALMER • JEFFREY L. PARKE • KEVIN W. PARKER • NATHAN T. PARKER • NANCY L. PARSONS • BARTON L. PAULHAMUS • DONNA C. PAULHAMUS • ASHLEY L. PAYNE • DAVID E. PEACOCK • KIM A. PERKOSKI • MARGARET R. PERRY • JEFFREY A. PETERSON • KAREEM M. PETTEWAY • JAMES S. PETTIGREW SR. • NAM C. PHAMDO • WILLIAM C. PHELPS III • DENTON W. PICKETT • ANDREW T. POAST • RICHARD R. PORTER • JOSEPH A. PRICE • SCOTT R. PRIETZ • ROBERT PUDELKA • LESLIE F. PUGH • CLARENCE E. PURVIS • ALEXANDRA M. QUINN • CATHY A. QUINN • LINDA L. RABER • LIANE B. RAMAC-THOMAS • JANICE A. RAMIREZ • FRANK O. RANDALL • ASEEM H. RAVAL • MINHAJ RAZA • BRIAN E. REARDON • HEATHER M. REARDON • RUSSELL J. REDMAN • RON E. REMILLARD • DANIEL M. RENFRO • KYONG-SOOK RHEE • EDGAR A. RHODES • WALTER W. RICE • BRANDON K. RICHARD • ROBERT A. RICHARDS • FRANCES J. RICHARDSON • JENNIFER ROBERTS • WILLIAM C. ROBINSON • CHRISTOPHER J. RODRIGUEZ • ROSE T. RODRIGUEZ • JEAN L. ROEHL • ERIC W. ROGALA • EDWARD J. ROTH • LORI A. ROWLAND • ANUPOMA S. ROZARIO • ROBERT W. RUBY • ROBERT A. RUMPF • MARC C. RUPINTA • BRUCE R. RUSSELL • JOHN J. RYAN JR. • MAGDA M. SAINA • EZEQUIEL G. SALAZAR • JOHN SAMSUNDAR • APRIL D. SAXON • PETER A. SCALA • MATTHEW G. SCARLETT • BARBARA A. SCELSI • MARK O. SCHLEGEL • BRIAN G. SCHNEIDER • DOUGLAS R. SCHUBERT • PETER A. SCHUMACHER • ROBERT C. SCHUYLER • BRYAN C. SCHWINN • BRUCE D. SCOTT JR. • ROBERT A. SEALOCK • CANDECE D. SELING • ELISA G. SHAPIRO • JOSEPH S. SHAW • R. J. SHEPHERD • DAVID J. SHIBILSKY • VERNON J. SILL JR. • CHARLETTE R. SILVA • DANIEL J. SILVERA • PETER R. SILVERGLATE • EDWARD A. SIMON • GORDON L. SISLER • REBECCA A. SKIDMORE • JENNIFER H. SKINNER • JONATHAN D. SKINNER • LAURIE A. SLATNISKE • LAMONT SLIGH • JACQUELINE SLOWE-CROSLAND • CARROL D. SMART • GEORGE A. SMITH JR. • ERICKA D. SMITH • MARY E. SMITHSON • ANNE J. SOLA • ROBERT T. SORANNO • MARY E. SOULES • TERRI L. SPITCAUFSKY • CHAD R. SPROUSE • BRIAN L. SPURGEON • DIPAK K. SRINIVASAN • RAMAKRISHNAN K. SRINIVASAN • RICHARD C. STEWART • JASON A. STIPES • CHRISTOPHER I. STONE • JANICE H. STRANGE • ROBYN M. STROSNIDER • JAMES R. STUTLER • KENNETH W. SUNDERLAND • JOHN M. SUTTON • DAWNA L. SWARTZ • MARIAN SWIRSKI • RAFAL P. SZCZEPANOWSKI • DAVID J. TACK • DAVID W. TART • RAEANNE L. TENNYSON • JAMES M. TEPE • ROGER E. THIBAUDEAU JR. • DENISE Y. THOMAS • MICHAEL K. THOMAS • RAJIV G. THOMAS • CHRISTOPHER L. THOMPSON • GREGORY L. THOMPSON • PATRICK L. THOMPSON • STEPHEN A. THOREN • NORMA L. TODD • BRUCE A. TOTH • JODI L. TRAUTMAN-PHELPS • GEORGE S. TRAVEZ • ROBERT S. TRESSLER • BARBARA J. TRUCKENBRODT • SIDNEY E. TURNER • WILLIAM M. TURNER • SCOTT M. TYSON • ABHA UPADHYAYA • CHRISTINA J. UY • ROBIN M. VAUGHAN • KENNETH E. VERBRUGGE • MICHAEL A. VERMILYE • JEFFREY M. VERTHEIN • GEORGE G. VETTICAD • PAMELA L. VIGDERHOUSE • JENNIFER A. VINCENT • RICHARD L. VIRGILIO • RICHARD W. VOGT • LIMING M. VOO • GLENN R. WAGNER SR. • JAMES R. WALRAVEN • JOSEPH A. WALTERS • CHARLOTTE H. WANG • THOMAS C. WANN • KEVIN M. WARREN • SHIRLEY A. WARREN • DONALD WATKINS • JO-ANN R. WEAVER • BRANDI A. WEESE • BRADFORD S. WEIR • RACHEL E. WEIR • PAUL A. WEISMAN • MICHELE B. WEISS • KAIDI WENG • PAUL R. WESCOAT JR. • DANIELLE M. WESOLEK • RONALD L. WHITE JR. • TIMOTHY L. WHITE SR. • BRIAN W. WHITE • FRED D. WHITING • KAREN M. WIEPRECHT • PENNY L. WILLIAMS JR. • DAVID T. WILLIAMS • DONNA WILLIAMS • ADEYINKA O. WINDAPO • NATHANIEL S. WINSTEAD • ROBERT W. WISE • MARY A. WITCHER • THOMAS D. WOLF • LEEHA H. WOOD • DENISE A. WORRELL • DONNA M. WORTMAN • JOANN N. WYATT • MICHAEL D. WYNNE • KWADWO A. YEBOAH • HAROLD D. YOUNG • TRACEY L. YOUNG • MATTHEW J. YOUNGMANN • FRANK A. ZAWADA • YONGLIANG ZHANG • DUNJA S. ZIOMEK

As we celebrate our 75th anniversary, we extend our gratitude to the government sponsors and industry partners with whom we have collaborated since our founding in 1942. Our success and value as a national resource depend on the strong relationships we have built with these groups, and we look forward to addressing future challenges together.

Defining Innovations

A History of The Johns Hopkins University Applied Physics Laboratory

Russ Banham

The Johns Hopkins University Applied Physics Laboratory

11100 Johns Hopkins Road, Laurel, Maryland 20723-6099

240-228-5000

www.jhuapl.edu

Printed in the United States of America

21 20 19 18 17   1 2 3 4 5

ISBN 978-0-9983158-0-5

Library of Congress Cataloging-in-Publication Data

Names: Banham, Russ, author. | Johns Hopkins University. Applied Physics
   Laboratory, issuing body.
Title: Defining innovations : a history of the Johns Hopkins University
   Applied Physics Laboratory / Russ Banham.
Description: Laurel, Maryland : The Johns Hopkins University Applied Physics
   Laboratory, [2017] | Includes index.
Identifiers: LCCN 2016050873| ISBN 9780998315805 (hardcover) | ISBN
   099831580X (hardcover) | ISBN 9780998315812 (pdf) | ISBN 0998315818 (pdf)
Subjects: LCSH: Johns Hopkins University. Applied Physics
   Laboratory--History.
Classification: LCC QC51.U62 B36 2017 | DDC 620.0072/075281--dc23LC record available at https://lccn.loc.gov/2016050873

DISTRIBUTION STATEMENT A. Approved for public release; distribution is unlimited.

On the cover: The images on the cover of this book represent a sample of the Laboratory's many critical contributions during its first 75 years. See page 138 for information about these milestones.

On the inside cover pages: Listed alphabetically by the year they joined APL are the names of the more than 15,000 people who have worked at the Lab since its founding. The names are printed across photos that symbolize the connection between the Laboratory's past, present, and future.

FSC
www.fsc.org
MIX
Paper from
responsible sources
FSC® C005744

Contents

From the University

At my installation as president of Johns Hopkins University in 2009, I spoke of the extraordinary and inexorable link between the values upon which we were founded as our nation's first research university and the unique experiment that is America, with its "can-do" pragmatism, boundless optimism, lofty ambition, and brave daring.

These ideals are exemplified across our divisions, but nowhere more so than at our Applied Physics Laboratory. For the past 75 years, the Lab and its staff members have tackled many of our nation's most complex and critical scientific challenges, spanning the oceans' depths to the outer reaches of space.

From its pioneering efforts to perfect a fuze that helped turn the tide of World War II and development of the world's first global satellite navigation system in the 1960s, to its more recent creation of the world's most advanced prosthetic limb, APL has epitomized the culture of innovation, experimentation, and persistence we aspire to as a university. APL's engineers and scientists have laid the foundation for space exploration missions that have visited every planet in our solar system. They also are responsible for generations of advanced technologies and systems that protect our nation and those who serve it, and secure the cyber networks we rely on in our everyday lives.

We are truly proud of all these achievements as well as the Lab's ongoing work to ensure the security of our nation and its citizens even as it advances knowledge at the frontiers of science and engineering.

Ronald J. Daniels
President, Johns Hopkins University

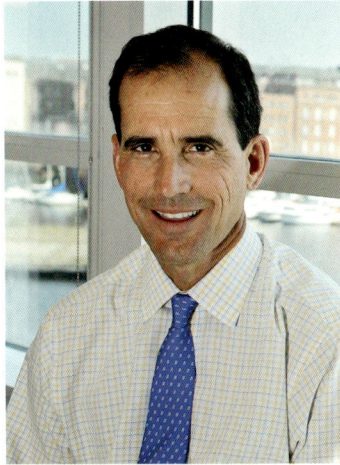

From the Board

On the inside cover pages of this book are the names of more than 15,000 men and women who, since 1942, have dedicated themselves to the security of our nation and the pursuit of scientific discovery through their work at the Johns Hopkins University Applied Physics Laboratory.

Since joining the APL board of managers, I have had the opportunity to meet some of these people, and I can tell you without reservation that they are among our nation's most talented and dedicated engineers, scientists, and professionals. Like those who preceded them, they work on many of the most technically complex and critical challenges facing our nation. They are skillfully led and supported by an enthusiastic executive team that shares their passion for public service.

On behalf of my board colleagues, myself, and the generations of board members who preceded us, I want to share the tremendous pride we feel in all who have so ably and nobly served this very special organization during the past 75 years. Each board member shares a special relationship with APL, and we are exceedingly proud of our association with the Lab and its work as part of the Johns Hopkins University community.

As the proud father of an active duty Marine Corps officer, I feel a deep and personal connection to the dedicated men and women who defend our nation and protect freedom around the globe. I take comfort and pride in knowing that APL is providing our military forces with the proven, reliable technologies and capabilities they need to succeed in their many vitally important missions—and keeping America ahead of its adversaries.

As we mark this important milestone in the history of this great enterprise, we reflect proudly on the Lab's many past achievements and look forward confidently to the new challenges and opportunities we will face together.

Michael D. Hankin
Chair, APL Board of Managers

From the Director

The Johns Hopkins University Applied Physics Laboratory has always been a special place, entrusted by our sponsors to analyze and solve many of the nation's most complex national security and space exploration challenges. Although much has changed as APL evolved from a relatively small makeshift laboratory established in the early days of World War II into the dynamic research and development organization we are today, much remains the same.

Having spent the majority of my professional career at the Lab, I have witnessed the incredible transformation that has taken place during the past three decades. I believe APL's founders would be proud of the organization we have become. Today, our contributions to the nation are as vital as ever, and the scope and impact of our work have expanded to include many new sponsors and mission areas as we pioneer the frontiers of science and technology.

Although we are a much more complex and diverse organization today, we continue to nurture the spirit of innovation and culture of experimentation that characterized the Lab's early years. We also continue to create systems engineering solutions that repeatedly deliver new capabilities to the nation's warfighters. Perhaps most important, we remain guided by our founders' deep commitment to trusted service to our sponsors and the nation.

In the 75 years of its existence, the Lab and its staff members have been responsible for thousands of critical contributions to our nation's most critical challenges, along with a smaller number of *defining innovations*—game-changing developments that profoundly advanced science, engineering, and military capabilities. We celebrate and honor these with this book.

It is equally important to note that the history of the Lab continues to be written. The impact and value of many of APL's most important contributions were not initially obvious. In several cases, it took years for these defining innovations to be widely adopted and recognized for their true impact and significance.

Undoubtedly, many of the big ideas being pursued at the Lab today will lead to major advances in national security, space exploration, health, and, more generally, broader areas of science and engineering. In recent years, we have invested significant attention and resources to ensure they do. Today, our engineers, scientists, analysts, administrative professionals, and support staff collaborate more freely and openly than ever before with each other and an ever-broadening array of Johns Hopkins and external partners, and are encouraged to take risks in the pursuit of potentially game-changing ideas. They do so with enthusiasm, purpose, and a sense of urgency.

As we look to the future, our nation faces a wide variety of dynamic threats, including the proliferation of highly capable weapons, concerns about homeland protection, and the spread of terrorism. Rapidly evolving technologies, combined with the interconnectedness of the global community, make these threats more complex and less predictable than any we have ever faced.

Despite the uncertainties and challenges—or, perhaps, because of them—we are pursuing major advances in fields that range from autonomous systems, synthetic biology, and quantum computing to cybersecurity, precision medicine, and surface and undersea warfare. We also continue to grapple with complex technical challenges that include protecting our space-based assets, enhancing the resilience and capabilities of deployed systems, developing hypersonic technologies, and creating systems to predict and prevent the spread of infectious disease. As always, we lean forward to face new challenges, because that is what we do at the Applied Physics Laboratory.

Our innovations are united and driven by a core purpose: to make critical contributions to critical challenges, whenever they arise and wherever they are needed. As we reflect on our past, we envision our future, a future grounded in our core values. We will continue to operate with unquestionable integrity and achieve game-changing impact through the application of our world-class expertise in our enduring commitment to provide trusted service to the nation. Ours is a future in which we continuously strive to achieve more in a highly collaborative, fulfilling (even fun!) environment. And as we continue on our quest to create defining innovations that ensure our nation's preeminence in the 21st century, we will always seek to be bold, do great things, and make the world a better place.

During my tenure, I have had the opportunity to work with and get to know some of the most talented and dedicated people anywhere, and I feel a deep sense of pride for all that we and our predecessors have accomplished. I am hopeful that those who are present when APL celebrates its centennial in 2042 will consider those of us serving today worthy representatives of the many thousands of men and women who so capably served our nation during the Lab's first 75 years.

Ralph D. Semmel
Director, APL

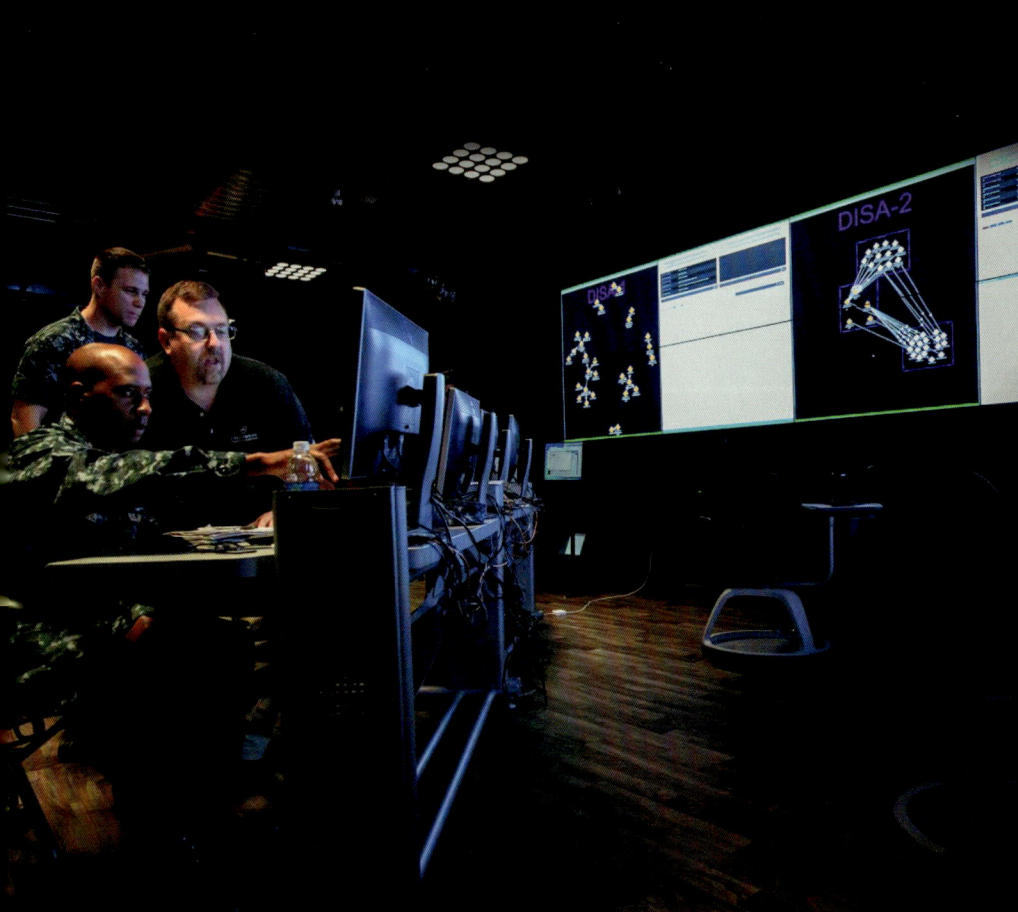

Chapter 1

Critical Contributions to Critical Challenges

Widely known among U.S. government and military officials, the Johns Hopkins University Applied Physics Laboratory (APL) is an indispensable research and development center. For the past 75 years, it has contributed immeasurably to the nation's security, the exploration of space, and the betterment of humankind.

Launched by the U.S. government with a small group of scientists and engineers tasked with a vital top-secret mission at the outset of World War II, the Lab has evolved into one of the nation's premier research and development centers. More than 6,000 technical and administrative professionals are employed at its campus in Laurel, Maryland.

For more than seven decades, government sponsors have turned to APL to solve some of the most critical challenges facing the nation. The Lab's scientists, engineers, and analysts serve the government as both trusted advisors and technical experts, who also develop and prototype new capabilities that safeguard the nation and push the boundaries of science and engineering. Their innovation, resourcefulness, and unquestioned dedication to solving the most complicated technical problems are unsurpassed.

In fact, so sensitive is the Lab's work in support of national security that this book can feature only a portion of its many historic achievements and programs. Broadly, work at APL is divided into 12 separate mission areas: Air and Missile Defense, Civil Space, Cyber Operations, Homeland Protection, National Health, National Security Analysis, National Security Space, Precision Strike, Research and Exploratory Development, Sea Control, Special Operations, and Strategic Deterrence. Together, staff members in these mission areas conduct more than 1,100 ongoing research and development projects for a wide variety of government sponsors.

Over the decades, APL has pushed through innumerable scientific, engineering, technical, and technological barriers. Staff members have been awarded numerous patents for their unclassified work, and more than 30 companies have spun off from APL technologies and products—six in just the past two years.

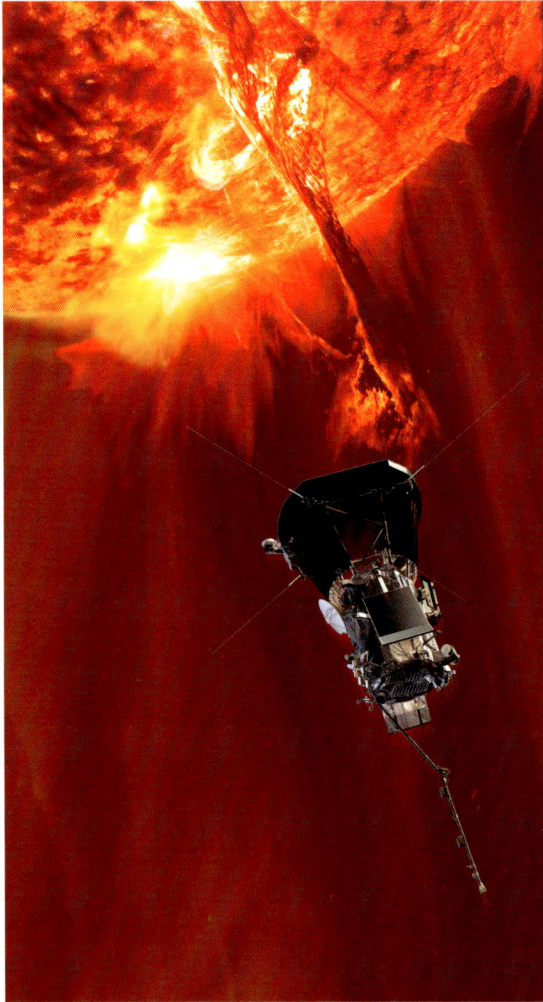

Artist concept of Solar Probe Plus, NASA's mission to touch the sun. APL scientists and engineers are building this robotic spacecraft, which will, for the first time, explore the corona of the sun.

In a 2002 *Johns Hopkins APL Technical Digest* article, APL's former director Alexander Kossiakoff pointed out the Lab's distinct difference from other research institutions—its singular focus on solving operational problems through systems engineering principles and practices, and its dedication to unraveling the entire puzzle and not just a part of it. APL does not simply deliver a solution the sponsor wants; it often delivers solutions they had not realized were possible.

The Lab's staff members are relied on to provide objective, independent technical advice to U.S. government officials, which is why having independent institutions like APL is vital. The Lab's not-for-profit status and university affiliation liberate its staff members to go beyond business metrics to deliver the decisive advantage a sponsor seeks—and sponsors rarely push back at the Lab's suggestion of a new direction. Because so many of APL's projects are integral to the nation's defense and the security and health of all Americans, this truth telling is all the more important and far-reaching.

APL also has the deep technical domain expertise to provide world-class problem-solving for the government. Its staff is practiced in defining the nation's most complex technology challenges and then designing, developing, testing, evaluating, and, in some cases, literally building the solutions from scratch. Their dedication to solving sponsors' needs has made APL a treasured national resource, widely regarded for delivering boldly imaginative solutions to the nation's most complex national security issues and perplexing space exploration challenges.

On APL's roughly 450-acre primary campus and its smaller campus in the nearby Montpelier complex, more than 24 buildings house more than two million square feet of specialized laboratory and office space. In one building, scientists and engineers are presently engaged in designing and building a spacecraft that will probe the corona of the sun, the closest approach ever to our solar system's star. In another lab, researchers and technicians are creating the materials for this spacecraft, using state-of-the-art additive and subtractive manufacturing equipment. Across campus in a room with giant wall-to-wall computer screens, a group of technologists is working on improvements to the country's cyber-threat situational awareness.

Down the road from that building, staff members are engaged in developing more capable cruise missiles, while some colleagues are absorbed in ways to enhance the detection of an adversary's submarines and others are conceiving solutions to defend against evolving ballistic missile threats. While many of the research and development projects at the Lab have been underway for decades, sponsors often turn to APL with urgent requests for new operational capabilities. In both cases, APL is well known for making critical contributions to sponsors' most critical challenges.

Lab staff members, and the thousands of others in government, industry, and academia with whom they partner, appreciate the gravity of their activities. They are entrusted with the safety and security of every American, as well as millions of other people across the planet depending on U.S. military readiness and broad scientific and technical advances. Although staff members are engaged in different missions, they also come together in joint activities to accomplish pressing national goals, contributing their intellects and expertise to myriad projects on behalf of us all.

LEFT: *Analysts and engineers like Elisha Peterson, standing, work to improve cybersecurity through research in APL's LIVE (Live data, Integration, Validation, and Experimentation) Lab.*

BELOW: *Lab engineers are leading key development activities for Standard Missile-2, Standard Missile-3, and Standard Missile-6, the Navy's primary air and missile defense weapons. A Standard Missile-6 is shown here launching from a Navy vessel in June 2014.* (U.S. NAVY)

APL was founded on a singular government need during World War II—to protect the Navy fleet, which was under severe attacks from the air. With American lives at stake, the urgency of this mission impelled a small group of scientists and engineers to unite their respective knowledge and skills in pursuit of a solution. The criticality of the situation demanded constant development and testing by the men and women of APL, followed by more of the same. No stones could be left unturned in the hunt for solutions. None were.

Army Private First Class Harold Pukl, 36th Division, U.S. 7th Army, puts a proximity fuze on a 155-mm shell in France on April 6, 1945.
(SIGNAL CORPS)

Chapter 2

Answering the Nation's Call

The war in Europe escalated in the early months of 1940, and in June President Franklin D. Roosevelt formed the National Defense Research Committee (NDRC) to rally the effort to re-equip the armed services. At the time, the country was distressingly unprepared for the exigencies of battle, its minimal military might comprising mostly surplus World War I materiel. Soliciting the aid of American scientists and U.S. industry to help develop more sophisticated military equipment, Roosevelt stated that the NDRC would supplement the U.S. Army's and U.S. Navy's ongoing research into "the use of mechanisms and devices of warfare."

Roosevelt appointed Vannevar Bush, president of the Carnegie Institution of Washington, as chairman of the NDRC. Trained as an electrical engineer at the Massachusetts Institute of Technology, Bush was known for his decisiveness and willingness to defy tradition, characteristics deemed important for leading a group of mostly university-affiliated scientists and engineers in the development of innovative military technologies. Bush organized the NDRC into several divisions, each composed of multiple sections working on different armaments or their constituent parts. Section A-1, for example, undertook research into explosives, while Section C-2 studied pyrotechnics.

A crucial area of research was developing a new type of fuze to increase the effectiveness of Allied anti-aircraft guns. Two types of fuzes were in use—the timed fuze, which was triggered to explode at a preset time after firing, and the contact fuze, which exploded upon contact with an object. Neither fuze was proving to be effective at downing elusive modern aircraft that could make sharp turns and steep ascents and descents. Naval gunners often used hundreds of rounds of ammunition before hitting a single plane.

The work of developing the new fuze fell to the NDRC's Section T, led by Merle A. Tuve, a physicist at the Carnegie Institution. Tuve had received his Ph.D. in physics from Johns Hopkins University and was a pioneer in the use of pulsed radio waves to examine the layers of the Earth's ionosphere. As its name implied, the section was intentionally named after its leader.

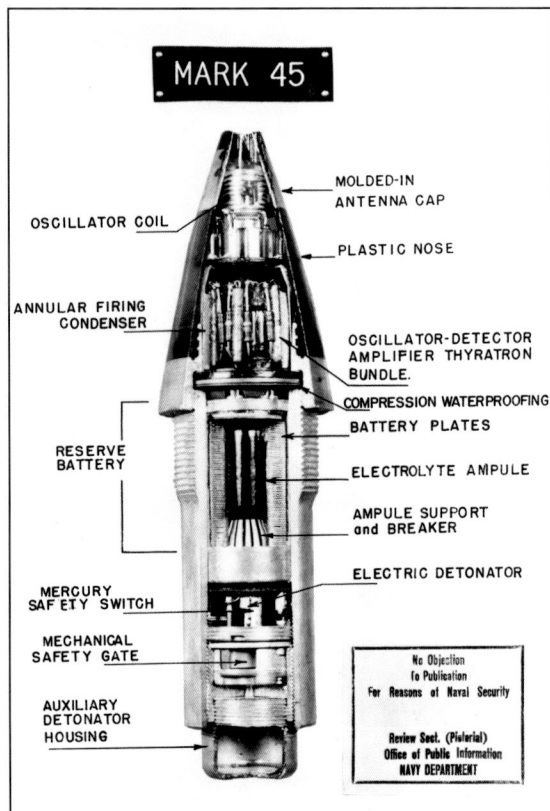

Knowing they needed to quickly develop a better fuze, Tuve set up five research sections to conduct separate feasibility studies. The job of Section T was to oversee the research and development conducted by these teams of scientists and also to supervise production of the fuze. "This was probably the first time that a comprehensive production job of this sort was steered by a small civilian group, with distinguished officers providing the liaison," Tuve said in 1962.

In the months leading up to Pearl Harbor, Tuve determined that a radio-influenced fuze was the most promising approach. When a shell was fired, a tiny radio transmitter-receiver in the fuze would send out electromagnetic waves. When the reflected radio waves indicated the target was within range, the fuze would trigger the explosive.

"(Tuve) knew that if a proximity fuze could be developed, it would be one of the most important projects imaginable, when and if the United States entered the war," wrote Ralph B. Baldwin, a former senior physicist at APL and author of *The Deadly Fuze: The Secret Weapon of World War II*. Baldwin's book is widely considered the definitive story of the fuze's development.

Proximity fuzes were not a new concept. British scientists had been working on them for several years, and the British government filed a provisional British patent for the invention in early 1942. However, no one had yet succeeded in overcoming the damage to the fuze caused by the shock of the gun's firing. Subjected to 20,000 times the force of gravity and centrifugal forces as strong as 475 rotations

per second, the glass vacuum tube in the fuze's electronics disintegrated. Another drawback was the short shelf life of the miniature dry cell batteries used to power the fuze's electronics, requiring their continual replacement at sea, possibly at a time of great urgency.

Of utmost concern, however, was the possibility that the fuze would trigger an explosion in the gun barrel. Were this to occur in combat, the casualties would be high, and the loss of lives might cause Navy gunners thereafter to refuse to fire proximity-fuzed shells. Some means of ensuring the shell traveled a safe distance before detonating was needed.

Tuve was not intimidated. Described by colleagues as dynamic and relentless, he was determined to create a practical proximity fuze as quickly as possible. On December 6, 1941, one day before Japan's attack on Pearl Harbor, Tuve wrote the Office of Scientific Research and Development that Section T faced an "imperative" need for "enlargement" to transform the experimental fuze into a workable weapon for mass production. He insisted that his division would need to increase by "three to five times."

To manage this effort, Tuve recommended the Carnegie Institution be the home for this expanded team of researchers. This choice was not surprising, given the relationship both he and Vannevar Bush shared with the scientific organization. Tuve also provided a list of alternative organizations that might host this research effort, among them his alma mater, Johns Hopkins University. "It is believed that Johns Hopkins could be persuaded to accept the undertaking for a laboratory near Washington," he wrote. Tuve concluded his message with an ominous warning, written in all capital letters: "THE TIME IS SHORTER THAN WE THINK."

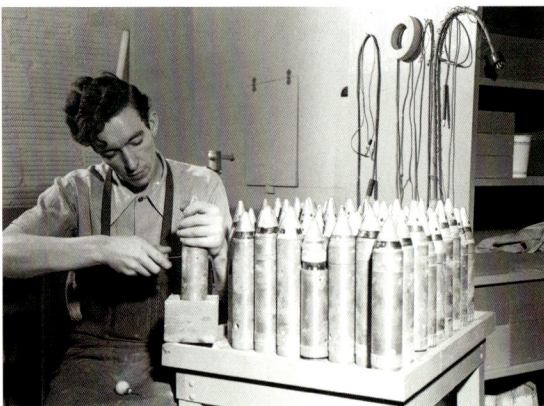

Pearl Harbor: A New Sense of Urgency

On December 7, 1941, the U.S. Pacific Fleet was attacked at Pearl Harbor. A day later, Roosevelt declared war on Japan. With America now officially at war, the resolve to produce a more viable fuze intensified. The need was so dire that the Navy's Bureau of Ordnance set the bar for deployment in the field at only a 50 percent rate of effectiveness.

But even this standard was formidable. According to Baldwin, "(The) prevailing opinion (was) that proximity fuzes could not be made in time to be of use in the war," he wrote.

Section T was undaunted. "I don't want any damn fool in this organization to save money," Tuve instructed his staff. "I want him to save time." To get an improved fuze into the combat theater as soon as possible, Section T personnel worked 16-hour days.

Motivated by the importance of their mission, the section's scientists and engineers had their first success: reducing the breakage rate by cushioning the vacuum tubes. In January 1942, these prototype fuzes were tested at a secret Navy facility located on a farm in southern Maryland. They were installed in five-inch anti-aircraft shells and fired vertically into the sky. Fifty-two percent survived the firing impact and maintained radio transmission during the flight.

In the meantime, Tuve's recommendation to the NDRC to enlarge Section T progressed. Given the potential conflict of interest Vannevar Bush, who was at the time head of the NDRC and president of the Carnegie Institution, would face in taking on such a large government contract, he

solicited the interest of Isaiah Bowman, president of Johns Hopkins University. Bowman brought the matter to the university's board of trustees, which signed a direct research contract with the Navy on March 10, 1942. The trustees agreed to sponsor Section T even without understanding the exact nature of the work to be conducted. All they knew was that the project was vital to the Allied cause.

The contract called for the university to provide laboratory space, equipment, testing facilities, and additional scientific and engineering personnel. Tuve changed the name of Section T to the Applied Physics Laboratory, a title he felt underlined the practical nature of the organization's work. APL was created to exist only through the end of the war.

Because of the secret nature of APL's work, the fuze was referred to as the VT, or variable time, fuze, to conceal its true capability. The project also required a research and development facility that would not raise suspicions, so a rather nondescript brick building at 8621 Georgia Avenue in Silver Spring, Maryland, a suburb on the outskirts of Washington, D.C., was chosen to house the facility. The building had previously accommodated an automobile dealership known as the Wolfe Motor Company. The large "USED CARS" sign out front was left in place as a means of concealment.

The facility opened on May 1, 1942, and shortly thereafter a staff of more than 200 employees occupied the building. The dealership's interior was partitioned into offices and lab workspaces. In subsequent years, APL would branch out into adjacent buildings and add two additional stories to the main structure.

Nighttime test firing of the proximity fuze from a Navy 6-pounder gun at Newtown Neck, Maryland.

Shrouded in Secrecy

Personnel were regularly warned not to tell area residents nor anyone else about the nature of their work. The staff had two primary tasks: to improve the design of the proximity fuze and to resize the fuze for use in different artillery shells. To achieve these goals, they drew on the scientific, engineering, and production expertise of dozens of universities and industrial laboratories that had agreed to assist the war effort.

Although the breakage rates of the glass vacuum tubes had been reduced, APL sought to significantly reduce this rate. To further cushion the tube, the staff members encased it in small rubber cups that were embedded in a special wax compound. To determine the efficacy of this concept, they dropped the tubes from the roof of the headquarters building to a concrete driveway below. The results were extremely encouraging.

To address the short shelf life of the dry cell battery powering the fuze's electronics, APL engineers later incorporated an innovative wet cell battery developed by the National Carbon Company. The battery stored electrolyte in a glass ampule that broke when the round was fired. The broken ampule then released the electrolyte, and the centrifugal force generated by the rotation of the projectile forced the liquid acid between thin plates, activating the battery.

The final challenge was eliminating the chance of a shell exploding in the gun muzzle, and the team did this by designing, developing, and installing an innovative mercury time-delay switch. The switch to trigger the fuze was opened by the centrifugal force caused by the firing of a shell, eliminating the possibility that it would detonate in the gun.

In August 1942, APL tested these refinements at sea on USS *Cleveland* by firing at unmanned aerial drones. The results were promising—in four rounds, three drones were downed. As a result, the Navy ordered full-scale production of the proximity fuze by Crosley Corporation, a maker of low-price radios. Crosley was one of several industry partners that had agreed to provide APL manufacturing capacity for the war effort. Within a month, more than 400 fuzes were being produced per day.

The goal was to quickly dispatch the fuzes to the Pacific Fleet, where Japanese aircraft were inflicting devastating aerial strikes on U.S. and Allied ships. Due to the project's secret nature, only a few high-ranking naval officers were aware of the fuze's development, and none knew how to deploy the fuze in combat. The commanders also had significant concerns over the fuze's safety and reliability. Because APL had developed the new technology, the staff members felt it was up to them to prove its efficacy and to facilitate its use in the field. Five APL scientists, among them physicist James A. Van Allen—who later discovered the radiation belts encircling the Earth—volunteered to demonstrate the proximity fuze in actual combat. The scientists were quickly commissioned as naval officers to help with fielding of the fuze.

Our Garage Story

Like many innovative technology companies, APL started out in a humble garage. The Lab's first headquarters at 8621 Georgia Avenue in Silver Spring, Maryland, was in a used car dealership formerly owned by the Wolfe Motor Company, Inc.

Above the front entrance was a large rectangular sign reading "USED CARS." Since the work going on inside the building was a closely guarded wartime secret, the sign stayed in place. So did the primitive potbelly stove that heated the environs.

Over the next few years, the building grew, with new sections added as the size of the staff grew to support the expanded scope of work. An adjacent building was added and two new floors were added in 1943 and 1944 to provide additional space. Still, local residents had no real idea of what was going on inside the old Wolfe Motor Company. The shades were drawn at all times of the day, and the staff was warned never to tell anyone what they were up to.

Rumors circulated that the building was an experimental medical facility, not surprising since the security guard greeted many a staff member as "doctor." Others thought it was a mortuary. Apparently, a coffin-like box containing experimental vacuum tubes was mistaken for the real thing.

Eventually, the "USED CARS" sign was replaced with one that let everyone know the name of the resident: Applied Physics Laboratory. A modern-looking lobby was installed, complete with an American flag. The structure started to look like an average office building.

The Silver Spring office remained an operational part of the Laboratory until the mid-1970s, when operations were consolidated at the Howard County campus.

USS Helena, *shown here later in the war, achieved the fuze's first combat success by downing two enemy aircraft in the Pacific in January 1943.* (U.S. Navy)

The Fuze in Action

On January 5, 1943, a group of Japanese Aichi dive bombers attacked USS *Helena*. The Navy cruiser was one of several ships patrolling the southern coast of Guadalcanal as part of Allied forces' first major offensive against Japan. The *Helena* had 500 rounds of proximity-fuzed five-inch Navy anti-aircraft projectiles on board—and the APL scientists to guide their use. Navy gunners fired at one of the Japanese planes, downing it with just the second salvo.

While the successful strike was a euphoric moment for the Navy and APL, the good news was short-lived. Nearly 50 percent of the projectiles failed to reach their targets. This was not due to the fuze technology, but a result of the Navy's Mk 1 gun directors—the systems that sighted a target and then aimed the gun. Each Mk 1 required a crew of 16 men and consumed an average of 40 seconds to track a target by using mechanical computations, making it nearly impossible to follow the erratic flight path of a sharply turning Japanese plane.

Without prompting by the Navy, APL staff members took on the urgent task of improving the gun director. Their hard work and willingness to solve the problem led to the development of the Mk 57 gun director, which required only one man to operate and was able to lock on to a target in a mere 4.7 seconds. The Mk 57 was ready for combat use in 1944, and its deployment on USS *Missouri* was a resounding success.

The new gun director was a critical contribution to the war effort, combating the growing number of Kamikaze suicide attacks on the fleet. By locking on to targets at much greater distances, the Mk 57 was able to detect and down a Japanese plane before it could begin attack runs on Navy ships.

Although APL's assignment was to create a new fuze, Tuve and his staff went far beyond this initial task, believing their true mission was to develop a better means of shooting down enemy planes. This was the first example of APL's commitment to holistically solving problems beyond the immediate task.

In the end, proximity fuze projectiles proved many times more effective than other types. Although the Navy used proximity fuzes throughout the war, the Army was resistant to their use because of concerns that a dud fuze might be retrieved and studied by German scientists. However, by 1944, the Army changed its stance and started incorporating the fuze in ground combat, causing shells to detonate above ground level, with devastating effect on enemy troops. By the war's end, more than 23 million proximity fuzes were produced, with the Army ultimately using twice as many as the Navy.

Reports from German prisoners characterized the Allies' artillery fire as the most destructive they had ever encountered. In its most important profound single use, the fuze is credited with protecting the vital access route of General George S. Patton's 3rd Army to assist the capture of Bastogne, France, during the Battle of the Bulge, thwarting five German divisions. "The new shell with the funny fuse is devastating," Patton later wrote in a letter to the chief of ordnance at the War Department. "I am glad that you all thought of it first."

By "you all," Patton was referring to Merle Tuve and his colleagues at APL, the Army and Navy Ordnance bureaus, and the many industry partners who had worked so tenaciously to develop the fuze—although even Patton did not know who they were at the time, given the top-secret nature of the work.

The success of the fuze in the Pacific prompted similar praise from Navy Secretary James V. Forrestal. "The proximity fuze has helped blaze the trail to Japan," he said. "Without the protection this ingenious device has given the surface ships of the fleet, our westward push could not have been so swift, and the cost in men and ships would have been immeasurably greater."

Military historians later judged the proximity fuze as one of the three most significant technological developments of the war, along with radar and the atomic bomb. This *defining innovation* helped establish the Laboratory as a valuable national resource and laid the foundation for a unique and trusted relationship with the U.S. Navy that continues today. Further, the development of the proximity fuze had a profound effect on future weapon developments. To this day, most offensive and defensive munitions of all types, except "hit-to-kill" weapons, employ proximity fuzes to trigger munitions.

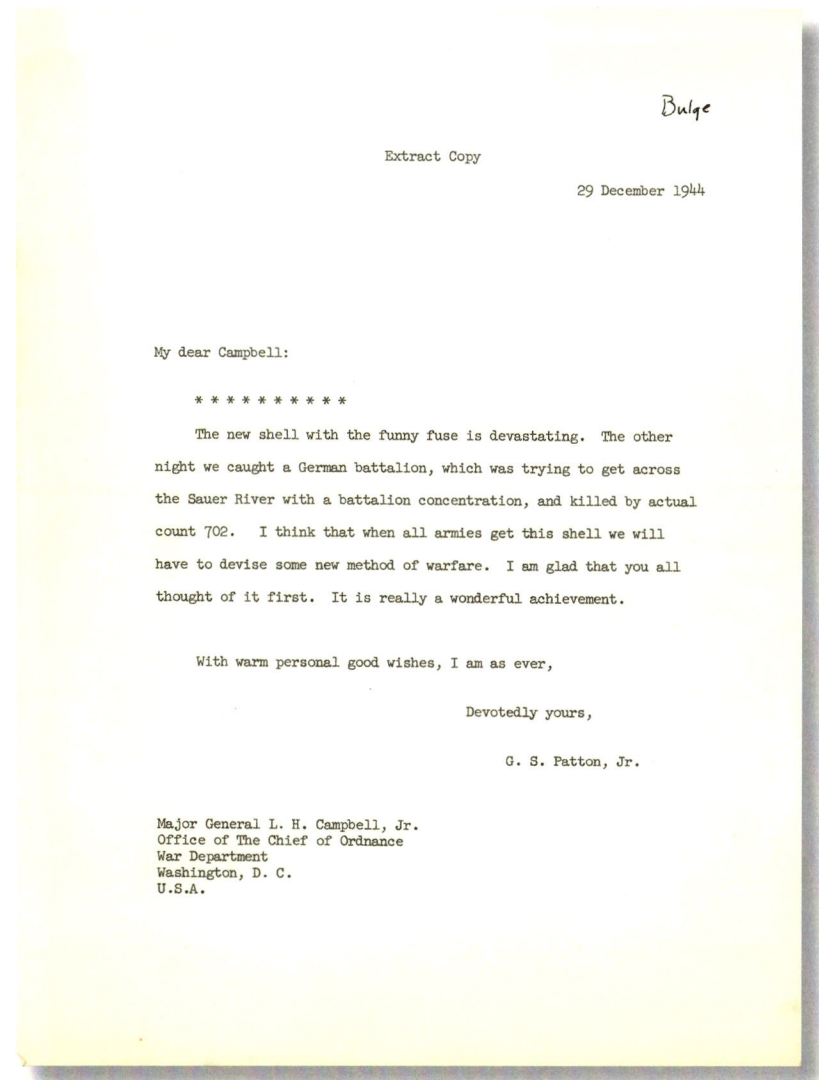

Letter from General George S. Patton describing the effectiveness of the fuze in ground combat during the Battle of the Bulge in 1944.

Cobra ramjet missile testing at Fort Miles, Delaware, Rocket Range.

Chapter 3

The Birthplace of Navy Air Defense Missiles

As World War II wound down, APL faced an uncertain future. The original plan was to dismantle the Lab once its service to the war effort had concluded. But the war was not yet over and Nazi Germany was still developing next-generation weapons. Navy officials began to reconsider this decision.

A key concern was Germany's capacity to deploy rocket-propelled ship-seeking missiles from high-flying aircraft. Should a plane with such missiles approach a Navy vessel, quickly veer out of anti-aircraft range, and launch a projectile, the fleet would be vulnerable to tremendous losses.

Through its work on the proximity fuze and Mk 57 gun director, APL had demonstrated unusual competence for warfare analysis and the delivery of end-to-end solutions. APL staff members also excelled at analyzing complex challenges and providing comprehensive engineering solutions. These were the capabilities the Navy needed to deal with the emerging threat.

In a memo to Navy officials, Merle Tuve highlighted the threat. "(A) Navy tactical situation may arise if the enemy adopts guided missiles for attack against task forces from airplanes just beyond the limited range of anti-aircraft," Tuve wrote Vannevar Bush in July 1944. "The problem must be faced before very long if we hope for real defense against future air attacks."

In a subsequent analysis conducted for the Navy's Bureau of Ordnance, APL concluded the best defense would be a rocket-launched anti-aircraft missile traveling at supersonic speed that could converge on, overtake, and destroy an enemy plane. In response, the Ordnance Bureau requested that APL supervise and coordinate the development of a missile with those characteristics.

The challenges were many. At the time, radar guidance technology was nominal, the techniques of supersonic flight were largely unknown, and there was no rocket capable of carrying a warhead large enough to destroy a plane. And there was the accelerated timeline. "[Fleet Admiral Ernest] King has directed that this program be carried forward on an urgent basis," Tuve wrote Bush in December 1944. "This is not to be an ordinary project."

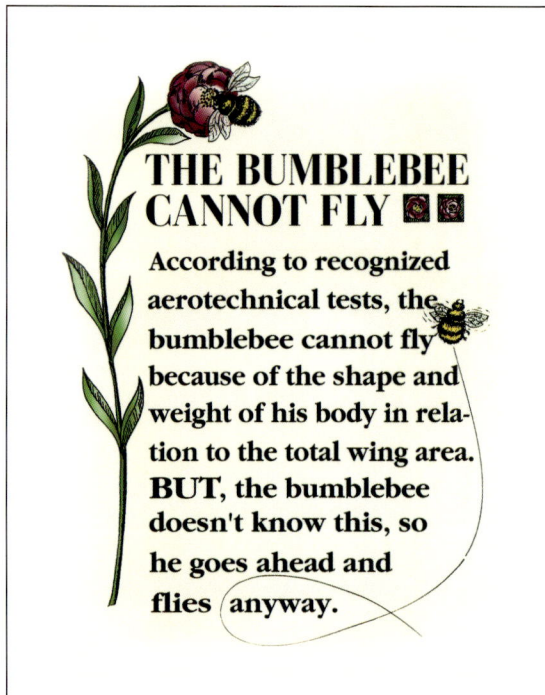

RIGHT: *Lab engineers prepare a Cobra ramjet missile for launch and testing at Fort Miles, Delaware. Beginning in the mid-1940s, the site was used for fuze and ramjet testing conducted by the Laboratory.*

BELOW: *In late 1944, Merle Tuve spotted a poster like this hanging in the office of Navy Captain Carroll Tyler, special assistant to the director of the Office of Scientific Research and Development. The poster inspired Tuve, who was well aware that he and his team faced a challenge to develop a guided missile, to name the program Bumblebee.*

THE BUMBLEBEE CANNOT FLY

According to recognized aerotechnical tests, the bumblebee cannot fly because of the shape and weight of his body in relation to the total wing area. BUT, the bumblebee doesn't know this, so he goes ahead and flies anyway.

A few days later, the Johns Hopkins University board of trustees signed the contract authorizing APL to begin work on this new challenge, called Task F. APL's assignment was to create a long-range radar-guided anti-aircraft missile, the nation's first. The proposed missile was dubbed Talos, in recognition of the giant bronze automaton that protected Crete in Greek mythology, also once again reflecting Merle Tuve's initial. To assist the staff's pursuit of this goal, APL signed associated contracts with nine universities and 12 industrial companies. The partners would provide additional research and engineering, as well as production capabilities.

The Bumblebee Flies

Task F certainly was not an "ordinary project." To attack high-speed air targets before they launched a weapon at a Navy vessel, APL would have to devise a missile with greater horsepower and lighter weight than current engines allowed. The missile would need to carry a 600-pound warhead over a range of 10 miles at altitudes as high as 30,000 feet and be highly maneuverable to be able to track and destroy a fast pitching, rolling, and darting plane. Added to these demands was the need for the missile to be produced in sufficient quantities and at a reasonable cost.

The solution that emerged over a period of months was an air-breathing ramjet engine to achieve the requisite performance. Conceived by French engineer René Lorin in 1908, a ramjet uses an engine's forward motion to compress incoming air to help propel the vehicle. Once in flight, the incoming air

LEFT: *Ralph Gibson (who later became APL director), Rear Admiral A. G. Nobel (USN), Carl Mitman of the Smithsonian, and APL's Wilbur Goss with a Smithsonian display on the "flying stovepipe" ramjet engine.*

BELOW: *The crew readies a Cobra ramjet missile for installation in a launch ramp at Fort Miles. Now part of Cape Henlopen State Park, Fort Miles was a World War II coastal defense site tasked with defending the mouth of the Delaware Bay.*

from the forward motion mixes with a kerosene-based fuel to produce thrust. Because ramjets cannot produce thrust at zero airspeed, they require liftoff from a rocket. APL estimated that a ramjet-powered missile would also require just one-fifth of the fuel weight carried by a conventional liquid-propelled rocket, making it far more lightweight than a typical missile.

There was only one hitch: No one had actually ever built a workable supersonic ramjet engine. Like the proximity fuze, the theory behind the concept was brilliant, but its development would be problematic.

Recognizing the immensity of the challenges, Tuve wryly code-named the project Bumblebee, based on a quotation he had come across: "The bumblebee cannot fly. According to recognized aerotechnical tests, the bumblebee cannot fly because of the shape and weight of his body in relation to the total wing area. But, the bumblebee doesn't know this, so he goes ahead and flies anyway."

It was an apt description of the impossible task APL now confronted. The staff members nonetheless took on the assignment with great enthusiasm and remarkable confidence in their scientific capabilities and diligence. Given the steep challenges, this "can-do" spirit of optimism was needed.

As the Lab ventured into this new technical area—the development of a missile-based air defense system—its technical research and systems analysis capabilities were called on to greater depth. Little was known at the time about the field of supersonic aerodynamics. The few wind tunnels that existed were too small to furnish reliable test results on a supersonic engine.

In 1945, the Lab began Bumblebee test operations at Island Beach, New Jersey. More than 300 people created and tested the world's first ramjet missiles, built from airplane exhaust tailpipes and booster rockets.

Improvisations, Innovations, and "Flying Stovepipes"

At APL's request, the Navy's Ordnance Bureau agreed to find and fund a suitable test site for the Lab's engineers and physicists to conduct aerodynamic and propulsion tests. In the early spring of 1945, the Bumblebee team, consisting of more than 300 people, gathered at the test site, a stretch of deserted coastline along Barnegat Bay in Island Beach, New Jersey.

There they built an 80-foot by 40-foot concrete pad that was topped with a 30-foot-long missile launcher fabricated from wooden beams. The staff also built primitive observation shacks behind nearby dunes, from which they could safely watch the missile firings. The field test headquarters consisted of an abandoned Coast Guard station that supplied water and electricity.

Improvisation was the order of the day. The first ramjet missiles were assembled from six-inch airplane exhaust tailpipes with a circular inlet for incoming air. The missiles were attached to standard high-velocity booster rockets. Tests were verified through observation. Early rockets performed unreliably, but each error was information that informed the development of the next set of missiles. They operated under the "Build a little, test a little, learn a lot" principle, articulated decades later by Rear Admiral Wayne E. Meyer, a key proponent of the Navy Aegis program.

The D-40 Cannonball

Imagine spherical missiles 15 to 22 inches in diameter and weighing 150 to 300 pounds that could be fired at a speed of between 500 and 800 miles per hour. Imagine no more: The Cannonball missiles, conceived by APL's Randolph Rae in the early 1950s, seem right out of a sci-fi movie from the era, but they actually existed, and even better—they worked.

Each of the three types of Cannonball missiles designed, developed, and built at the Lab carried two types of warheads and were created to destroy oncoming tanks. Using early guided missile technology, which was also developed at APL, the Cannonballs were sent "aloft" in several field tests. One observer of the exercises remarked that the midsize missile rose only about three feet off the ground,

sprouted "little flames," and took off "across the fields and hedgerows like a scared rabbit," before "plunging through the bull's-eye of a target 2,000 yards away." (The maximum range of the largest of the three missile types was more than 3,000 yards.)

The tests proved the efficacy of the solid-fueled spherical missiles, attracting the interest of both the U.S. Navy and the U.S. Marine Corps. Although the U.S. Army had funded the Cannonball only for development as an anti-tank missile, the Navy approved the construction of 15 missiles to be carried aboard submarines as anti-ship missiles. APL constructed approximately 50 Cannonballs, officially known as the D-40 A, B, and C missiles, between 1953 and 1956.

In the late 1950s, the budget-conscious Eisenhower administration winnowed down the field of missiles for production. This led to the decision to cancel the costly Cannonball, which was deemed both too expensive and too bulky to operate in combat.

Researchers lower a large-scale ramjet engine into the high-altitude test chamber at the APL-designed and -developed Ordnance Aerophysics Laboratory in Daingerfield, Texas, where it could be tested at conditions that simulated flight.

In May 1945, the war in Europe drew to a close with Germany's unconditional surrender. APL's contract with the Ordnance Bureau effectively ended, meaning that this promising work was now in jeopardy. Despite enthusiasm for the Bumblebee test program, the lingering questions over the future of APL required a resolution. The board of trustees at Johns Hopkins University was divided on the question of renewing the association with the Navy in peacetime. Nevertheless, both parties' awareness of the national necessity of continuing the ramjet research resulted in an extension of the contract for another year.

It was the right decision. In June 1945, a ramjet missile made its first successful flight, maintaining a supersonic speed of nearly 1,200 miles per hour for more than five miles before splashing satisfyingly into Barnegat Bay. An observer described it as looking like a "flying stovepipe." Area fishermen reported hearing a sonic boom. "All of us who watched the firing knew what we had seen could be done again, on a larger scale," said Wilbur H. Goss, an APL physicist whom Tuve had appointed to lead the top-secret research effort.

With the Navy's backing, APL opened a new test facility in Forest Grove, Maryland, two miles north of the headquarters building at 8621 Georgia Avenue. There they simulated flying velocities at nearly twice the speed of sound. The Lab also was given permission to help design and develop the Navy's first supersonic wind tunnel in a vacant factory in Daingerfield, Texas.

Serendipitously, a 100,000-cubic-foot blower had been left behind by the previous tenant. APL incorporated the blower into the wind tunnel's design. It would become the country's largest and most advanced supersonic propulsion test facility, permitting the study of aerodynamic principles at speeds of 2,000 miles per hour.

To more precisely calculate the aerodynamic forces of jet engine thrust and drag, the government gave APL and its contractor partners several deconstructed German Vergeltungswaffe-1 (V-1) flying bombs, the first jet-powered cruise missiles. The V-1s, known as "doodlebugs" in England and as "buzz bombs" by American service members, had been captured during the waning days of the war. APL's engineers and physicists studied the missiles and used early digital computers to evaluate the aerodynamic forces at play. Their insights were incorporated in subsequent rounds of missile launches into Barnegat Bay.

Gathering scientific data was a constant challenge. Tests of the ramjet-powered missiles ended up with many of the projectiles lost in the Atlantic Ocean, making it impossible for researchers to determine what went wrong mid-flight and how to correct this flaw. To gather more experimental data, APL turned to telemetry, an automated communications process whereby measurements made of an object at remote points are transmitted by radio waves. At the same time, the speed of the missile was measured by radar, and its movements were captured on film running at 60 frames per second. Using modeling, the team translated the various data points into valuable engineering information.

The development of the anti-aircraft missile now stretched across three states—the facilities in Forest Grove, Maryland; Daingerfield, Texas; and Island Beach, New Jersey. As this crucial research and testing progressed, the means of war were about to change dramatically.

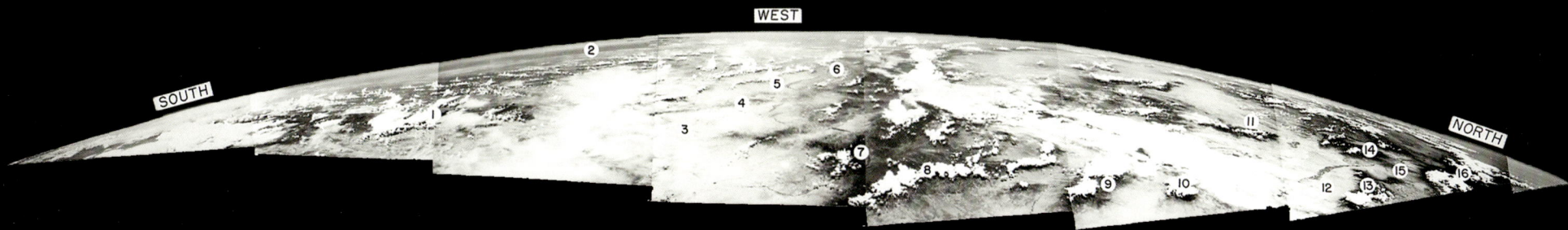

First View of the Curvature of Earth from Space

At the end of the war, the U.S. Army captured hundreds of partially assembled German Vergeltungswaffe-2 (V-2) rockets, from which 25 complete rockets were assembled for test purposes. Aware that several APL scientists like James Van Allen, who had recently returned from serving as a U.S. Navy ordnance and gunnery officer during the war, were interested in high-altitude research, APL Director Merle Tuve accepted an Army offer to support its rocket research program. Tuve's decision would propel APL into a new area of research—satellite development.

Standing nearly 46 feet tall and with 28 tons of thrust, the V-2 was the world's first long-range ballistic missile. It reached a speed of 3,400 miles per hour and a maximum altitude of 114 miles. When the Germans launched a test of the rocket in June 1944, the V-2 became the first human-made object to breach the boundary of space.

Van Allen and his team developed an astonishing variety of measuring instruments like sensors, spectrometers, and Geiger-Mueller counters, which were embedded in the V-2's nose cone. The instruments brought back the first photos of the curvature of the Earth as well as illuminating data on the cosmic ray particles that bombarded the planet. The findings revealed that secondary particles called mesons were far more abundant than previously thought. Ultimately, this work would lead to the discovery of the radiation belts encircling the Earth, named the Van Allen Belts in Van Allen's honor, years after he left the Lab for a position at the University of Iowa.

Access to the V-2 rockets also gave APL physicists and engineers experience developing liquid-propellant rockets. Because of the finite number of these rockets, Tuve recommended that the Ordnance Bureau fund a project for APL to develop a simpler version of the gargantuan V-2 for experimental purposes. The request was granted, resulting in the Aerobee rocket, a 20-foot-long, 1,650-pound liquid-fueled missile that could carry a payload of 150 pounds of equipment 70 miles into the upper atmosphere. More than 3,000 of the Aerobee rockets were eventually built in partnership with Aerojet Corporation.

This was humankind's first view of the curvature of the Earth, a composite of a photo sequence shot approximately 60 miles above the surface by an APL camera installed on a V-2 rocket, launched at White Sands Proving Ground, New Mexico, July 26, 1948. The vista extends 2,700 miles from Mexico to Nebraska, approximately 800,000 square miles, with the following annotated reference points: 1 = Mexico; 2 = Gulf of California; 3 = Lordsburg, New Mexico; 4 = Peloncillo Mountains; 5 = Gila River; 6 = San Carlos Reservoir; 7 = Mogollon Mountains; 8 = Black Range; 9 = San Mateo Mountains; 10 = Magadalena Mountains; 11 = Mt. Taylor; 12 = Albuquerque; 13 = Sandia Mountains; 14 = Valle Grande Mountains; 15 = Rio Grande; 16 = Sangre de Cristo Mountains.

Marking the extension of APL's contract with the Navy in 1946 are (left to right) Lawrence Hafstad (APL director from 1946 to 1947), Merle Tuve (APL director from 1942 to 1946), D. Luke Hopkins (Johns Hopkins University board of trustees), and Isaiah Bowman (Johns Hopkins University president).

The dropping of atomic bombs on the cities of Hiroshima and Nagasaki resulted in Japan's unconditional surrender on August 15, 1945, followed by the formal armistice signing on September 2. The Atomic Age had begun.

A Post-War Magnet for Talent

With the United States now a global superpower, the Navy sought to continue its relationship with APL. In October 1946, Navy Secretary James Forrestal wrote Johns Hopkins President Isaiah Bowman to request another contract extension, citing the "extremely important" work being conducted in the Bumblebee project. A few days later, Bowman replied that the board of trustees had authorized to extend the APL contract through the end of June 1947.

This was exhilarating news for the staff, which comprised a core group of 250 key scientists, mathematicians, and engineers, among them four propulsion experts from the Allegany Ballistics Laboratory (known as Section H during the war) who would have significant impact on the Laboratory in later years. Ralph Gibson was the British-born deputy chief of Section H, and Alexander Kossiakoff, his assistant director of research. On leave from their university posts during the war, the scientists had planned to return to their teaching positions, but they were invigorated by their wartime experiences. According to Kossiakoff, they thrived on the thrill of development, rather than doing just scientific research. Also joining APL from the Allegany Ballistics Laboratory was a chemist, Frank McClure, and mathematician Richard Kershner. In time, these men would play significant roles in APL's future.

The tests of the ramjet engine at Island Beach progressed steadily. Nevertheless, more research was needed to develop the missile's guidance system. It is one thing for a supersonic missile to destroy a stationary object a mile away, but hitting a moving target required vastly more refined controls.

Among the various options studied, a radar beam-riding guidance system stood out as the optimal technology. With this system, a single radar beam detects the target and determines the general

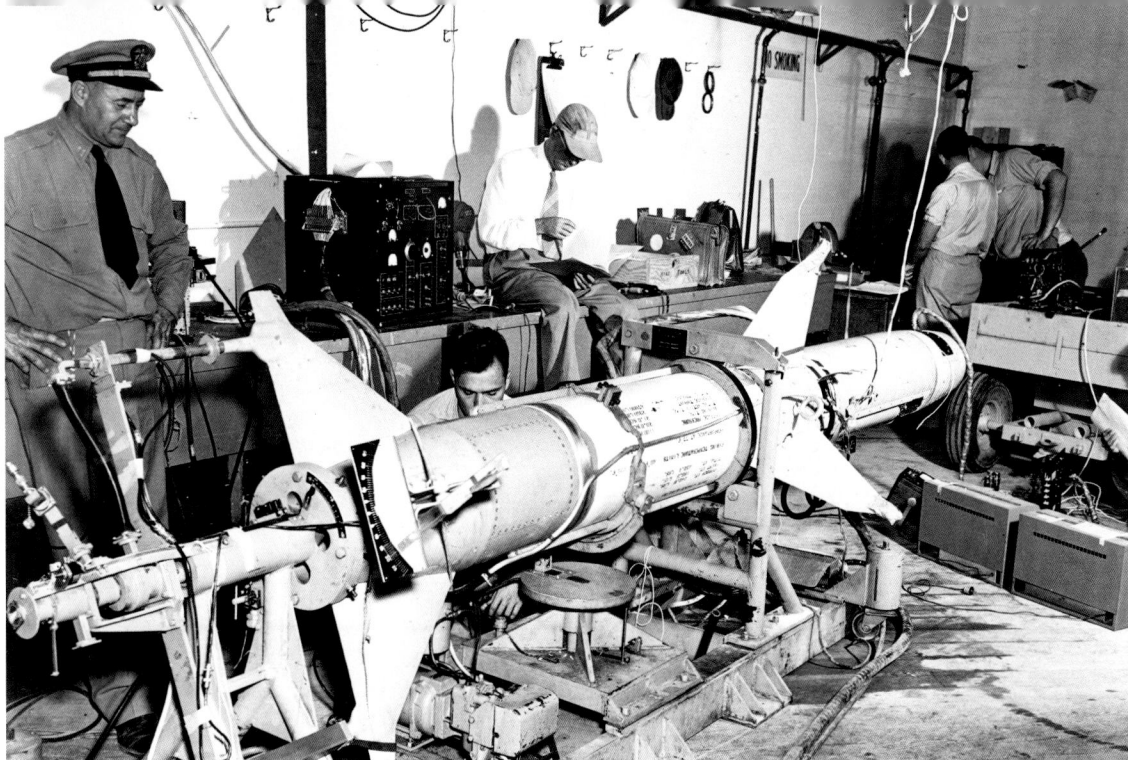

The STV-3B undergoing system testing. The successful launch of this fixed-wing control test vehicle laid the foundation for the guidance, flight stabilization, and aerodynamics of future high-speed missiles.

direction toward which the missile should be launched. Once fired, the missile comes in contact with another beam from a second radar system, which is also pointed at the target. When the missile reaches the center of this beam, it encounters a third narrowly focused beam that guides it toward the target. A radio receiver in the missile's tail section translates the various signals from the beams into control commands that adjust the projectile's course.

Although the researchers believed this was the best option, they considered it an interim step until something better came along. As they continued to perfect the concept, their work nurtured the development of a series of Bumblebee supersonic test vehicles (STVs), culminating in a supersonic beam-rider test vehicle known as the STV-3. The successful launch of this fixed-wing control test vehicle laid the foundation for the guidance, flight stabilization, and aerodynamics of future high-speed missiles.

By the end of the decade, the wide-ranging knowledge gleaned from the Lab's myriad projects would coalesce into establishing APL as the leading guided-missile research and development center in the United States. Meanwhile, the need for this work was becoming increasingly important, as political and military tensions between the two newly emerged superpowers, the United States and the Soviet Union, had escalated into posturing just short of open warfare.

In this hostile environment, American officials and their Soviet counterparts concurred that the best defense against the other was containment—a massive buildup of nuclear weapons and other armaments that would keep the other side wary and at bay. This assured destruction doctrine held that if both the United States and the Soviet Union were armed with an equal nuclear capability, neither country would have an incentive to initiate a conflict.

A sailor aboard USS Boston (CAG 1) stands by the missile-loading hatch as a Terrier launcher slews into the sun to point its missiles skyward. (U.S. Navy)

Chapter 4

Sailing into the Cold War

The onset of the Cold War solidified the need for APL's valued contributions, particularly in the area of missile development. The government increasingly counted on the Lab's scientific and engineering skills to help Navy officials analyze technical problems, propose innovative solutions, and bring together the intellectual and industrial talents needed to solve intricate challenges.

In April 1948, APL was given the high-priority task of rapidly transforming its supersonic test vehicle, STV-3, with its solid rocket motor, into a working interim shipboard weapon system. A spin-off from the Talos missile, development of the new missile—dubbed Terrier—was a priority, even as longer-range efforts to develop Talos continued. Convair, an aircraft-manufacturing company, won the government contract to produce the new missile.

Although APL was initially sponsored to oversee Terrier's flight tests, planning, and analysis, its role expanded significantly when production problems threatened the program. A team of 25 engineers led by mathematician Richard Kershner was assigned to unravel the predicament.

At Convair's manufacturing facility, the APL team applied its systems engineering expertise to make step-by-step adjustments to the system's design and engineering. A particularly frustrating problem was the need for the missile to be disassembled whenever a component malfunctioned, creating manufacturing bottlenecks. To fix a faulty receiver, for instance, engineers had to take apart the hydraulic system first.

The APL team proposed a solution to redesign the missile as a series of functionally independent sections, with a separate power section, warhead section, guidance and control section, and so on, today known as modular design. To demonstrate the viability of this solution, the Lab offered to oversee a pilot test program to develop 10 such missiles, which the Navy accepted. Eight of the nine APL-built missiles, designated Terrier 1B, were successful in test flights, clearing the way for the acceptance of the new missile's design.

RIGHT: *At 3:00 a.m. on a June 1946 morning, engineers paused to mark the first successful operation of the Ordnance Aerophysics Laboratory wind tunnel in Daingerfield, Texas. Test section design and tunnel operation were under the direction of Al Eaton, standing fifth from right.*

BELOW: *Ralph Gibson, the Lab's longest-serving director (1948–1969). Gibson's career spanned some of the nation's most inspired technological advances in both defense and general science. His accolades included the Medal for Distinguished Public Service, the Defense Department's highest civilian award.*

Subsequent tests, however, revealed a vexing and persistent problem. The missile rolled in the opposite direction than had been predicted by existing aerodynamic theory. On the APL team was a young aerodynamicist named Alvin Eaton, who had joined the Lab in 1945. One evening in 1947 in a hotel bar, two colleagues challenged Eaton to solve the reverse-roll problem. After his co-workers retired to their rooms, he remained at the bar, working up some diagrams in pencil on a series of cocktail napkins.

As he worked, Eaton came to the conclusion that a strong interaction of pressure fields at the missile's wing–body juncture was occurring, causing the reverse roll. He awoke his Convair colleagues and used makeshift materials, including lampblack and oil and tiny silk tufts, to demonstrate the principle. Eaton not only showed them the reasons for the reverse roll, but he also showed how to control the problem via the use of flippers or fins situated at the ends of the tail surface. Eaton substantiated the feasibility of his theory through wind tunnel tests. Al Eaton's discovery that missiles could be steered with tail control surfaces also significantly reduced the size of missiles for compact shipboard storage. The small dorsal fins he developed are recognizable features on all Navy Standard Missiles to this day.

This unyielding approach to solving technical problems was APL's hallmark. Carl O. Bostrom, an experimental physicist who joined APL in 1960 and eventually became director, commented, "It is never enough to know that a technique or device works in principle. The real-world environment will inevitably frustrate the effort. ... More often than not, innovation is needs-driven."

Like other members of the staff, Bostrom believed that APL's activities should not end in the laboratory but should also include follow-up testing, evaluation, and physical participation in the Navy's fleet exercises to make observations and adjustments. Undoubtedly, this approach earned APL a reputation as a trusted source of competent and objective technical assessment and evaluation. The Navy appreciated that the Lab persevered until a problem was solved, or proven insoluble.

As initial tests of the Terrier were being conducted over the California desert, Soviet-backed North Korean troops stormed the 38th parallel into South Korea in June 1950. Just five years after the end of World War II, the United States was engaged in another armed conflict. The urgency of the war now dictated the accelerated development and deployment of the surface-to-air Terrier missile.

The First Guided-Missile Cruiser

In January 1953, APL oversaw successful at-sea tests of the Terrier aboard USS *Mississippi*, prompting the Navy to immediately put the missiles into large-scale production. In November 1955, the cruiser USS *Boston* was armed with Terriers, becoming the world's first guided-missile ship. APL had once again demonstrated an uncanny ability to solve the Navy's needs under extremely trying conditions in an incredibly short period of time.

During the same period, work progressed on the longer-range, supersonic, surface-to-air Talos ramjet-propelled missile. Because of its initial weight of 7,000 pounds, it was dubbed the Navy's "big missile." Under the direction of Wilbur Goss, the Lab initiated efforts to develop an experimental prototype of Talos and built test facilities to analyze data on the missile's air inlets, combustors, and guidance system.

One goal of the project was to design and develop a radar-assisted homing missile guidance system that could provide greater accuracy at longer ranges and lower altitudes than the beam-riding guidance system used in Terrier. This would allow the Navy to overcome an ongoing issue with the experimental missile. When it approached two or more planes flying closely together, the beam radar guidance system received conflicting signals from both targets and could not determine which one to attack.

APL's engineers resolved the issue by incorporating missile seeker technology from Raytheon's Sparrow air-to-air missile, as described in APL's *The First Forty Years*. The Navy requested that APL develop a Talos missile that could carry a tactical nuclear warhead. The U.S. Air Force also expressed interest in developing a land-based Talos system that would defend Strategic Air Command (SAC) bases against enemy bombers, but it never deployed Talos for this purpose.

By December 1953, APL had successfully flight-tested the first longer-range ramjet-powered Talos missile carrying a simulated nuclear warhead, just 18 months after the program commenced. Five years later, Talos entered service aboard the missile cruiser USS *Galveston*. By the mid-1960s, Talos was the principal air defense armament on six additional ships.

The Lab's many collaborations with the Navy and private industry on Terrier and Talos provided matchless first-hand knowledge about the behavior of shipboard missile systems and the problems that could arise in the use of these weapons. As more guided-missile ships came into commission,

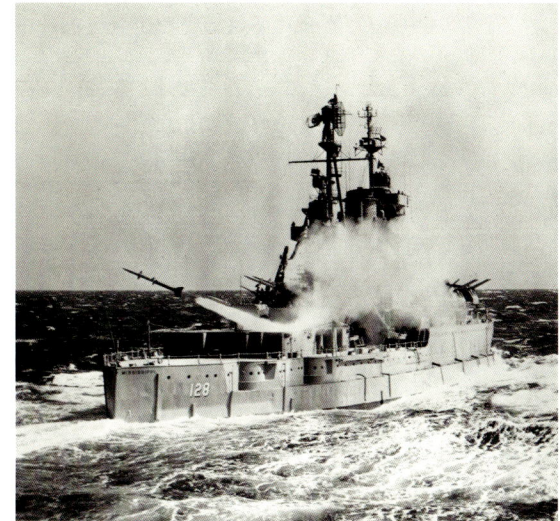

A Terrier missile roars off the aft launcher of USS Mississippi (BB 41), *which was modified in 1952 to carry two dual-arm missile launchers to permit testing of Terrier under more realistic at-sea conditions.*

APL's involvement with them expanded. Both Talos and Terrier had been developed for large Navy cruisers and destroyers, but not for smaller ships. At the Navy's request, APL established a small-ship guided-missile study group in March 1954 to design and develop Tartar, a compact, short-range weapon system.

APL's design for the smaller missile called for eliminating some of the separable components used in Terrier and Talos. For example, the booster and sustainer rockets in Terrier were replaced with a single dual-thrust motor in Tartar. Other aspects of the design were similarly graceful. The missile was controlled and steered by dorsal fins that unfolded immediately upon the launch, and the shipboard turret could store 40 missiles and launch them in rapid succession. The design was also cost-effective: Both Tartar and Terrier shared the same guidance and control components, permitting these components to be manufactured on a single production line. By 1960, the first Tartar-armed midsize ship was operating at sea.

All three missile systems—Terrier, Talos, and Tartar, which were named in honor of Merle Tuve and his Section T—drew on manual and computer simulations by the Lab's Assessment Division to analyze their effectiveness. The Lab's analytic models incorporated the systems' radar detection and tracking, missile trajectories, weapon delivery accuracy, and warhead damage measurements. These findings contributed to substantial improvements in the 3T missile systems, as they became known, offering a measure of relief to the U.S. government, which was extremely concerned about the Soviet Union's buildup of nuclear weapons. The combination of technical solutions in propulsion, guidance and control, aerodynamics, homing, and fusion not only led to the first Navy surface-to-air missiles but also is the *defining innovation* that is integral to modern air and missile defense systems.

The U.S. Navy was also focused on developing capabilities to launch a response attack from a submarine armed with nuclear warhead–equipped missiles to deter the threat of a Soviet preemptive nuclear strike against the United States. Submarine-launched ballistic missiles provided a significant deterrent advantage over land-based missiles because of the vessels' mobility and quiet acoustic signature, allowing them to avoid detection in vast ocean patrol areas. Ballistic missile submarines soon became a key element of the assured destruction policy of nuclear deterrence.

In 1957, the Navy's Special Projects Office (SP) was formed to develop a submarine-launched strategic weapons system. The office turned to APL to assess whether the existing liquid-fueled Jupiter intermediate-range missile might be suitable for the mission. The Navy wanted the system ready for launch no later than mid-1960.

The breakneck schedule was far from the project's only challenge. Because the Jupiter missiles stood 44 feet tall and weighed 160,000 pounds, adapting them to operate inside a submarine was daunting. The bottle-shaped rocket also was much bigger than anything previously tested and evaluated by the staff, and its guidance system had to be exceptionally precise and durable to withstand the shock of an undersea launch and the subsequent acceleration. This Jupiter design was not suitable for a submarine, and the Navy decided to abandon the Jupiter program in favor of a solid-fueled missile system for submarines, which evolved into the Polaris system. This shorter-range alternative with a solid rocket motor stood at 28 feet tall and was only 28,000 pounds.

"(Polaris) was just miles beyond anything that had ever been attempted," Kossiakoff said. "They were expecting a lot of things that were very high risk to work out all at the same time."

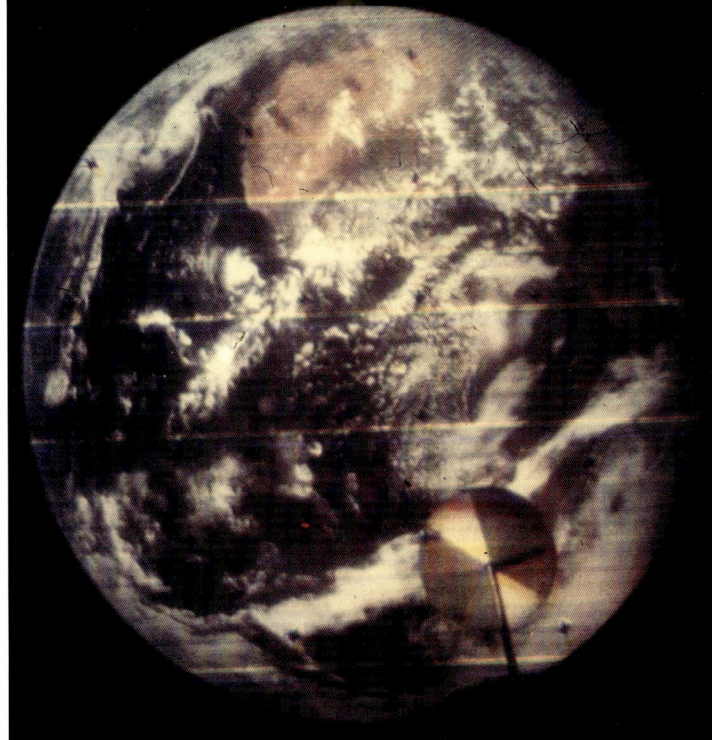

First Color Photo of Earth from Space

DODGE, the Department of Defense Gravity Experiment, was a satellite sent into orbit to study and demonstrate gravity-gradient stabilization, a procedure to keep one face of the satellite always pointing at the Earth. To help make certain that the satellite was pointing toward our planet, DODGE carried a camera, and by rotating three color filters in front of the lens, it was able to produce the first color picture ever made of the whole Earth. The photographs were featured in the November 1967 issue of *National Geographic*.

TOP LEFT: *Smoke billows below a Polaris missile during a test launch in April 1964, one of only two surface launches ever made in the history of the U.S. fleet ballistic missile program.*

It was these very high expectations that led the Navy to APL in the first place. However, the initial full-scale tests of Polaris at Cape Canaveral, Florida, were dismal failures, with the missiles breaking up a few seconds after their launch, the remnants floating in the nearby Banana River. Area residents dubbed the projectile a "snake killer."

The missile was sent back to the drawing board. Under Kershner's direction, APL conducted evaluations of the ground and flight test data to determine the reasons for the mishaps. The problem was jamming of the control system, a finding that led to a series of design changes subsequently implemented by the system contractor, Lockheed Missiles and Space Company.

In April 1959, the Polaris AX-6 missile was successfully launched at Cape Canaveral, traveling a distance of 300 miles. As one newspaper reported, "A smoke-belching Polaris rocket roared skyward today on its best launching to date. The rumble of the engines was heard for about one and a half minutes after the missile knifed through the clouds." The next step was to launch a Polaris missile from a submerged vessel. Several submarines already under construction were quickly adapted for this purpose.

On July 20, 1960, a Polaris missile was successfully launched from USS *George Washington*, making the vessel the Navy's first ballistic missile submarine. An hour and a half later, a second missile also fired perfectly. Both tests demonstrated the ability of Polaris to transition from underwater launch to powered flight. According to a prepared statement from the Navy, it was a "great step forward." More than that, their success in delivering a new capability from a concept in such a remarkably short time is a testament to the teamwork and ingenuity of APL, the Navy, and its industry partners.

Transit: The World's First Satellite Navigation System

In addition to defense of the Navy's surface fleet and strategic nuclear deterrence, the third of APL's burgeoning focus areas emerged from Merle Tuve's prescient decision to permit James Van Allen and other Lab scientists to pursue high-altitude research through the development of various measurement instruments. Just in time, too; the Soviet Union's launch of the first satellite, Sputnik, in October 1957, startled the United States, which had fully expected to launch its own satellite first.

The government had previously established a secret special presidential committee to evaluate opportunities in the field of satellite technology. This committee would later evolve into the Advanced Research Projects Agency (ARPA) and eventually into the Defense Advanced Research Projects Agency (DARPA). Unfortunately, the committee's efforts in space lagged behind the scientific accomplishments of the Soviets. APL would play an important role as the United States quickly entered the Space Age.

Intrigued by Sputnik's orbit around Earth, two young APL physicists, William Guier and George Weiffenbach, developed the first successful method of tracking satellites. Using an available 20-megahertz receiver, the physicists carefully observed and recorded the Doppler shift in signals that Sputnik transmitted.

Wilfred Zimmerman (left), David Moss, and James Smola test a mechanism designed to prevent the Transit 1A satellite from spinning while in orbit.

RIGHT: *George Weiffenbach (left), Frank McClure, and William Guier—who invented the concept of satellite navigation—study a map showing Transit satellite orbit passes.*

BELOW: *Technicians in APL's Computing Center process the Doppler information sent to it by six Transit receiving stations across the globe.* (U.S. NAVY)

"(They) decided that it would be fun to listen to the beeps that it was emitting, so they set up a receiver," Kossiakoff recalled. "Being accustomed to taking observations, they recorded the beeps, and as the satellite passed overhead, they heard the Doppler effect. When the satellite was approaching, the beep had a high pitch, and as it was receding, it dropped down to a low pitch, so it made sort of an S-curve on the plot. They also happened to be very skilled at complex calculations. We had these big computers. They said, 'I wonder what we could learn by studying the exact shape of that curve?'" What they learned was that they could precisely determine Sputnik's orbit solely by taking the Doppler measurements as the satellite passed over APL's campus.

Guier and Weiffenbach discussed their Doppler tracking results with Frank McClure, chairman of APL's research program. McClure, who was engaged in the Polaris strategic submarine program on behalf of the Navy, realized that the men's discovery might solve the problem submarines face in precisely determining their locations in the oceans of the world, as Kossiakoff explained, "by turning the thing around."

In other words, since it was possible to determine from the ground where a satellite was in its orbit, it might also be possible to determine locations on Earth from satellites in orbit. As McClure put it in saltier terms in a 1958 interview, "If you can find the orbit of a satellite (with Doppler tracking), you sure as hell can find the listening station on Earth from the orbit." Guier and Weiffenbach had effectively solved a major Navy dilemma—the worldwide navigation of Polaris submarines. The accuracy of this type of navigation system far surpassed that of any previous system.

As always, APL was eager to take a concept through to its completion. In a meeting with officials from ARPA, McClure expressed his opinion that the Lab had the solution to the navigation problem and wanted to demonstrate it by actually building a satellite and trying it out. "They gave us start-up funds, and sure enough, (we) built a satellite using the same people that built guided missiles," Kossiakoff recalled.

The Lab was a fitting choice for the project, which the Navy subsequently funded in full. The staff had significant experience building complicated, durable electronic equipment that fit in a small space and also could withstand the impact from the launch and acceleration by rockets. Just two and a half years after Sputnik shot through the skies, APL created the world's first navigational satellite, which the Lab dubbed Transit, still naming projects with a "T" in honor of Merle Tuve.

The prototype satellite, the Transit 1A, was launched on a Thor Able rocket in September 1959. Although it failed to reach orbit, all other aspects of the launch were successful. This gave APL enough confidence to establish a Space Development Division, headed by Kershner, on Christmas Eve 1959.

Just four and a half months after the new division was established, Transit 1B was launched at Cape Canaveral by a three-stage Thor Able-Star rocket. The satellite made it safely into orbit, albeit at a lower orbit than was planned. Nevertheless, the satellite performed well enough for the Navy to continue funding APL's design and building of additional experimental Transit satellites.

With characteristic diligence and perseverance, staff members produced a series of Transit satellites. The spacecraft entered service as the Navy Navigation Satellite System in 1964; four years later, an operational constellation of satellites and on-orbit spares was in place. APL's multifaceted work comprised the design and development of the satellites, shipboard receivers, and a network of ground stations. The system provided positional accuracy on Earth within 100 meters. This *defining innovation*, called Transit, was the forerunner of modern Global Positioning System (GPS) technology that is ubiquitous today.

A New Home in Howard County

To accommodate the Lab's growing and varied workload, the staff progressively grew to a point where it became distressingly obvious that the space at 8621 Georgia Avenue and the two nearby buildings in Silver Spring were insufficient. There was another drawback. "As Silver Spring grew and settled, the countryside around that laboratory became filled with houses," Kossiakoff recalled in a March 2000 interview. "The residents complained bitterly that there was too much disturbance going on."

The search for much larger accommodations began and ended in 1953 with the purchase of 290 acres in Howard County, Maryland, about 15 miles northeast of the original headquarters site.

Staff members move Transit 1B to its launch vehicle. The satellite launched on April 13, 1960, and despite not reaching ideal orbit, it proved that the concept of satellite navigation would work.

Butler Buildings

About 20 "Butler" buildings, 40 feet wide, 100 feet long, and 13 feet tall, were erected on campus from 1955 to 1959. Although intended to serve as temporary structures to augment space and efficiency (at the time, only Building 1 existed on campus), most remained the site of important Lab research for the next five decades. In 1986, plans were announced to demolish eight of the buildings to make way for Building 13. The rest remained until a demolition event on August 1, 2008, marked by a celebration of the buildings' history—and of the "Central Green" to come.

TOP RIGHT: *Walt Verdier (left), supervisor of the Contracts and Budgets Group, and Director Ralph Gibson watch the ground being leveled for the first building to be constructed on the Howard County site in 1953.*

Johns Hopkins University agreed to assume one-third of the land's cost, and the Navy agreed to amortize the remainder. At $300 per acre, the property was inexpensive and its large footprint provided ample room for future growth.

In 1954, the first building on the site, a $1.8 million, 63,000-square-foot structure known as the "new laboratory," was ready for occupancy. Within months of the building's dedication ceremonies, Johns Hopkins University's board of trustees approved the construction of a $1 million addition to the main structure. A dozen prefabricated sheet-metal "Butler" buildings were acquired and stationed on the APL campus to house the Terrier and Talos test and engineering facilities. In subsequent years, the Forest Grove operations were relocated to these buildings.

Once a clandestine operation in a former automobile dealership disguised with a "USED CARS" sign, APL was now revealed to the world as a sophisticated research and development laboratory. While most of the work going on at the new campus still remained classified, the new headquarters played an important role in the recruitment of many esteemed scientists, engineers, and technicians. For one thing, it actually looked like a major research facility, which it was. But even more important in attracting high-quality candidates was how APL differentiated itself from other research and development organizations. Job candidates were told they would have the opportunity to apply the results of their work to practical problems of national importance, in a university environment.

The opportunity to perform groundbreaking research in the name of patriotic public service resonated with many engineers and scientists, both young and old. This new generation of innovators would play a pivotal role at the Lab as it continued to grow and tackle ever more critical challenges.

Early Autonomy:
Ferdinand and the Beast

APL can trace its expanding knowledge and leadership in robotics and autonomy to a pair of "automatons" affectionately known as Ferdinand and the Beast. The APL scientists (such as John Chubbuck, shown here with Ferdinand) who built the robots in the early 1960s wanted to create a machine that could operate without human assistance in a natural environment, rather than in one constructed especially for it. Based on the state of electronics and artificial intelligence at the time, the robots' sole purpose was to survive by navigating APL's hallways.

And survive they did: Using touch-sensor systems, the cylindrical Beast and its older, smaller, square-shaped "brother" Ferdinand avoided doorjambs, vending machines, stairs, open doorways, and other obstacles to locate electrical outlets and recharge their batteries.

The Beast later acquired sonic guidance and optical recognition systems, an early sign of the quick development and adaptation infused throughout APL's current work, the same characteristics that are leading to autonomous and robotic technologies capable of supporting combat and exploring the seas and skies, in addition to protecting troops and improving lives.

More recently, APL has made significant advances in battlefield and homeland protection with the Advanced Explosive Ordnance Disposal Robotic System (AEODRS), a program to develop a family of interoperable and interchangeable robotic systems.

The guided-missile cruiser USS Ticonderoga (CG 47) was the first Navy warship to feature the Aegis Combat System, which allows the ship to track and engage multiple airborne threats.

Chapter 5

From Rockets and Missiles to Strategy and Systems

In the 1960s and 1970s, APL's core efforts on behalf of the U.S. Navy, to design and develop guided missiles, evaluate the sea-based strategic deterrent force, and develop a satellite navigation system, evolved to innovatively solving new, extremely complex technical problems.

As before, the Lab applied a systems engineering approach to a sponsor's problems and needs. Rather than simply build something to specifications, APL's engineers and scientists evaluated the all-encompassing goal and then designed, developed, and, in some cases, manufactured what was required to achieve it, in collaboration with industry partners. This work was followed by rigorous tests and analyses of the system to ensure the end solution comprehensively addressed the overall operational objective.

APL worked closely with the Navy officers and technical personnel, as well as with the private companies that transitioned the Lab's experimental prototypes into production articles. When technical and production issues surfaced, APL's expertise was available to industry to help solve these problems. To conduct tests and train operators in the use of a system, staff members were regularly dispatched to Navy surface ships and submarines, in some cases for weeks at a time.

The Laboratory's singular approach to solving problems and its track record of success continued to make it a go-to organization for many of the Navy's complex operational needs. The Cold War had entered a new phase of hostilities in the late 1960s, marked by the escalating conflict in Vietnam. U.S. policymakers gradually increased the country's involvement in this war to contain the spread of communism and curtail Soviet expansion. At the same time, the Soviet Union continued to enlarge its nuclear arsenal.

The Navy had three specific concerns that APL could address: attacks by low-altitude anti-ship missiles evading radar detection, the use of electronic countermeasures to jam communications and radar systems, and the launch of multiple missiles simultaneously. Existing U.S. defensive systems could not respond in time to these tactics. APL would be called on to address all three issues.

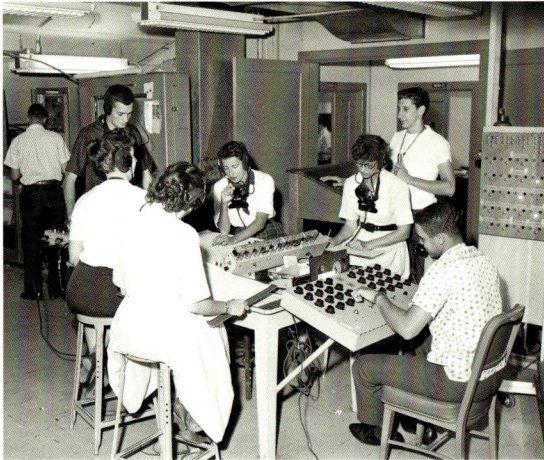

In the early 1960s, the Navy was readying a large number of new U.S. surface ships for service. The ships would carry advanced versions of the Terrier extended-range missile and the Tartar medium-range missile. More than 26 Terrier-armed vessels were near completion, and to protect these vessels at sea, the Navy requested that the Lab undertake a comprehensive study of the Soviet air threat.

Warfare Analysis: Defining Threats and Capabilities

APL's Assessment Division, which had been overseeing warfare analyses since it began as Central Laboratory Assessment in the late 1940s, developed a computerized version of the Navy's air defense, dubbed Program 323, which allowed for more quantitative assessments than had been previously possible. The effort was among the first large digital computer simulations of naval air defense. To assist the Navy in its use, the Lab conducted an analytical war game of a Soviet missile attack against a U.S. carrier battle group.

These heightened analyses were just the first step in the Lab's approach to the Navy's needs. The overarching goal was to develop a comprehensive shipboard weapons system that could be used to eliminate or reduce the adversary's air threat. This new ship defense system would rely on powerful computers and a more effective type of radar to detect and track missiles launched by enemy ships and submarines. Other objectives were to obtain a better understanding of electronic countermeasures designed to jam or deceive radar, sonar, or other detection systems as well as the electronic counter-countermeasures that would minimize the effect of the countermeasures.

During its maiden cruise off the coast of Virginia, USS Albany *(CG 10)—the first cruiser to be armed solely with guided missiles—simultaneously fires three air defense missiles (two Talos and one Tartar).*

It was a tall order, even for APL. The Navy tasked the Lab to put together a plan for a new ship defense surveillance system that could detect, identify, track, and destroy an incoming missile. The challenges were many and complex. For instance, radar systems at the time were subject to interference caused by the weather, sea movements, encumbrances on land, and the electronic countermeasures taken by an adversary to saturate a radar receiver with "noise," or incorrect information. These impediments made it difficult to determine whether or not an adversary's missile had actually been detected—obviously not a reliable baseline for ship safety and security.

The staff members were entrusted to test their hypotheses, analyze the data, and issue a final report on suggested recommendations. To assist this work, full-scale replicas of the Terrier and Talos fire-control systems—the components that come together to assist a weapons system to hit a target—were built at the campus. Their assessment, led by Alvin Schulz, who later became an associate director at the Lab, suggested the development of a futuristic integrated weapons control system that could spot, pursue, and destroy an adversary's missiles while eliminating most countermeasures and counter-countermeasures. The report indicated that these much-needed capabilities could be achieved through the development of a phased-array radar system utilizing electronic beam scanning to identify an incoming missile.

Transit's Technology Innovations

During the 1960s and 1970s, the Lab designed, built, tested, and operated numerous satellites for the Transit navigation system. Fully operational in 1964 with a constellation of five primary satellites, the system vastly improved the ability of U.S. submarines around the globe to accurately determine their positions.

Navigation was not Transit's sole purpose, however. Its satellites carried instruments to measure the Earth's geodetic and magnetic properties and to serve purposes of astronomy.

APL pioneered many advances in satellite design and operation. Much of this work was in response to big challenges, such as keeping satellites facing Earth so their signals could be received without interruption. In addressing the issue, APL applied principles that used Earth's gravitational field to keep the spacecraft's antennae always pointing Earthward for proper control and stabilization.

Another challenge was the constant spinning of satellites once launched. The incessant rotation made it difficult for scientists to accurately measure the spacecraft's Doppler signals to place the satellite in geosynchronous orbit. To combat the problem, APL incorporated a de-spinning mechanism similar to a yo-yo toy. After launch, weights at the end of tethers were ejected from each side of the rotating spacecraft to neutralize the spin.

Other innovations included an ultra-stable quartz crystal oscillator to maintain precise radio frequencies and the use of dual frequencies to overcome the signal-distorting effects of the Earth's atmosphere. Transit satellites were among the first spacecraft to be controlled from ground command and the first with onboard computers and microprocessors to store digital data. Transit also served as the world's first satellite-based navigation system, making it the precursor to the modern GPS (Global Positioning System).

In 1967, APL released use of the Transit system to private industry, where it became the reference system for ocean navigation, oil surveying, international boundaries, and other critical measurements, continuing to serve into the 2000s.

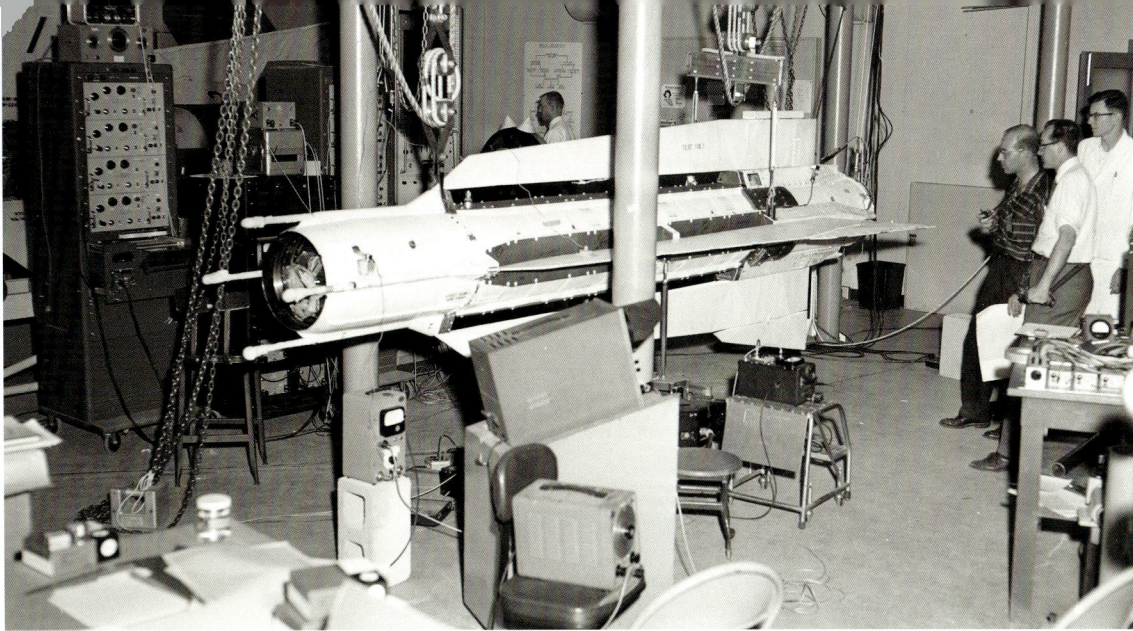

First Effort to Build a Navy Phased-Array Radar

In the 1960s, radars typically relied on a single movable antenna that mechanically rotated 360 degrees, and it was becoming increasingly clear that such radars would be unable to detect, track, and guide U.S. surface-to-air missiles against multiple attacking enemy aircraft or missiles. To address this critical challenge, APL developed a phased-array radar concept for the Navy. The earliest design grouped together a number of antenna "feeds" via a special microwave lens to transmit and receive multiple signals simultaneously. This allowed for more precise analyses by analog computing, which could interpret the wave interactions among these signals and form directive antenna beams. Each second, the radar antenna conducted 360-degree scans of the horizon with its beams, tracking up to 10 targets at intervals of 1/10th of a second—an amazing accomplishment.

Through this work, APL also introduced a practical way to filter out clutter and jamming. Most important, the Lab's multifunction phased-array radar was designed to guide 20 U.S. missiles to multiple targets at the same time. This new ship defense system offered a decisive advantage over existing systems. Its capabilities were so formidable that the Navy named it Typhon, after the monstrous giant and most deadly being of Greek mythology.

"Typhon was the first attempt to recognize that the anti-aircraft warfare problem was a total package," said Alvin Eaton, Typhon project supervisor at APL, in a 1962 interview. "You had to consider finding potential targets, sorting them out, defining which of the things you saw were proper targets for engagement, setting up an engagement process, and actually executing the engagements."

At the Navy's request, APL subsequently designed and developed two different Typhon prototype missiles: a long-range ramjet to strike an aircraft before it released its weapons and a medium-range solid-rocket missile that could be fired in rapid sequence, one missile every 10 seconds. Due to the complexity and ambitiousness of this innovation, the new system experienced significant technical and production problems, causing unexpected delays and cost overruns.

The Big Dish Goes Up

APL's "big dish," a 60-foot-diameter satellite antenna, opened for operations on March 15, 1963. Constructed of fiberglass and aluminum, the big reflector, which was designed for APL by the Philco Corporation's Western Development Division, was placed atop a two-million-pound concrete base, which supports a 45-foot-tall pedestal. The antenna can command satellites, receive signals, and track space probes as far as 230 million miles from Earth. The antenna's first job was to communicate with the Lab's Transit satellites, and it has sent commands to and received data from dozens of spacecraft over the past five decades.

TOP LEFT: *A Typhon missile undergoing testing at APL's Environmental Test Laboratory.*

RIGHT: *This small facility, placed on the roof of Building 6, housed a prototype of the Lab's Advanced Multifunction Array Radar (AMFAR) system. AMFAR's successor, the AN/SPY-1, became the primary radar for the Aegis Combat System.*

BELOW: *This view of the AMFAR prototype with panels removed shows the interior microwave and electronics elements of the system. Instead of a large, rotating dish, AMFAR used electronics to send out radar beams at any angle in microseconds.*

"In truth, the radar was somewhat ahead of its time," said Eaton. "We were postulating the use of techniques that weren't quite ready. We had done that before in Talos, Terrier, and Tartar development, but this was different. It required substantial improvements in particular elements and in overall system control."

Because of government budget constraints and continuing radar design issues, the Navy made the difficult decision in 1963 to terminate further Typhon development. Although this was a blow to the morale of those working on this effort, a silver lining appeared two years later. The Navy authorized the development of an advanced surface missile system (ASMS) that called for a new design approach for a phased-array radar system, providing another opportunity to achieve the objectives of Typhon.

As this work progressed, a Soviet-made cruise missile fired from an Egyptian patrol boat in 1967 sank the Israeli destroyer *Eilat*. The action compelled the Department of Defense (DoD) to approve additional funding for the Navy to produce the ASMS integrated naval weapons combat system in a shorter time frame.

Other geopolitical factors also soon came into play. In 1968, American forces reached their peak in Vietnam, following the Tet Offensive, during which 80,000 North Vietnamese regular army troops and Viet Cong attacked in an attempt to overthrow the South Vietnamese government. With tensions rising between the superpowers, ASMS was now deemed absolutely crucial to the Navy's defense strategy.

Looking ahead, the Navy could see the end of the service life of the Talos cruisers in the 1980s, followed by the end of the Terrier and Tartar guided-missile destroyers in the 1990s. ASMS would supersede these programs as the nation's next-generation advanced air defense system. In 1969, ASMS was renamed Aegis, for the shield of the ancient Greek god Zeus. Aegis would "shield" a new Navy fleet comprising a series of technologically advanced ships with a revolutionary combat system that integrated radar, guidance, control, and propulsion technology.

The Navy requested that APL conduct experiments and analyses to develop the radar detection and tracking technology for Aegis. Recent enhancements in solid-state electronics and digital computers assisted the Lab's creation of an Advanced Multifunction Array Radar (AMFAR) system in 1969, led by Chester Phillips, Bill Zinger, Theodore Cheston, and Joe Frank. For this design "phase shifters" had been invented to digitally control, via computer, the combination of signals among radiating elements making up the array to form directional antenna beams.

AMFAR could electronically send out a radar beam at any angle in microseconds, rather than waiting for a large, cumbersome radar dish to complete a rotation. In fact, this electronic agility was so fast that the array allowed the radar to do many things very quickly and could interweave the data, allowing radars on ships to keep up with a massive missile attack and shoot down the missiles before they arrived. APL effectively demonstrated that a full-scale system with AMFAR's design could satisfy the Aegis system's operational requirements for surveillance, tracking, and missile guidance via the AN/SPY-1 system.

The Navy selected RCA Missile and Surface Radar Division (today part of Lockheed Martin) as the contractor to build the revolutionary naval combat system, with APL serving as the technical advisor. APL's primary task was to examine the contractor's design to ensure it was simple to operate at sea and satisfied the Navy's technical requirements. If not, the Lab was given leeway to propose alternative approaches more likely to meet the technical requirements and to conduct critical evaluations of the proposed alternatives.

AMFAR, a *defining innovation*, was so well designed that RCA adopted its architecture and key components, including the phase shifters. The AMFAR design remains a recognizable feature of today's Aegis SPY-1 radar configuration; this radar lies behind the signature octagonal plate visible on the superstructures of ships that carry the Aegis Combat System.

Meanwhile, APL was simultaneously involved in another project to develop an automatic detection and tracking system upgrade to the Navy's Terrier and Tartar missile defense systems to better distinguish between actual targets and interference. The IADT (Integrated, Automated Detection and Tracking) system fused data from the signal returns of multiple onboard ship radars to automatically detect and follow large numbers of aircraft and cruise missiles in the at-sea environment, with fewer false radar contacts, faster speeds of identification, and more precise target locks. In 1978, APL's design (designated the AN/SYS-1 system) was successfully tested on USS *Towers*. The second IADT system, AN/SYS-2, was positively demonstrated in 1982 aboard USS *Mahan*.

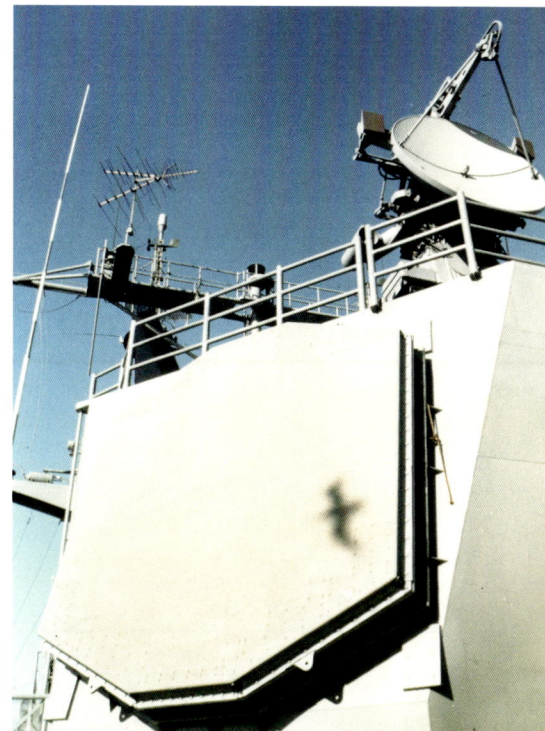

Encased by its signature octagonal cover plate, the AN/SPY-1 phased-array radar antenna is shown installed aboard USS Norton Sound *(AVM 1) for operational testing.*

RIGHT: *A Harpoon missile seeker undergoing testing in the anechoic chamber at APL's Guidance Systems Evaluation Laboratory (GSEL).*

BELOW: *The Harpoon anti-ship missile was designed to be launched from Navy ships, submarines, and aircraft; here, a P-3C Orion anti-submarine and maritime surveillance aircraft carries four Harpoons under its wings and fuselage. APL validated the sea-skimming anti-ship missile's guidance and seeker systems in low-level flights over the open ocean made in a World War II–era B-25 bomber.* (U.S. NAVY)

The Lab's contributions to the AN/SPY-1 radar system for the new Aegis ships, and the AN/SYS automated detection and tracking systems for Terrier and Tartar, encouraged the Navy in 1978 to designate APL as the technical direction agent for the Battle Group Anti-Air Warfare Coordination (BGAAWC) program, focused on ensuring interoperability among the ships.

The Navy hoped to use such advanced automation and integration to coordinate the defense of the entire fleet against large-scale raids by aircraft and cruise missiles; the latter utilized high-G maneuvers under the cover of self-screening and high-powered jammers. Such deceptive practices would overwhelm the tracking capability of a single radar. To tackle this intricate threat, the Navy hoped to integrate the radar and fire-control systems of different ships to direct multiple vessels in a wide-ranging battle group to carry out a mission on a synchronized basis.

Prior to this program, APL's primary task was to design combat systems for individual ship operations. At the Navy's behest, the Lab now focused on developing a way to collect, distribute, and weave together the missile target information of several ships in a theater to coordinate the weapon to target across the entire battle group. In succeeding years and decades, APL would inch ever closer to achieving this powerful networked air defense.

Precision Strike Systems: Harpoon and Tomahawk

The 1967 sinking of the Israeli ship *Eilat* also convinced the Navy that it needed to quickly develop its own cruise missiles. Work subsequently progressed to produce what would become the medium-range anti-ship Harpoon missile and the longer-range Tomahawk cruise missile, both of which would

Exploiting Undersea Physics: Advanced Sonar Arrays

APL has long been at the forefront of testing and evaluating sensor systems at sea to ensure the high performance, accuracy, and reliability of towed sonar arrays. From the beginning of the SSBN Security Technology Program (SSTP), the Lab has followed a rigorous methodology for planning and executing large-scale ocean tests, a true team effort comprising numerous scientists, engineers, and support personnel working toward a common goal.

When DoD experiments with long-line towed sonar arrays in the early 1970s failed to achieve the high gain they were designed for, APL developed the tests, prototypes, models, and detailed ocean physics and engineering analyses needed to unlock the potential of this revolutionary technology application.

APL's groundbreaking undersea research and development resulted in a *defining innovation* that provided the foundation for the powerful long-range towed arrays in use throughout the U.S. Navy today aboard submarines, surface combatants, and surveillance platforms. In addition, this innovation informed the stealth design requirements for multiple generations of U.S. submarines.

This work continues through research and development for providing cross-platform systems that integrate multiple sensors into a network to improve the effectiveness of anti-submarine warfare. For example, a major technical issue with this concept has been the communications bandwidth needed to transmit significant amounts of data produced by multiple sensors. In response, APL staff members developed an original set of data compression algorithms.

APL's SSTP efforts in nonacoustics over the past 40 years have resulted in the development of increasingly smaller and more sensitive, accurate, and reliable sensors measuring the ocean's temperature, conductivity, fluorescence, and acoustic and optical properties. The Lab's continual design improvements have led to significantly enhanced sensor performance and higher reliability in the unforgiving ocean environment.

A Harpoon missile launches from USS Lockwood *(DE 1064) in 1973. Lab engineers made key contributions to the Harpoon targeting system, electronics, propulsion system, and airframe.* (U.S. NAVY)

become vital precision strike systems for the Navy. APL scientists and engineers played a number of key roles in each program, especially in missile guidance and accuracy.

In developing the Harpoon, the Navy wanted a missile that could be launched from ships, submarines, and aircraft. APL was selected to head several important design studies, and Martin Barylski led an APL team that made critical contributions to understanding radar backscattering from the sea and its effect on the selection of active radar seeker parameters against ship targets. Engineers at APL designed multi-frequency radars and instrumentation to collect data on sea clutter, target radar cross-section, and radar track point. This equipment was installed in a World War II–era B-25 bomber flown as low as 50 feet over the water. Laboratory engineers flew in the aircraft as test conductors during various test phases, playing a key role in validating the missile's accuracy in low-level flights over the open ocean and presenting data that was compared with competing seeker concepts. The resulting targeting system was so precise that the missile was immediately put into production by McDonnell Douglas, which was selected to develop and build the missile.

Another concern of the Navy's was the potential for an adversary to use sophisticated jamming and deception techniques to misdirect a Harpoon cruise missile. To limit this possibility, the Navy solicited APL's countermeasure technology expertise in guidance-testing the missile system. Other APL-led studies helped determine the propulsion system and airframe selected for Harpoon, which was flight certified in 1976.

Collaborative Leadership

By 1966, Ralph Gibson, who had served as Lab director since 1948, and Johns Hopkins University President Milton Eisenhower were nearing retirement. To ensure a smooth transition, they agreed that an outstanding choice to succeed Gibson would be Alexander Kossiakoff, then the Lab's associate director. Frank McClure was selected to fill the position being vacated by Kossiakoff.

During the transition, which unexpectedly lasted two years, Kossiakoff was appointed assistant director and McClure associate director. In effect, three people filled two positions. Fortunately, what might have been an awkward situation for some organizations was a benefit to the Lab because of the leaders' close working relationships. The timing allowed Gibson to focus on external relations with sponsors and Congress, while Kossiakoff and McClure focused on Lab operations. During this same period, APL negotiated and signed a new trust agreement with the Navy, ensuring the Lab's continuing technology development role. Shown in the photo (from left) are Alexander Kossiakoff, Rear Admiral Arthur Gralla, William Mautz (standing), Ralph Gibson, Henry Porter (standing), A. L. Gordon, Stuart Janney Jr., and Frank McClure at the signing of the agreement.

When he retired in 1969, Gibson had served as director for 21 years, an achievement that will probably never be bested. During his tenure, APL expanded from early missile development to broader systems across the fleet, and he enthusiastically supported development of Transit, the world's first satellite-based global navigation system. He also fostered collaborations with the Johns Hopkins School of Medicine.

Like Gibson, Alexander Kossiakoff was an expert in the new field of rocket propulsion and also joined APL after working at the Allegany Ballistics Laboratory. After the war, he led efforts to improve missile designs and development, most notably on the use of modular missile design for the Terrier missile. Though he stepped down as director in 1980, Kossiakoff continued making valuable contributions to the Lab as its chief scientist. His commitment to education is recognized in the large auditorium and classroom facility that bears his name—the Kossiakoff Center, which was dedicated in 1983 on APL's campus.

Frank McClure, who played a major role in the development of the Transit satellite navigation system for the Navy, went on to serve as the first director of APL's Research Center from 1949 to 1972. The center achieved international recognition in numerous research areas in physics and chemistry, and the 1,000 papers published during his tenure as director are a tribute to his extraordinary scientific leadership.

APL also worked on the guidance accuracy of the longer-range Tomahawk cruise missile, which initially had a range of 250 miles. The Navy wanted the missile to become a longer-range nuclear strike weapon that could navigate heavily defended environments and strike strategic targets. Achieving these goals required a means to autonomously verify and adjust the missile's location en route to a target. APL engineers attacked the problem using terrain-contour matching (TERCOM) technology, which matches a missile's onboard altimeter readings to elevation maps stored in its computer. The Lab developed algorithms to reliably predict which ground areas provided a correct match.

To improve the accuracy of conventionally armed Tomahawks, APL created another set of algorithms to effectively use Digital Scene Matching Area Correlator (DSMAC) technology. The algorithms compared images taken by a camera on the missile to scenes stored in the missile's computer. Based on the success of APL's initial work on Tomahawk, the Navy appointed the Lab the technical direction agent for the Tomahawk program in 1982.

This *defining innovation*—the application of TERCOM and DSMAC to create the world's first long-range precision-guided weapon that could fly at low altitude over variable terrain to its selected target—has been a key element of the U.S. arsenal since the early 1990s. TERCOM and DSMAC remain operational on Tomahawk for use if GPS is not available.

SSBN Security: Protecting Our Nation's Sea-Based Strategic Deterrent

By the late 1960s, Russian technological advances were placing U.S. strategic bomber and intercontinental ballistic missile forces at risk, increasing the nation's reliance on its submarine-launched

ballistic missile force to provide a credible deterrent. However, it was not known whether these submarines could remain undetected to survive a nuclear first strike and retaliate. In response, DoD established the SSBN Security Technology Program (SSTP), with APL as the lead laboratory, to ensure survivability of the nuclear-armed submarine force by virtue of its stealth.

The initial APL team recognized the limitations of relying too heavily on intelligence, and they avoided hasty decisions to implement "obvious" or "easy" countermeasures, often based on unreliable assessments. Instead, they created an innovative approach that relied on rigorous modeling, analysis, and testing to authoritatively assess and address the art of the possible in undersea detection, which was the key to submarine survival.

The program was driven by what the laws of physics and the limits of technology allowed. All relevant undersea phenomenologies, such as acoustics and hydrodynamics, were investigated to identify vulnerabilities and explore uncertainties associated with them. Rigorously applying the scientific method, APL physicists and engineers conducted at-sea testing to resolve uncertainties, allowing them to authoritatively determine whether or not a vulnerability existed.

Since this program started, APL has conducted more than 200 scientific sea tests and more than 190 tactical exercises, investigating more than 50 ocean phenomenologies to detect and correct vulnerabilities in the stealth of U.S. submarines. Early on, national policymakers gained confidence in the survivability of our sea-based deterrent, and the prospect of a renewed nuclear arms race was averted. Forty-seven years later, a survivable sea-based deterrent continues to deter adversaries and dissuade potential adversaries.

Tensions Rise at Home During the Vietnam Conflict

While the Lab continued to make a number of significant technical contributions to the nation, this period was one of great social upheaval across the nation and the world. The Vietnam War resulted in anti-war demonstrations across the country and strident protests at Johns Hopkins University about the institution's support of APL's wartime contributions. It was a challenging time at the Lab, but under the leadership of Director Kossiakoff, APL had established a clear role as a national technical and scientific resource.

In 1968, the board of trustees affirmed the criticality of the Lab's work, noting that these efforts extended beyond national security. As the executive committee of the board wrote, "APL has made and can continue to make highly significant contributions to the advancement of general science and technology." The committee further cited the joint programs and mutually beneficial interactions between APL and other divisions of the university, making the Lab "appropriate to the central purpose" of Johns Hopkins. Certainly, the Navy considered APL's contributions to be invaluable. "There is no other organization in the U.S. with experience in the problems of the Navy which has the breadth of demonstrated capability in science and engineering which is found at APL," Assistant Secretary of the Navy Robert Frosch commented in 1971.

Four years later, the two-decade Vietnam War finally ended. Questions lingered about the university's continuing support of APL, and then another institutional challenge surfaced in 1976. DoD conducted a study to examine the efficacy of the nine nonprofit federal contract research centers (FCRCs) that had provided the department with analyses and evaluations since 1950, assisting its planning, research and technology development, and systems engineering and technical direction. APL was an FCRC at the time, and this study would influence the U.S. Congress in limiting the mission scope and size of projects undertaken by the FCRCs.

As a result of the study, Congress concluded that APL and a similar laboratory at Penn State University should no longer be considered FCRCs. Rather, the Lab should contract with DoD under the procurement procedures that were traditionally in place for universities. This was a highly positive development.

As Malcolm R. Currie, undersecretary of defense for research and engineering at DoD and the author of the study, reported to Congress: "University laboratories function as creative sources of new technology and vital ties to the university community. They have developed capabilities in their specialty areas, which are not paralleled by other organizations in industry or government. Universities attract staffs of outstanding quality and provide an environment of professionalism and objectivity. They fill essential missions for the [military] services and the services strongly support their use."

While the report recommended the imposition of controls on the remaining FCRCs, the message regarding APL was clear: The Lab's work was so singularly important to the nation that it required a degree of flexibility not afforded by FCRC regulations.

Electronic Warfare

On July 24, 1965, the United States lost its first aircraft to a Soviet-built SA-2 surface-to-air missile system in the skies over Vietnam. The next day, the director of defense for research and engineering asked APL to study the situation and recommend ways to counter this threat. APL completed an initial assessment within two weeks and recommended changes to tactics and the development of electronic countermeasures.

To validate these changes, APL developed a test range facility in partnership with the Navy's primary operational testing organization, known as Echo Range, at China Lake, California. In the years since, APL has played a large role in the design and development of systems to support the

Navy EA-6B Prowler electronic warfare aircraft (shown flying over USS *John F. Kennedy* in the Navy photo above), as well as its successor, the EA-18 Growler. Both aircraft are designed and equipped to suppress enemy defenses in support of U.S. and allied offensive operations.

When the Air Force decided to build its own jamming capability in the EF-111A in 1983, APL performed similar tasks, leading to related self-protection jamming and decoy technologies and tactics.

These efforts expanded to include developing countermeasures against enemy weapon systems and counter-countermeasures to prevent enemy systems from

defeating U.S. systems. APL continues to be deeply involved in Navy electronic warfare operations through its work with the Jammer Technique Optimization (JATO) group. This consortium of military, government, and independent research and development organizations provides engineering, development, and test support to evaluate, validate, and operate radar and communications jamming techniques. Among JATO's more recent successes is APL's development of a jamming capability for the U.S. Marine Corps to defeat the use of improvised explosive devices (IEDs) in Iraq.

APL continues to support the Navy, Air Force, and Marine Corps in developing and operating countermeasure systems.

At the radar display, Director Alexander Kossiakoff (seated) and James Austin of the Fleet Systems Department, who later led the Submarine Technology Department, view combat information from SYS-1, whose development they led. The SYS-1 software combines data from multiple radars, allowing earlier detection of threats.

Space Technology–Inspired Medical Devices

Beginning in the 1960s, APL's pursuit of new technologies to solve medical problems yielded several important breakthroughs, including the world's first rechargeable pacemaker, an implantable defibrillator, and an implantable insulin medication system. Like many Lab medical device innovations, these devices grew from technology developed for space missions that relied on the miniaturization of advanced, highly reliable electronics. These devices were developed in partnership with Johns Hopkins Medicine.

To build a rechargeable pacemaker, APL engineers had to overcome the issue of deterioration of electronic components by body fluids. To do so, they developed the first hermetically sealed pacemaker, applying reliability and assurance techniques used to validate spacecraft. They also leveraged their expertise in telemetry to remotely collect performance data. In the 11 years of the device's use, nearly 6,000 people were implanted with it.

The implantable defibrillator was born from a Johns Hopkins School of Medicine request for APL's assistance in applying its microelectronics expertise. The resulting Automatic Implantable Cardiac Defibrillator could both detect the onset of fibrillation and respond to it. The battery-powered device, about the size of a computer mouse, was successfully implanted for the first time in 1980. Subsequent clinical studies indicated that the thousands of patients implanted with the device more than doubled their life expectancy after receiving the defibrillator.

By the 1980s, APL's biomedical engineers had developed a Programmable Implantable Medication System (PIMS) to automatically deliver correct doses of insulin. A project in partnership with Novo Pharmaceutical in Denmark, which perfected a motion-resistant form of insulin, PIMS was first successfully implanted in 1985. Within the next half-dozen years, the insulin pump was implanted in hundreds of patients worldwide. PIMS was such a revolutionary advancement that it resulted in the most claims for a U.S. patent in the history of the Patent Office, up to that time.

Dr. Kenneth B. Lewis (left), Johns Hopkins Medicine cardiologist, and APL's Robert Fischell, developers of a rechargeable pacemaker. They look on as Helen Chambers—the first recipient of the pacemaker—performs her weekly recharging in this 1978 photo.

Space-Based Missile Defense Becomes a Priority

A more urgent and crucial mission for the Lab originated in 1983, when President Ronald Reagan announced his decision to create the Strategic Defense Initiative (SDI), a space-based missile defense system designed to protect the United States from attack by both intercontinental and submarine-launched ballistic missiles. Reagan had long opposed the strategic offense nuclear deterrence doctrine of mutual assured destruction. Conversely, SDI was a strategic *defense* alternative centered on the development of a "shield" that would intercept Soviet missiles in the air before they could strike U.S. targets. Because part of this defense system would be in space, the media dubbed the imaginative initiative "Star Wars."

To oversee SDI, Reagan established the Strategic Defense Initiative Office (SDIO) in 1984. With an urgent mission and a limited technical staff, the office reached out to APL and other organizations with experience in developing space systems and weapons systems. The Lab was well stocked in both regards. By this time, APL had gained a collective 20,000 years of experience among its staff members

LEFT: *Assembly of the Delta 181 follow-up space-based missile defense experiment; APL later conducted the Delta 183 experiment.*

BELOW: *Carl Bostrom, then head of the Space Department, became director in 1980 and would lead the Lab through some of its most crucial Cold War–era work and growth. During his tenure as director, the Lab was given technical direction agent roles for Tomahawk and other systems; he also oversaw creation of the Lab's Naval Warfare Analysis Department. He retired in 1992.*

working in missile systems, satellites, and related fields. Of APL's 1,600 staff members at the time, 1,000 were engineers.

The SDIO requested that APL design and develop a prototype missile interceptor that could demonstrate the feasibility to destroy an intercontinental ballistic missile (ICBM) during powered flight. Although the 14-month timetable given the Lab was tight, the staff enthusiastically took on the assignment, excited about the inherent challenges of the task.

From the beginning, a key concern for the "Star Wars" program was the need to maintain compliance with the Anti-Ballistic Missile Treaty of 1972, which limited the United States and the Soviet Union each to a single ground-based site from which to launch defensive missiles at incoming ICBMs. To meet the conditions under the treaty, APL would need to create an interceptor that launched in a suborbital phase, thereby obviating the single ground-based launch site rule.

The Exdrone

Unmanned aerial vehicles (UAVs), or drones, are ubiquitous today, with more than a million sold to industry and the public in the United States in 2015. APL has long been at the forefront of drone development, thanks to the efforts of Maynard Hill, a metallurgist who spent much of his time at the Lab in the 1980s designing and developing a series of drones.

Hill became interested in drones in the mid-1960s, when he worked for the U.S. Air Force on meteorological investigations of clear air turbulence. From 1964 through 1971, he established 13 different records for radio-controlled aeromodels and invented a method of stabilizing aircraft through the use of the electrostatic field that exists in the atmosphere. Shown here in this 1974 photo are (left to right) Maynard Hill (Remotely Piloted Vehicle program manager), Robert Givens, Melvin Newcomer, William Charbonneau, and Raymond Cole.

At APL, Hill designed the BQM-147A Expendable Drone, or Exdrone, now known as the U.S. Marine Corps' Dragon Drone. The Corps reached out to APL in 1986 to build a low-cost, small piston-powered UAV that could be used as an "expendable jammer" in battlefield electronic warfare.

The Exdrone went into service just in time to help the Marines drive the Iraqis out of Kuwait City in the Gulf War.

Launched by a pneumatic railgun, the 89-pound Exdrone is flown by a pilot on the ground to a cruising altitude as high as 10,000 feet, although the mission altitude typically hovers around 3,500 feet above ground. The top speed is 100 miles per hour and the maximum flight time is about 2 hours. The payload consists of a color television camera, infrared cameras, and a communications jammer. When a mission concludes, the autopilot guides the drone to cease operation, at which point a parachute is ejected to recover the UAV at a preset recovery area.

APL formed a design team that included scientists and engineers from the Lab's Space and Fleet Systems departments. It was led by John Dassoulas and Mike Griffin, who later served as head of APL's Space Department and went on to become NASA administrator. The team considered the development of a tactical missile using active homing guidance as the interceptor. This conventional radar would guide the missile to within 100 feet of the target missile, at which point the warhead would explode and saturate the environment with lethal pellets. APL selected the McDonnell Douglas two-stage Delta vehicle as the rocket booster, giving the project its name—Delta 180, as the 180th Delta II booster in production. Hughes Corporation soon joined the team to build the interceptor with McDonnell Douglas.

As the 14-month deadline neared, APL altered the design for the experimental interceptor, coming up with a new and radical concept in which a single rocket would launch two spacecraft in orbit. Each would fly off in a different direction and then, at a distance of about 135 miles, they would turn and face each other, nose to nose, as if in a duel. At approximately 35 miles, the terminal radar homing system on the intercepting spacecraft would then track the target vehicle, guiding the missile toward it.

On September 5, 1986, a scant two months beyond the incredibly tight deadline, the experimental Delta 180 carrying the inventive APL-designed and -built missile sensor package was launched from Cape Canaveral. Less than three hours later, the interceptor scored a direct hit with a test missile. The following year, President Reagan awarded a Presidential Commendation to APL for the Delta 180 program.

During this period, a stream of SDIO contracts flowed into APL's Space and Fleet Systems departments, including improvements to the Delta program resulting in the Delta 181 and 183 experiments. APL space-related research during the 1980s encompassed many nonmilitary projects as well. One was the development of radar altimeter satellites on behalf of NASA. APL was engaged in multiple altimeter projects, including one to make high-precision measurements of ocean-surface topography and another aboard the Geodynamics Experimental Ocean Satellite C (GEOS C) to demonstrate the first satellite-to-satellite tracking capability. APL also developed the GEOSAT (U.S. Navy Geodetic Satellite) radar altimeter, which measured the distance from a satellite to the surface of the sea within a remarkable five centimeters, and the Ocean Topography Experiment (TOPEX)/Poseidon radar altimeter, which took the first continuous global measurements of oceanic surfaces.

From Desert Shield to Desert Storm

Back on Earth, APL was tasked to assist the armed forces in another war, mercifully a brief one, following Iraq's invasion of Kuwait in October 1990. Iraq's military prowess dwarfed that of Kuwait, and within 12 hours Iraq effectively controlled the small country. Iraqi leader Saddam Hussein defended the invasion on grounds that Kuwait was an Iraqi territory advancing an anti-Iraq conspiracy.

In the United States, the invasion stirred concerns of an Iraqi threat to Saudi Arabia, a key ally and major supplier of oil. Hussein had excoriated the Saudis as the illegitimate guardians of the holy

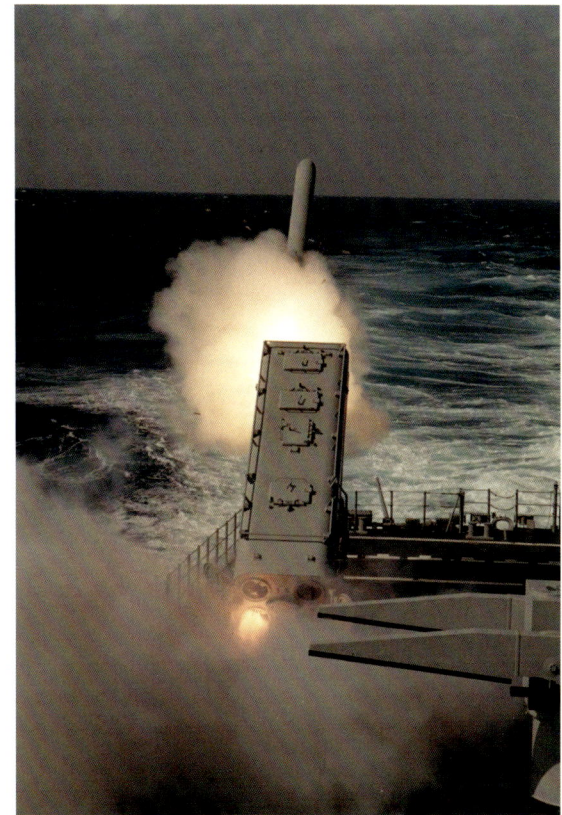

A Tomahawk land-attack missile (TLAM) is launched from USS Mississippi (CGN 40) during Operation Desert Storm. (U.S. NAVY)

A TLAM is fired toward an Iraqi target from the battleship USS Missouri *(BB 63) at the start of Operation Desert Storm in 1991. Accuracy improvements made by APL allowed Tomahawk to precisely strike military targets.* (U.S. NAVY)

city of Mecca. At the behest of the Saudi monarch, King Fahd, the United States launched a defensive mission code-named Operation Desert Shield, sending troops to the country.

When Saddam Hussein refused to comply with a United Nations resolution requiring the withdrawal of Iraqi forces from Kuwait, a U.S.-led coalition took action to eject the Iraqi forces. To support what threatened to become a major conflict, the Navy dispatched two battle groups and the battleships USS *Missouri* and USS *Wisconsin* to the Persian Gulf. Beginning in January 1991, an extensive aerial bombing campaign was launched against Iraq, backed by the United Nations and a coalition force of U.S. allies, including the United Kingdom, France, and Canada.

Because the Navy was first on the scene in the Gulf War, APL's contributions were in abundance. Within the first few minutes of Operation Desert Storm, Tomahawk missiles launched from USS *Missouri*, USS *Wisconsin*, and other ships struck with incredible precision at strategic Iraqi targets. APL's technical demonstration of the Tomahawk's accuracy and reliability gave the Navy all the assurance it needed to deploy the long-range strike missile in combat for the first time.

Throughout the short conflict, battleships, cruisers, destroyers, and submarines in the Persian Gulf, the Mediterranean, and the Red Sea also launched Tomahawks at Iraq's surface-to-air missile sites, electrical power facilities, and even Saddam Hussein's presidential palace. Altogether, 297 Tomahawks were fired, of which 282 hit their targets, a resounding demonstration of APL's missile guidance capabilities.

During Operation Desert Storm, the United States demonstrated a number of technologies that had been in development for many years—among them, radar-evading stealth technology, precision-guided munitions, and GPS technology. In one of the shortest conflicts in modern history, the Gulf War ended in less than six weeks, on February 28, 1991.

The U.S. and allied success during this short conflict generated enormous media coverage. Although it received less media attention, another important development was taking shape aboard Navy ships in the Persian Gulf. As sailors watched Iraqi Scud-B missiles being launched into Saudi Arabia and other countries in the region, it became clear that Aegis ships in the Gulf could track these missiles. This realization accelerated Navy efforts to develop an Aegis sea-based theater ballistic missile defense system that, years later, would further evolve into a land-based ballistic missile defense system called Aegis Ashore.

Chapter 7

Transitions, Evolutions, and Revolutions

In the post–Cold War period of the 1990s, the U.S. government sharply curtailed defense spending. Although the impact was felt across APL's sponsored programs, the Lab continued to pursue game-changing developments that were underway at the time, and many new innovations, on behalf of sponsors.

Representative of these efforts was the continued work to bring the Cooperative Engagement Capability (CEC) into operational service. Having developed the ingenious concept for this new capability and the sensor networking technologies at the heart of the system, APL and the Navy were convinced CEC could solve the critical challenge posed by the threat of advanced air and missile attacks expected to emerge in the late 1980s.

As a means to help demonstrate the revolutionary advance this capability offered over existing radar technology, APL, along with contractors, developed an early prototype CEC unit to "try out" at its campus in 1987. The Lab took a cue from its early days when staff members assessed the breakage rate of cushioned vacuum tubes for use in the radio proximity fuze by dropping them from the roof of the Wolfe Motor Company in Silver Spring. To test CEC, APL mounted CEC hardware on several campus buildings that served as mock "ships" for use in a land-based system demonstration.

"The system worked very well using raw radar data that had been collected at sea as inputs into the prototype CEC system, and senior Navy officials visited APL to observe the demonstration of the system," said Jerry Krill who was APL's CEC systems engineer at the time. "The Navy accepted the results of the test and approved our taking the next generation of prototypes to sea for testing on Aegis cruisers."

In 1990, prototype CEC equipment and software were tested for the first time at sea against a variety of proxies representing threat missiles and aircraft. The test involved two Aegis ships; the land-based Aegis system at Wallops Island, Virginia; a land-based Tartar system at Dam Neck, Virginia; and other assets in various locations in the region. This event is referred to today as Demo 90. APL's revolutionary real-time sensor networking system passed.

Ship Self-Defense System

While the Aegis Combat System provides an unparalleled level of air defense capability, ships with large flight decks—aircraft carriers and amphibious landing vessels—are less suitable for installation of the large AN/SPY-1 radars needed for Aegis. To protect those vessels, APL played a major role in the development of the Ship Self-Defense System (SSDS). SSDS is an automated combat direction system that integrates with already developed sensor and weapon systems, including the Evolved Sea Sparrow Missile (ESSM) and predecessors like the Sea Sparrow (RIM-7P) missile, shown in the Navy photo above being launched from the amphibious assault ship USS *Boxer* (LHD 4) during a 2013 missile firing exercise; the Rolling Airframe Missile (RAM); and the Phalanx Close-In Weapon System (CIWS). The APL-designed software architecture was based on many years of experience dealing with Navy combat systems, tactical software, and sensor integration development. SSDS can use data provided from the Lab-designed CEC to track and engage targets.

As a result of the demo's success, CEC became a major acquisition program. Because it was a high-priority program, Congress directed accelerated development and testing to get CEC to initial operational capability by 1995. Formal acquisition processes and testing would catch up after this initial fielding.

Four years later, the Navy dedicated an entire battle group to assessing CEC's effectiveness in what was one of the Navy's most complex tests ever. The radar sensors representing four types of combat systems on five different vessels—two Aegis ships and three ships of the USS *Dwight D. Eisenhower* Carrier Battle Group—were integrated into the network. The test was an unqualified triumph.

Despite intensive electronic countermeasures against the radar sensors, all the CEC units independently constructed an identical target identification and track picture. Using data from all sensors, the units were able to cooperatively engage representative threat targets. After Navy warfare centers certified the system for operation in collaboration with the combat system and CEC prime contractors, a formal test in 1995 led to the declaration of initial operational capability. The Navy made the decision to introduce CEC to the fleet on an accelerated full-scale basis. It was a great moment for everyone working on the project at APL. Although CEC acquisition and testing would continue, ever-changing combat system upgrades among Aegis and non-Aegis ships, as well as major changes to tactical data link systems, slowed progress considerably. Final certification of operation and technical suitability and full-rate production did not occur until after 2000.

Increasing Oversight and Government Regulation

Even as these innovations continued across the Lab, the government's sharp budget cuts began to take a toll. The Cold War had thawed and the Berlin Wall that had separated communist East Germany and democratic West Germany since 1961 was torn down in 1990, paving the way for German reunification. With the perception of peace at hand, the public clamored for substantial cutbacks in military funding and the closure of military bases. APL was susceptible to these geopolitical forces.

Since its beginning, APL had engaged in a single sole-source, noncompetitive contract with the Navy, from which all assignments originated. If another military branch or federal agency sought service from the Lab, it first had to request funding authorization from the Navy. Once approved, the Navy amended this work into its sole-source contract with APL.

The Lab's director at the time, Carl Bostrom, recalled the belt-tightening and additional administrative requirements being placed on the Lab. "The government increased documentation pressure in making sure it was getting what it paid for," he said. "It was becoming increasingly difficult to meet compliance obligations." APL decided to branch out in contracting, and a separate contract with the Strategic Defense Initiative Office (SDIO) became the second APL contract with the government.

By the middle of the decade, the situation had reached a tipping point. The government's acquisition policy shifted to greater reliance on the big defense contractors, which were named lead system integrators on large, multifaceted programs. Along with this new role, the large defense contractors were given greater authority to assign tasks performed by research and development centers, including

APL, which had traditionally worked directly for sponsors to avoid conflicts of interest. When the Defense Department informed the Lab that the lead system integrators would now serve as intermediaries, APL voiced its concern, citing the dire impact this would have on the Lab's ability to provide unbiased, independent technical advice.

"We objected," said Ruth Nimmo, APL's assistant director for operations. "If we had to work for the contractors, we might not be able to objectively evaluate their technologies and systems."

It was not an easy determination, but APL ultimately declined to participate in certain aspects of the new acquisition program. Russ Gingras was among those who supported APL's decision. "We have something here to uphold as crucial—our ability to provide objective analyses and technical evaluations for our government sponsors, free from conflict of interest," Gingras responded. "The Lab must retain the complete trust of government to always act in its best interest. It's the heart of our trusted service to the nation, and we are not going to undermine it."

"A line needed to be drawn in the sand," said Stuart S. Janney III, who at the time was chair of the APL board of managers and a member of the Johns Hopkins University committee that oversees APL. "We had to respond and we did, stating the case that APL was too valuable to national security to put its work on hold." APL's traditional sponsors, such as the Navy, felt the same way and continued to fund the staff's work through the traditional process. Over time it became apparent that the new acquisition reform program was not as efficient, cost-effective, or productive as the government had hoped.

In 1996, Undersecretary of Defense for Acquisition and Technology Paul Kaminski, who understood the value of the independent, objective technical advice and core capabilities provided by

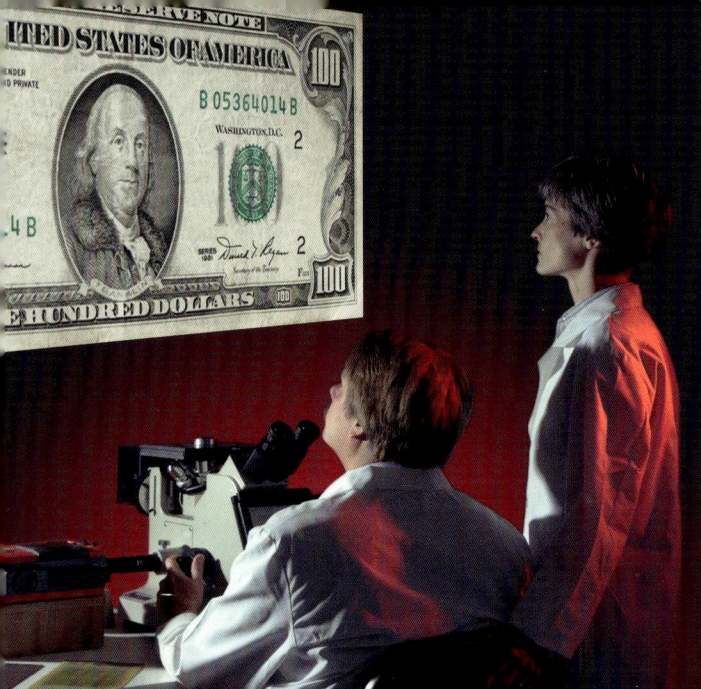

Securities Technology Institute

Between 1994 and 2000, APL operated a Securities Technology Institute (STI) for the U.S. Department of the Treasury Bureau of Engraving and Printing. STI was tasked with developing advanced counterfeit deterrence technologies for future versions of U.S. currency. The program arose in response to advances in reprographic technology and computer graphics (notably color copiers, scanners, and color laser printers), which had greatly increased the tools available to traditional counterfeiters and created a new class of "casual" counterfeiters.

TOP RIGHT: *Senior Navy leaders participate in Warfare Analysis Laboratory Exercises, or WALEXs (led here by defense systems analyst Russ Gingras, who later became APL chief of staff), to explore future system needs and priorities in post–Cold War scenarios.*

organizations such as APL, solved the dilemma. He created a new category of research organizations called university-affiliated research centers, or UARCs, that would directly serve DoD sponsors. APL elected to adopt the new designation.

UARCs would apply their government-recognized core capabilities in support of national priorities for government sponsors, allowing them to continually exercise and enhance the nation's essential engineering and technology development capabilities. To avoid potential or perceived conflicts of interest, these centers would not be allowed to compete against, nor work for, private industry or, in most cases, to perform commercial work. UARCs were also recognized for their collaboration with the educational and research resources available in their affiliated universities.

Despite these changes, the reduced military spending continued to have a broad effect on government-funded research and development programs. "This was a difficult time for the Lab," said Nick Langhauser, who joined APL in 1991 and is today chief financial officer. "Although we had some flexibility, this was a painful and stressful time as we were forced to adjust to broader fiscal realities."

In the face of this period of upheaval, the urgent missions facing the Lab kept up morale. APL's Warfare Analysis Laboratory (WAL) had a more prominent and visible role than before. Throughout the decade, its analysts assumed greater responsibilities for helping senior government decision-makers tackle increasingly vexing problems, constructing war rooms on campus to address future geopolitical situations and related threats. In this work, APL staff members assessed counterterrorism methods, theater missile defense, strike warfare, and other growing warfare challenges.

To achieve viable concepts for ballistic missile defense systems, WAL analysts conducted more than 20 large-scale war games for the Defense Department. But the most important advancement during the decade was expanding the scope of warfare analysis from naval warfare to joint operations, as embodied in the new Joint Warfare Analysis Department and its WAL. Previously, most analysis activities had focused on single-service needs; the emphasis now was on examining the requirements, capabilities, and concepts for joint warfare by all the armed services.

During this same time, scientists and engineers in APL's Space Department were in the midst of building APL's 56th satellite, the Midcourse Space Experiment (MSX), a massive 5,500-pound spacecraft. APL's groundbreaking hyperspectral imaging technology was on board the satellite to help identify, detect, and track ballistic missiles during their midcourse incoming flight phase.

Following SDIO's Delta 183 program, MSX was launched in 1996. After completing its mission the following year, the satellite was transitioned to the Air Force, where it continued to provide service. In subsequent years, APL refined its hyperspectral imaging technologies to discern such minuscule details on the surface of the Earth as different plant types and mineral compounds.

Revolutionizing Planetary Exploration

The Lab's nonmilitary space contributions grew substantially during the 1990s, despite the government's budget constraints. In 1992, NASA Administrator Daniel Goldin issued his "Faster, Better, Cheaper" directive, which threatened to eliminate or considerably slow development of the multi-billion-dollar flagship missions to explore the solar system.

Undeterred, Stamatios "Tom" Krimigis, head of APL's Space Department at the time, welcomed the opportunity to compete for missions to design, build, and operate a lower-cost spacecraft. Krimigis had joined the Lab's staff in 1968 and was one of the world's leading space scientists. He was determined to upend the widespread assumption that spacecraft design, development, and construction were synonymous with high costs.

With indispensable backing from Maryland senator Barbara Mikulski, a tireless champion of NASA, Krimigis and the Space Department leveraged the Lab's work on several NASA-sponsored missions to propose a program for affordable missions to explore the solar system. The program, called the Discovery program, established stringent cost caps for each of its missions, beginning with the first spacecraft in the series, the Near Earth Asteroid Rendezvous (NEAR) satellite. APL was able to design, build, and deliver the NEAR space probe one month ahead of schedule and $38 million under budget. "NASA wanted 'faster, better, and cheaper' and we gave them what they wanted," Krimigis said.

NEAR rocketed into space from Cape Canaveral in February 1996 on a three-year journey to orbit and investigate the composition, structure, and magnetic properties of 433 Eros, the second largest near-Earth asteroid (approximately 21.4 × 7.0 × 7.0 miles). Despite several technical mishaps that almost resulted in the loss of the spacecraft, NEAR Shoemaker, renamed to honor asteroid impact scientist Eugene Shoemaker, entered the asteroid's orbit one year later than planned on February 14, 2000. The Valentine's Day rendezvous was chosen, as Eros was named for the Greek god of love.

APL engineers stand in front of the massive 5,500-pound MSX, the largest spacecraft ever built at the Lab. Hyperspectral imaging technology allowed MSX to show how to identify, detect, and track ballistic missiles during the midcourse incoming flight phase.

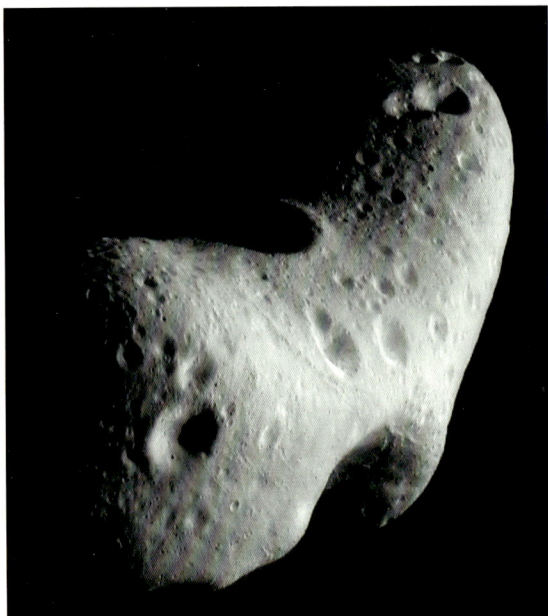

RIGHT: *Director Rich Roca (left), Space Department Head Tom Krimigis, NASA Administrator Dan Goldin, and Senator Barbara Mikulski (Md.) in the NEAR Shoemaker Mission Operations Center as the spacecraft approached the asteroid Eros for its first encounter, in 2000.*

BELOW: *The asteroid Eros, in an image created from six separate photos taken from the NEAR Shoemaker spacecraft while it was 124 miles above the rocky surface. On February 12, 2001, the APL team softly landed the spacecraft on the asteroid's surface, a feat that had never before been accomplished.*

The mission was a complete success. The space probe transmitted astonishing images and data indicating that the asteroid's surface featured some smooth, flat areas, while other areas were strewn with boulders. Unlike the planets in our solar system, Eros had not experienced widespread melting and differentiation into distinct layers. In the end, the NEAR Shoemaker spacecraft returned 10 times more data than was anticipated.

After completing its planned mission on February 12, 2001, something startling transpired. Unbeknownst to NASA and the public, APL's engineers had envisioned softly landing the spacecraft on the asteroid, a scientific and engineering feat that had never been attempted before. NASA approved and the landing was a success, with NEAR Shoemaker touching down at what equated to brisk walking speed. NASA extended the space probe's mission by another two weeks to obtain additional data. The decision proved to be worthwhile, as NEAR Shoemaker transmitted X-ray data from the surface, a bonanza for scientists eager to learn all they could about near-Earth bodies.

The NEAR mission's success not only cemented the Lab's qualifications as a leader in low-cost planetary exploration, but it also proved the viability of low-cost planetary science missions. This *defining innovation*—conceiving and proving the viability of low-cost planetary science missions—had a profound impact by inspiring NASA's Discovery and New Frontiers programs, allowing the United States to affordably complete its exploration of the solar system within 50 years. Thanks to Senator Mikulski's continuing advocacy of low-cost planetary science missions, APL would later design, build, and operate spacecraft on NASA missions to Mercury and Pluto.

The Lab contributed heavily to an urgent Navy need to improve submarine detection technologies, such as the broadband sonar display shown here in this 2006 photo of the Ohio-*class guided-missile submarine USS* Florida *(SSGN 728).* (U.S. Navy)

Exploiting Undersea Acoustic Technology and Systems

Elsewhere at the Lab, other staff members were engaged in their own crucial efforts on behalf of their sponsors and the warfighters who rely on these efforts. A major ongoing mission was to help the Navy vastly improve submarine sonar, tactical control, and information integration. In the preceding years, the Soviets had made acoustic improvements to their submarines, making them quieter and increasingly difficult to detect and track. These advancements threatened the undersea advantage the United States had enjoyed for decades.

"The government's technology development and acquisition processes were simply unable to keep pace with the threat," said Lisa Blodgett, an electrical engineer who joined APL in 1991 and today leads the Lab's Force Projection Sector. The U.S. Navy submarines' sonar and combat control systems were either approaching obsolescence or were outdated by the time they were deployed.

To help the Navy ensure, on a continuing basis, its undersea acoustic superiority, APL was enlisted to play significant leadership roles in several Navy efforts to transform its acquisition processes to an open architecture/open business model. In this model, software is developed independently from the hardware through the use of middleware, which acts as a bridge between an operating system and applications.

The new sonar acquisition program was called ARCI, for Acoustic Rapid Commercial Off-the-Shelf (COTS) Insertion. During the development phase, APL helped create and lead a peer-reviewed

In 1996, APL embarked on a major Navy initiative to incorporate the most advanced sonar and combat system capabilities during new submarine construction and overhaul, as well as backfitting these capabilities into existing platforms. With APL's partnership, this initiative has fundamentally changed the Navy's acquisition processes for submarine sonars and combat systems into a modern, agile, and innovative enterprise that has saved our nation billions of dollars in legacy acquisition costs. (U.S. Navy)

build–test–build program to introduce sonar system improvements and quantify the performance gains. APL staff members led major portions of the testing, in the laboratory and at sea, to quantify ARCI performance improvements. APL also created a partner program, the ARCI Engineering Measurements Program (AEMP), to analyze operational encounter data, facilitating understanding of operational system performance and data-driven improvements to ARCI.

ARCI was a brilliant concept that solved both immediate and long-term needs. Through the open architecture model, the Navy could purchase commercial off-the-shelf hardware and middleware to cost-effectively update the entire sonar system every one to two years, liberating it to rapidly respond to adversaries' potential quieting enhancements. And through the open business model, the Navy could leverage the collective insights from industry, small businesses, its own laboratories, and UARCs to ensure that opportunities and challenges were identified and addressed. Added up, the Navy could realize performance improvements in much less time and at vastly reduced costs.

ARCI fundamentally changed the Navy's submarine technology acquisition processes into a modern, agile, and innovative enterprise that incorporates the best available commercial technologies and practices. Today, ARCI provides our Navy submarine force with a decisive undersea advantage that has expanded to include surface ship sonar and surveillance systems. APL continues to provide the key leadership for rapid transition and improvements on the scale of full-platform sonar and combat control systems.

New Campus for a New Millennium

As the 20th century drew to a close, APL crafted its first site development master plan. The Lab had originally acquired a 290-acre site in Laurel, Maryland, in 1953 and subsequently added another 75 acres. In developing the master plan, the team established a vision of a unified campus with flexible building spaces. They objectively evaluated the use of existing facilities, resulting in the demolition of more than 500,000 square feet of space.

The first structures to meet this fate were the modular steel Butler buildings that served as APL's facilities and office space since the 1950s. The "tin shacks," as many staff members called them, were meant to be temporary and had long outlived their purpose. "No one missed them," said Ruth Nimmo, APL assistant director for operations. "Here we were doing this high-tech research in these outdated facilities that would flood and attract rats. The roofs were peaked and you had to walk sideways not to bang your head."

The master plan called for constructing more than a million square feet of new building space. "What was expected to be a 10-year construction program ended up taking more than 12 years," said Nimmo. "Right after we developed the master plan, September 11 happened and our growth curve exceeded our construction pace. We had to lease additional space ... we also acquired two additional parcels of land that now constitute our 90-acre south campus."

Meanwhile, the Lab recently celebrated the opening of the Intelligent Systems Center, a new facility in the Montpelier Office Complex, just east of the main campus, which was not on the original site development master plan. New construction continues apace. As this book goes to press, a new building is also planned for the south campus. "We've become inured here to the sounds of constant construction," said Nimmo.

The Laboratory has been a key technical leader within America's ballistic submarine fleet since the fleet's inception in 1957. Today, APL continues to serve a critical function in ensuring the accuracy and reliability of major systems of the nation's SSBNs, including the Trident II (D5) ballistic missile system, shown here during a 2016 test launch. (U.S. Navy)

Chapter 8

Keeping Pace with Evolving Threats

Of APL's many essential national security roles, few were as important as its responsibility for the independent test and evaluation of the U.S. Navy's Strategic Systems Program (SSP). The Lab's work was a key component increasing the capability of the nation's fleet of ballistic missile submarines and its sea-based missile weapons systems, the most survivable component of our nation's strategic deterrent force.

Since 1957, APL has provided crucial test and evaluation leadership to assure confidence in the reliability of the nation's submarine-launched ballistic missile systems. The Navy required absolute confidence that the system would perform as intended. The possibility that a nuclear-tipped ballistic missile would misfire or not engage the chosen target was too large a risk without this assurance.

With the new Trident missile system about to enter service, APL's focus extended to evaluating the system's accuracy. Through its meticulous testing, modeling, and analysis, APL ultimately was able to provide confidence in the missile's precision. The Lab's responsibility was to validate and monitor the error models for missile guidance as part of the Navy's System Flight Test Program, which was responsible for evaluating the Trident system's performance. APL conceived of a new instrumentation and processing suite that the Navy could use to estimate and validate the Trident missile guidance error model. Called SATRACK, it is a missile-borne instrumentation package that collects raw GPS data that can be combined with missile flight test telemetry and detailed error-estimation models to assess error contributors to the test missile's miss distance.

SATRACK met all the stringent guidance system evaluation requirements. For instance, it could detect small error contributors to a miss distance observed in the flight test program and then determine what went wrong. This information is used by the Navy SSP and its contractors to monitor, maintain, and improve system performance; it is also used by the U.S. Strategic Command, which is responsible for coordinating the necessary command and control capability to provide strike execution support. By validating the Trident system's accuracy, Strategic Command could confidently assign and allocate the Navy's sea-based strategic assets to adversarial targets.

In addition to conceiving the idea for SATRACK, APL created prototype instrumentation that collected data from both the operating missile and ground stations. The Lab also developed the pre-processing hardware and software and the post-processing data analytics to model and evaluate errors. APL's on-campus satellite tracking facility even served as a backup recording site for East Coast test flights.

SATRACK was first used in the late 1970s, and its success prompted the Navy to put the system into full service in March 1980. It soon became a key element of the nation's submarine-launched ballistic missile system, helping to maintain the nuclear deterrence strategy.

During Trident II's operational test and evaluation, the accuracy of the missile system was modeled and estimated with high confidence. The Lab's progressively improved models increased confidence in Trident II as a predictable and reliable sea-based weapons system capable of effectively engaging multiple targets. Able to determine the minimum number of weapons needed in different strike execution planning scenarios, APL's model-based parameter estimation methodology subsequently was extended to all phases and subsystems of the Trident II system.

By validating that a Trident II submarine-launched ballistic missile could accurately and reliably attack long-range targets that previously were not vulnerable to a sea-launched ballistic missile, APL had provided the government with an objective understanding of the Trident II (D5) weapon system's performance, informing both acquisition and planning decisions.

This APL *defining innovation* with SATRACK—the integration of technology and methodology to solve a vexing critical challenge—was quickly adopted by the Navy, cutting in half the number of flight tests required to precisely estimate weapon system accuracy, saving billions of dollars in flight test

For decades, Lab researchers have helped the Navy develop increasingly advanced long-range towed sonar arrays for submarines, ships, and surveillance platforms. Brooke Clayton is pictured here in APL's towed array fabrication facility.

costs. More significant, APL's developments enabled the Navy to successfully deploy Trident II and achieve an unparalleled level of accuracy that today ensures that U.S. Strategic Command is able to fulfill its mission.

Understanding Ocean Physics

As this crucial work continued, another part of APL was engaged in measures to ensure the security of U.S. strategic submarines (SSBNs) by making sure they could not be detected—an effort that later spawned another significant role for APL in detecting and tracking threat submarines.

In the 1960s, the primary way to locate an adversary's submarine was through the use of active and passive sonar arrays that relied on hydrophones—underwater "microphones"—for discerning sound waves in the water. To minimize noise interference from the propulsion systems located in the aft, or rear, part of a vessel, sonar arrays were positioned in the bow, or front—a location that made a submarine or surface ship vulnerable to threats from behind. In subsequent years, the Navy developed an alternative to this technology: a long-line towed sonar array with the ability to detect underwater threats at greater ranges, based on complex electronic beam forming.

The new technology worked fine, until Soviet submarines became quieter. "The Navy historically had an excellent undersea surveillance capability for tracking Soviet submarines in the Norwegian Sea, the North Atlantic, and the North Pacific, but new classes of Soviet submarines in the early 1980s were extremely hard to detect," said Dan Tyler, who joined APL as an electrical engineer in 1970 and led the Lab's Force Projection Sector from 1998 until 2015.

Given APL's highly regarded science and technology investigations and related at-sea testing associated with the SSBN Security Technology Program (SSTP), the Navy reached out to the Lab in 1985 to help restore the country's undersea surveillance capabilities. "We took on the assignment and formed an organizational structure to 'own' this new mission area," said Tyler. APL staff members conducted numerous tests to gauge the potential of an extended passive towed array of sensors to provide longer-range sonar coverage. This iterative process involved numerous cycles of design, fabrication, testing, and redesign, ultimately spanning multiple projects.

APL also played a major role for the Navy's program in developing low-frequency active sonar as an undersea surveillance capability impervious to submarine quieting. The team working on this program traveled around the world conducting at-sea tests in all waters, from Antarctica to Hawaii. In due course, APL's research into the physics of underwater sound waves provided the information needed for the Navy and other sponsors to develop long-range operational towed arrays on submarines, surface ships, and surveillance platforms. Such arrays pervade the fleet today, improving the vessels' detection capabilities while enhancing their stealth.

The Lab encountered major challenges during the design of the towed arrays, such as drag and the need for a large number of seawater-resistant insulated wires to transmit information from the sensors to the onboard analytical system. APL engineers worked with private contractors to construct a cable system overcoming these issues and, in the process, became the Navy's go-to research institution for these services.

"We did the fundamental physics on all these sensors, built them, prototyped the arrays, and then took them out to sea to provide hard data for understanding the physics and to measure detection performance," said Lisa Blodgett, who succeeded Tyler as head of the Force Projection Sector. "Nearly every towed array out there today stems from our work."

Extending Fleet Air and Missile Defenses

As APL's undersea research and development continued, so did its efforts to strengthen and extend the Navy's air and missile defenses. Even as the Navy and APL celebrated the success of the Cooperative Engagement Capability (CEC), they were interested in a new type of cooperative engagement that allowed engagements of targets far beyond the firing ship's radar horizon. The ambitious goal was to network multiple radar sensors at sea and especially in the air in such a way that a cruise missile attacking from beyond a ship's horizon could be successfully engaged and destroyed by that ship's missile.

To test and evaluate this intrepid idea, the Navy reached out to APL, a logical choice given its long experience as the technical direction agent for CEC, Aegis, and the Standard Missile program. The Lab led an Advanced Concept Technology Demonstration (ACTD) in which the Navy's existing air defense systems would be integrated to detect, track, and engage a cruise missile beyond the radar line of sight.

LEFT: *In 1996, APL was technical co-lead for the Navy for an Advanced Concept Technology Demonstration (ACTD)—referred to as Mountain Top—in which the existing air defense systems of the Navy, CEC, and a DARPA experimental airborne radar were integrated to detect, track, and engage cruise missiles beyond the radar's line of sight. The test involved numerous assets, including this radar station in Kokee State Park, Kauai, Hawaii.*

BELOW: *USS* Lake Erie *(CG 70), which fired and guided the Standard Missile-2 Block IIIA missiles that struck target drones. APL researchers and the crew of USS* Lake Erie *would team up again for another historic achievement 12 years later during Operation Burnt Frost.*

An initial challenge involved equipping aircraft with a radar system that could provide data on low-flying targets beyond the ship's horizon. Aegis would use this data for midcourse guidance of the Standard Missile-2 to send the ship-fired missile beyond the firing ship's radar horizon. The airborne radar would necessarily be much different from the much larger Aegis radar. Still, the problem for early feasibility testing was that the prototype airborne radar systems were much too heavy to be safely carried aloft by aircraft. APL's solution, jointly conceived with MIT Lincoln Laboratory, was to substitute something high in the sky to house the radar system—a mountaintop in Kauai, Hawaii—hence the ACTD's name, Mountain Top. The selected site was an abandoned NASA installation in Kokee State Park known as Site Alpha. The radar equipment was transported by truck up steep terrain to the summit, 3,800 feet above sea level, and lifted onto specially erected towers.

In 1996, the Mountain Top site, the prototype airborne radar, and modifications to CEC, Aegis, and the Standard Missile-2 were ready for testing. All the pieces were in place—Site Alpha, an Aegis ship stationed off the coastline, threat-representative drones, and two aircraft representing a more typical air traffic situation as mutual objects for CEC gridlock alignment. Using CEC, APL and its collaborating partners MIT Lincoln Laboratory, Raytheon, and Lockheed Martin networked the multiple ship and Site Alpha radars to form a composite airborne surveillance and fire-control radar capability.

RIGHT: *The BQM-74 drone cruise missile target that was recovered after being successfully engaged during the test known as Mountain Top. Damage to the left wingtip can be seen. The Mountain Top test was a key demonstration that eventually led to the development of Naval Integrated Fire Control – Counter Air (NIFC-CA).*

BELOW: *Civilian engineers operate radar consoles aboard a P-3 Orion aircraft that took part in Mountain Top.*

The demonstration was a resounding success, proving that it was possible to provide extended defense against land-attack cruise missiles that were launched from a distance beyond the horizon. Witnessing the historic event were Jerry Krill, APL's system lead for the project, and CEC's program manager, Conrad Grant, a physicist who joined the Lab in 1978 and had been one of the lead systems engineers for the Aegis Weapon System.

"Jerry and I were at the top of the mountain looking out across the horizon at the ship," recalled Grant, who would later serve as head of the Lab's Air and Missile Defense Sector and is now APL's chief engineer. "What was especially gratifying was that the early concept for battle group coordination had been the idea of Al Eaton more than 30 years before." Eaton was the same brilliant scientist who had figured out decades earlier why surface-to-air missiles rolled in a reverse direction at supersonic speeds, working out the solution on a series of cocktail napkins. "Al was in his late 70s at the time of Mountain Top and wasn't there with us, but he was immensely pleased to learn of the mission's success," Grant said.

As these many accounts depict, scientific inquiry at the Lab was extraordinarily diverse throughout the 1990s. However, ongoing reductions in defense spending brought about by the end of the Cold War prompted APL's leadership to consider broadening beyond its customary core competencies, widening its number of sponsors in order to secure more varied funding streams. In 1999, APL Director Gary Smith had just retired, and an interim director, Gene Hinman, was appointed as the university's board of trustees searched for a permanent successor to lead this crucial broadening effort. For the first time, the trustees looked outside of APL for the Lab's next leader.

Richard Roca (front), APL director from 2000 to 2010, leads a group including then-Chief of Naval Operations Admiral Vernon Clark (center, in uniform) to the 2003 Submarine Technology Symposium (STS) at the Kossiakoff Center. The symposium, hosted annually at APL since 1988, brings together leaders from across the undersea warfare community for technical collaboration. Also pictured are (left and right, second row) Rear Admiral Charlie Young, USN (now retired), and STS General Chair and then-Force Projection Department Head Dan Tyler.

New Leadership, New Perspective

To fill the top post, the board of trustees at Johns Hopkins University searched for someone with a seasoned business background, in addition to the customary scientific and technical credentials. In January 2000, Richard Roca, vice president at AT&T Laboratories with an academic background as a mechanical engineer, was hired as APL's director. At AT&T, Roca had led a staff of 2,000 people implementing the company's internet-based services.

Roca initiated his tenure by having frank discussions with current department leaders and staff, as well as sponsors of the Lab's work. As he recalled, "I kept my mouth shut and asked them what was good about APL and what concerned them about APL. These external and internal views were very similar, which was a good sign of what needed to be done."

Roca grasped that the Lab's organizational structure did not effectively allow it to promote its broad-based skill sets in a cohesive way, not only to enhance its value to long-standing sponsors but also to attract new sponsors with critical challenges.

The discussions helped formulate the new director's strategic approach. Among the immediate goals were to enhance teamwork, cross-pollinate the staff's scientific and engineering skill sets, better align APL with sponsors' current and evolving needs, and develop a more business-like approach to promoting the Lab's extraordinary capabilities. "I felt we needed to operate as more of a unified institution with a focused, enterprise-based strategic direction," Roca said.

The rapid and widespread increase in cybersecurity threats, and the nation's need to develop solutions and countermeasures, has been a major driving force in the Lab's focus and growth in the past decade. Shown here are Arjun Kalra (left), who recently retired, and Christopher Semon, of the Asymmetric Operations Sector, assigned to the Cyber Operations Mission Area.

The new director created a working group to consider what this optimal structure would look like. The members were asked to consider the specific missions of their sponsor sets and how they might redesign their respective organizations to better align with these needs. Every operation, facility, and person contributed to efforts to identify opportunities and challenges, and this input led to organizational adjustments.

At the time, Roca felt that APL's eight separate departments were missing opportunities to work across departmental lines to acquire new sponsors and challenging work. Because APL scientists and engineers understood what their traditional sponsors wanted so well, they intentionally focused on those sponsor needs.

The working group concluded that APL needed to marshal the resources of the Lab in a more integrated way to more comprehensively serve a sponsor's mission, and that the Lab should not shy away from promoting its broader capabilities.

"We had always done great work, but the staff members needed to stick their chests out a bit more in Washington, to tell people what we were now and ask if there was something else they needed us to do," said Stuart S. Janney III, longtime Johns Hopkins University trustee who served as APL board of managers chair from 1991 to 2014. "This is what private industry would do, but the Lab historically didn't think it was needed."

Coordination, however, required a higher level of communication across the Lab. To help this along, Roca decided to strengthen the departments with what he called business areas, later renamed

LEFT: *Building 26, shown here under construction, opened in June 2000 and included upgraded homes for APL's Warfare Analysis Laboratory (WAL) and Guidance Systems Evaluation Laboratory (GSEL).*

BELOW: *Building 17, shown soon after its opening in 2006, is now home to the Laboratory's Central Spark innovation space. One of the remaining Butler buildings from the 1950s can be seen in the lower right.*

mission areas. The heads of these areas would define the critical contributions they could provide to solve national challenges. If leaders needed skill sets outside their areas to contribute to a mission, they were encouraged to reach out across the Lab to recruit staff members with those skills. The success of this model would be determined by the extent of business each mission area engaged in with sponsors. "Although we had collaborated in the past, it was institutionalized now," said Russ Gingras.

In listening more closely to sponsor needs, it quickly became apparent to APL leadership that the government was struggling in determining how to defend its technology networks and systems against cyber threats. Through the years, these systems had become increasingly vulnerable to being hacked by adversaries.

The flexible access to, use of, and sharing of information is critical to the nation's security. Hundreds of thousands of globally interconnected computers, servers, routers, switches, fiber optic cables, and wireless communications systems provide critical support for national security and the country's economy, civil infrastructure, and public safety. A cyberattack could make this information vulnerable to theft or alteration, or deny legitimate users access to networks.

In the increasingly interconnected world, the various points of connection between the public internet and government and military networks create potential exposure risks. These points of weakness could have devastating consequences for the Navy and other government forces and agencies. In the future, APL would apply its broad-based military and technological expertise to assessing and mitigating this risk.

On August 1, 2008, demolition of the last of the Butler buildings began. These "temporary" structures had stood since the 1950s and were razed to make way for a "Central Green" space and more modern laboratory facilities on the Laboratory's main campus.

Modernization Continues

In addition to the organizational changes, strengthened areas of research, and new areas of focus, the restructuring also called for significant changes to campus facilities. For example, Building 26, which opened in June 2000, included upgraded homes for APL's Warfare Analysis Laboratory (WAL) and Guidance Systems Evaluation Laboratory (GSEL).

The reorganization concluded in mid-2001, although additional modifications followed. However, it would be another seven years before the prefabricated corrugated steel Butler buildings built in the 1950s would be torn down. In their place, much larger and more modern laboratory facilities, as well as a "Central Green" space, would sprout.

No one missed the Butler buildings, least of all Harry Charles, an electrical engineer who joined APL's Engineering Facilities Division in 1972, led the Technical Services Department, and is today the editor-in-chief of the *Johns Hopkins APL Technical Digest* and head of the APL Education Center. "I spent 17 years in one of them," Charles recalled. "I'm six feet, seven inches tall, four inches taller than the height of the upstairs ceiling. I've still got calluses on my scalp from banging my head."

As this chapter in APL's history came to a close, the efforts of former APL directors Gary Smith and Gene Hinman, as well as the steps being taken by the new director, Rich Roca, positioned APL as a more collaborative, cost-effective, and mission-focused organization. Though they likely had little awareness of how dramatically the national security situation was about to change, they each had done their jobs well in preparing the Lab for the future challenges it was about to face.

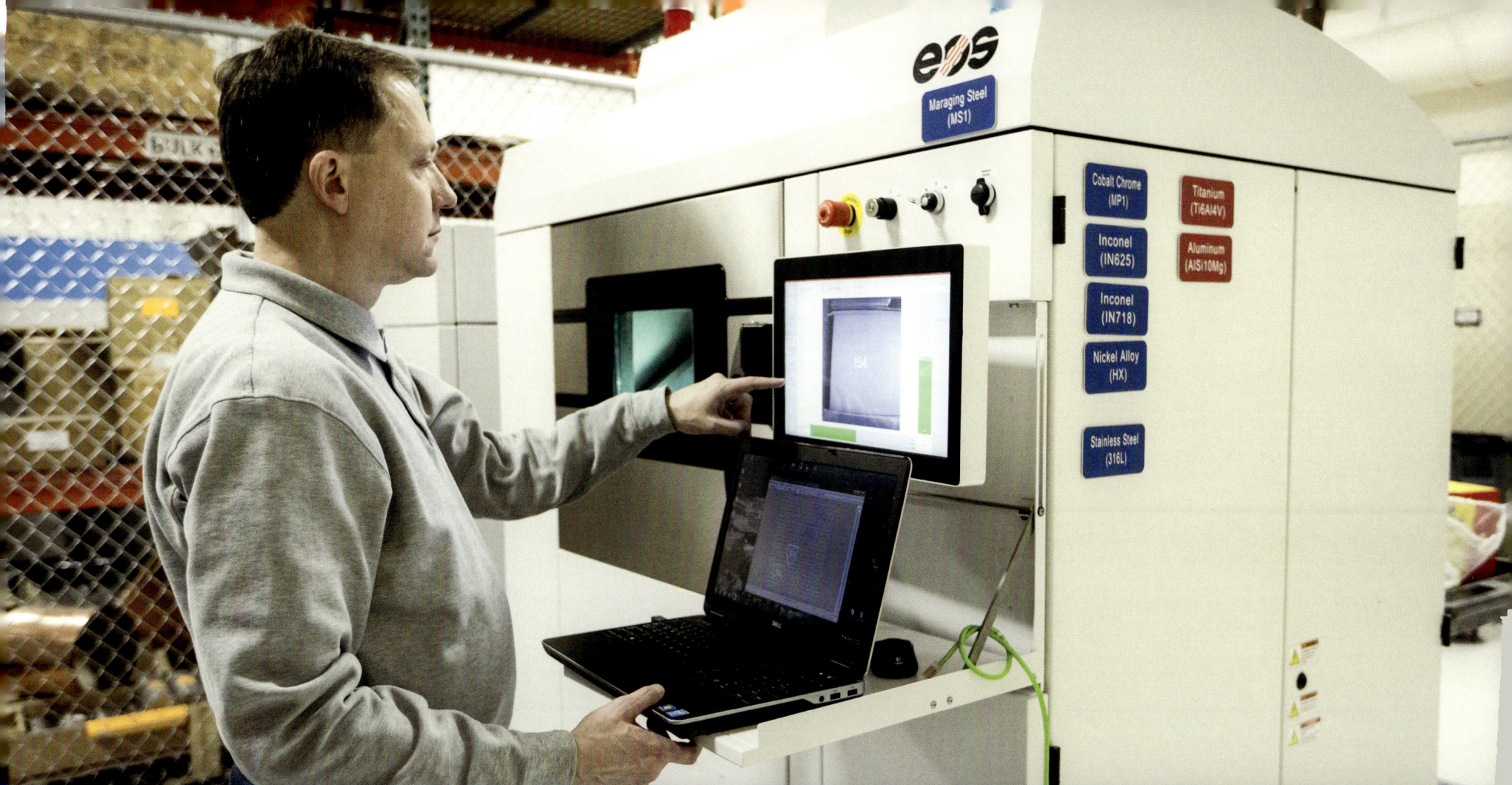

Advanced Mechanical Fabrication

Thirty years ago, several buildings on APL's campus were designated as fabrication shops, including three steel Butler buildings and the basements of other structures. In these buildings, APL technicians built and integrated hardware for programs across the Lab.

"We were scattered all over the place," said Paul Biermann, who joined the Lab in 1986 and is a materials and process engineer in the Research and Exploratory Development Department.

Today, this work is accomplished in a single 35,000-square-foot building that includes a state-of-the-art machine shop where staff members transform blocks of raw material into highly complex functional parts. In the Engineered Materials Lab, staff members mold, shape, bond, and cure polymer and composite materials to form a wide range of parts from spacecraft assemblies to high-fidelity human shapes.

That facility also houses a center of excellence focused on developing and applying the latest advances in additive manufacturing, a process in which digital three-dimensional designs are built by depositing materials in layers; shown here is John Slotwinski as he checks on the progress of metal parts being fabricated inside a metal powder bed fusion additive manufacturing system.

Those working in the facility team with scientists and engineers across the Lab to design and build a wide variety of components for sponsored and internally funded projects. Together, this facility and its staff members provide a tremendous capability to rapidly prototype and build highly complex devices.

The Advanced Mechanical Fabrication Lab has been involved in the development of 68 spacecraft over the years. "Two of them, MESSENGER to Mercury, and New Horizons to Pluto, have explored the far opposite extremes of the solar system," Biermann said. And soon, Solar Probe Plus will explore the sun dramatically closer than ever before. "That's pretty amazing."

Federal agents, firefighters, rescue workers, and engineers work at the Pentagon crash site on September 14, 2001, where a hijacked American Airlines flight slammed into the building on September 11. Staff member Ronald J. Vauk was at the Pentagon on naval reserve duty that morning and was killed in the attack. (DoD)

Chapter 9

Confronting the Realities of September 11

The September 11, 2001, terrorist attacks in New York and Washington, D.C., as well as the downing of the hijacked aircraft in Shanksville, Pennsylvania, shook the nation to its core and profoundly changed the threat environment at home and abroad. A number of APL staff members were at the Pentagon when the facility was attacked, and one, Ronald J. Vauk, a physicist in the Submarine Technology Department on Navy reserve assignment in the Naval Command Center, lost his life. The Lab's work to counter terrorism was suddenly and unexpectedly more personal.

"We received calls from across the government asking what APL could do for the country," said Doug Hudson, a former military officer who joined the Lab in 1998 and until recently served as director of special programs. "At the same time, the surge of loyalty felt here by staff members sparked inquiries to sponsors asking how we could help."

Eleven days after September 11, the U.S. government under President George W. Bush formed the Office of Homeland Security. The new agency was tasked to develop a comprehensive national strategy for safeguarding the nation against future acts of terrorism on American soil. Other federal agencies such as the Central Intelligence Agency, the National Security Agency (NSA), and the Federal Bureau of Investigation increased their focus on collecting and disseminating intelligence on possible plans of extremist elements in the United States and Europe.

Cyber warfare remained a key concern. Preventing the possibility that terrorists or other adversaries could steal state secrets or military technology and research to strike the nation's critical infrastructure or harm the U.S. economy became a top priority of federal agencies. The world had become tightly interconnected through the internet and wireless digital devices. There was fear that terrorists could harness these systems for command and control purposes. APL saw numerous requests for research and technical assistance from both traditional sponsors and new ones.

"We supported Homeland Security with its cybersecurity and other needs and entered into an engagement with the NSA to learn from them what the Navy needed for cybersecurity to protect its

In a 2001 ceremony marking the September 14 national day of mourning, APL staff members pause to remember Ron Vauk and the other victims of the September 11 terrorist attack across the country.

weapon systems," said Director Rich Roca. "Cyber threats were now a part of the equation, and we had to get better at dealing with them."

Roca reorganized the Lab to establish business areas, defined as portfolios of related programs that focused on sponsors' needs. APL's programs in information operations and defense communications were initially identified as business areas within the Power Projection Systems Department. Soon after September 11, Ralph Semmel, then deputy director of the Research and Technology Development Center, was selected to lead the Information Operations Business Area and then to lead the merger with Defense Communications to create the Infocentric Operations Business Area, which recognized cyber and related elements in communications and intelligence as a warfare area. The business area and corresponding branch of technical experts grew rapidly under Semmel, undergoing several transformations before being established as the Applied Information Sciences Department in 2005.

The new department led by Semmel had three principal tenets: defensive, to thwart adversaries from accessing U.S. government and military systems; offensive, to develop technologies that could be used against an adversary's systems; and intelligence-gathering, to determine how to collect and analyze wide-ranging information on enemy plans.

APL's substantial experience in developing military weapon systems in conjunction with its newer capabilities in cyber threat situational awareness resulted in unprecedented synergy in the area of cyber operations. "We worked to develop game-changing capabilities to stop or counter cyberattacks, while continuing to improve resiliency to detect and withstand such attacks," said Semmel.

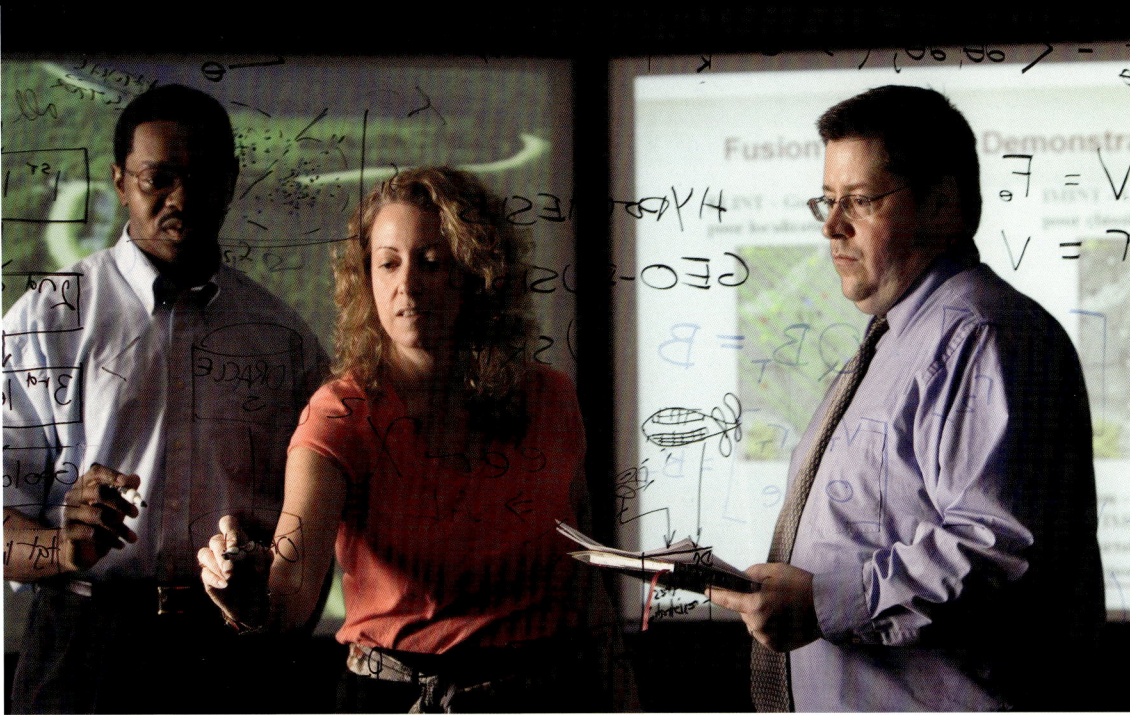

William Walton (left), Jacqueline Stock, and Christopher Boswell were part of the Laboratory research team that developed the Dynamic Time-Critical Warfighting Capability (DTCWC) system, which combines multiple data sources to identify and track mobile enemy targets.

As the Laboratory's work broadened, Roca commissioned a study in 2003 to explore what the world might look like 20 years in the future, in terms of critical challenges to national security. These forward-thinking musings, when reported to the Lab's executive council, resulted in a significant revision in the allocation of resources to business areas. The council decided to spend a larger portion of internal investment funds on asymmetric warfare capabilities, including cyber. "This required the Lab to reprioritize its traditional investments, and it started to pay off," said Ron Luman, who joined the Lab in 1978 as a staff mathematician, later served as head of its National Security Analysis Department, and is today APL chief of staff.

Although the Navy no longer confronted a "peer competitor" as it did in the days of the Soviet Union and the Cold War, it nonetheless encountered complex challenges that were rapidly expanding. One concern was the increasing possibility that adversaries would carry out unconventional warfare tactics in ports and the littoral zones, the relatively shallow waters near coastlines. In response, APL considered and developed technologies to help the Navy with surveillance systems and mine clearing.

The Lab had initiated a counterproliferation portfolio of programs in the 1990s that formed the core of what became another new post–September 11 business area, Homeland Protection. APL's projects for Homeland Security within this business area were wide-ranging, such as the development of a small sensor to detect biological threat substances in almost real time. Driving this work was the government's concern over Iraq's use of aflatoxin—a poisonous, cancer-causing chemical produced by certain molds—in violation of international rules of engagement. "To discern the presence of aflatoxin previously required bringing in a massive amount of lab equipment," said Jose Latimer, Homeland Protection mission area executive. "We quickly developed a suitcase-sized capability, based on work in our research center, that could be taken into the field to determine indications of its possible use."

APL served as technical direction agent for Tactical Tomahawk, the next generation of the U.S. Navy's Tomahawk cruise missile, shown here performing a successful functional ground test on May 17, 2002, at the Rocket Motor Test Facility located in Indian Head, Maryland. (U.S. NAVY)

Similar research was undertaken to develop small, portable systems that identified the presence of radiation and the chemical components used in explosive devices. With regard to explosives components, the Lab created a novel molecular imprinting technique to detect a particular substance. The molecularly imprinted polymers could be tailored to separate a particular target molecule from other molecules, thereby categorizing the constituent components.

Improvements in conventional weapons also were needed to reach terrorists operating in remote areas of the world. Tomahawk cruise missiles, long one of the Navy's primary long-range strike weapons, were now being updated to provide a more responsive capability to reach time-sensitive targets.

Plans were made to improve the Tomahawk missile, allowing it to loiter over an area while awaiting target designation or confirmation. Additionally, Navy commanders sought two-way communications that could provide battle damage assessment after a strike, and improvements that allowed steeper dive angles for upgraded weapon delivery accuracy and enhanced anti-jamming capabilities.

Tactical Tomahawk, as this new system was called, was designed to significantly increase the capability over the existing generation of the missile. Like earlier versions of the missile, the Tactical Tomahawk would be a long-range precision-guided strike weapon capable of being launched from surface ships and submarines. Following a preplanned route, the missile would travel hundreds of miles at subsonic speeds and could rapidly change targets while flying via a satellite-relayed command. Using ultrahigh-frequency satellite data streams, the missile would maintain two-way communications with operators, allowing it to receive commands and transmit status messages en route to a target.

As the technical direction agent for Tactical Tomahawk, APL led or participated in several government-contractor teams to achieve these aims. The Lab also created the guidance equations for the missile's terminal dive maneuver and successfully tested the missile's GPS resistance to jamming.

Tactical Tomahawk achieved initial operational capability in 2004. The following year, it completed the Navy's rigorous operational evaluation and was put into production.

During this same period, the Lab's fundamental responsibilities as the Navy's technical direction agent for Aegis and the Standard Missile program expanded into ballistic missile defense. The Lab had seven decades of accumulated knowledge and expertise in missile defense, dating back to World War II, which became the foundation of the Standard Missile-2 program, the Navy fleet's primary anti-air missile system.

In the late 1990s, the Navy looked to combine the extended-range Standard Missile (the Standard Missile-2 Block IV) with the Ballistic Missile Defense Organization's Lightweight Exo-Atmospheric Projectile (LEAP) to provide a "hit-to-kill" weapon from a surface ship, often compared to the challenge of hitting a bullet with a bullet.

APL led experiments for the Terrier and Aegis LEAP program, and MIT Lincoln Laboratory guided the development of the concepts for discrimination of the threat reentry vehicle from decoys and debris. For a congressionally directed joint service concept definition study in 1999, APL led the concept formulation working group, which recommended the architecture and development of a series of radars and missiles, setting a course for the evolution of Aegis Ballistic Missile Defense. This new missile, designated the Standard Missile-3, was the outcome of the Aegis LEAP intercept demonstration, and it resulted in a series of ballistic missile intercepts, the first of which occurred in January 2002.

By Presidential Directive, at the end of 2004, the Aegis Ballistic Missile Defense system was deployed in limited defensive operations status on Aegis cruisers and destroyers with the Standard Missile-3 Block I. Named the technical direction agent for this new system, APL concentrated its air and missile defense efforts on helping the Navy evaluate its ballistic missile defense capability through high-fidelity simulations of the end-to-end system, guiding the hardware and software tests of the kinetic kill vehicle in its Guidance Systems Evaluation Lab. APL also assisted with the planning and execution of flight tests. The Navy's operational forces were learning how to effectively deploy this complex capability and turned to APL to help with ship placements and radar search sectors against new threats. The Lab's mission was to assess the weapon system's ability to defend vital U.S. and allied naval assets against attacks by both cruise and ballistic missiles. APL was tasked not just to identify problems in these arenas but also to solve them through the development of innovative technologies and system improvements.

When North Korea launched a Taepodong missile that overflew Japan in 1998, Japan's interest in defending itself from ballistic missile attacks increased significantly. The country entered into a cooperative research program with the United States to develop the technologies necessary for an advanced version of the Standard Missile-3 Block I. In 2006, the United States launched a joint development program culminating in the Standard Missile-3 Block IIA, a larger missile that was compatible with the Navy's existing shipboard vertical launching system cells without modifications.

The Lab was named technical direction agent for the Aegis Ballistic Missile Defense System. Here, a developmental Standard Missile-3, designed to intercept short- to medium-range ballistic missile threats, is launched from the Pearl Harbor–based Aegis cruiser USS Lake Erie *on November 21, 2002.* (U.S. NAVY)

Another significant development in which APL collaborated effectively with the ballistic missile defense community, especially the Standard Missile-3 prime contractor, Raytheon, and the Aegis prime contractor, Lockheed Martin, resulted in an astonishing advancement in the guidance, navigation, and control of a missile in space. This same approach to continually enriching the value of the Navy's weapon systems was, after all, the type of innovative leadership that led to the development of the Tomahawk long-range, all-weather, subsonic cruise missile, engineered by the Lab to be capable of engaging a variety of surface targets.

APL also made continual improvements in submarine concealment and detection. For years, APL had led the design, development, testing, and evaluation of passive sonar systems that gathered data about an adversary's submarine from a variety of ship-towed sensor arrays, unmanned buoys, and underwater sensors. In the early 2000s, the Navy reached out to APL to improve the transfer of data among these different systems. The challenge was the large volume of information the systems produced, which made it difficult to send, share, and use the data in a short period of time. At the time, data compression algorithms that recoded the essence of the data so that it could fit through networks with limited communications bandwidth were not designed for sonar applications.

APL attacked the challenge with its typical curiosity and enterprising spirit, developing a unique compression algorithm specifically for passive sonar data. Preliminary at-sea tests of this passive sonar compression algorithm in 2005 demonstrated not only the algorithm's mission effectiveness but also its ability to transmit large amounts of critical information in a narrow communications bandwidth.

Scientific and technical limits also were overcome in APL's continuing efforts on behalf of NASA. From the Transit satellite system through the NEAR (Near Earth Asteroid Rendezvous), TIMED

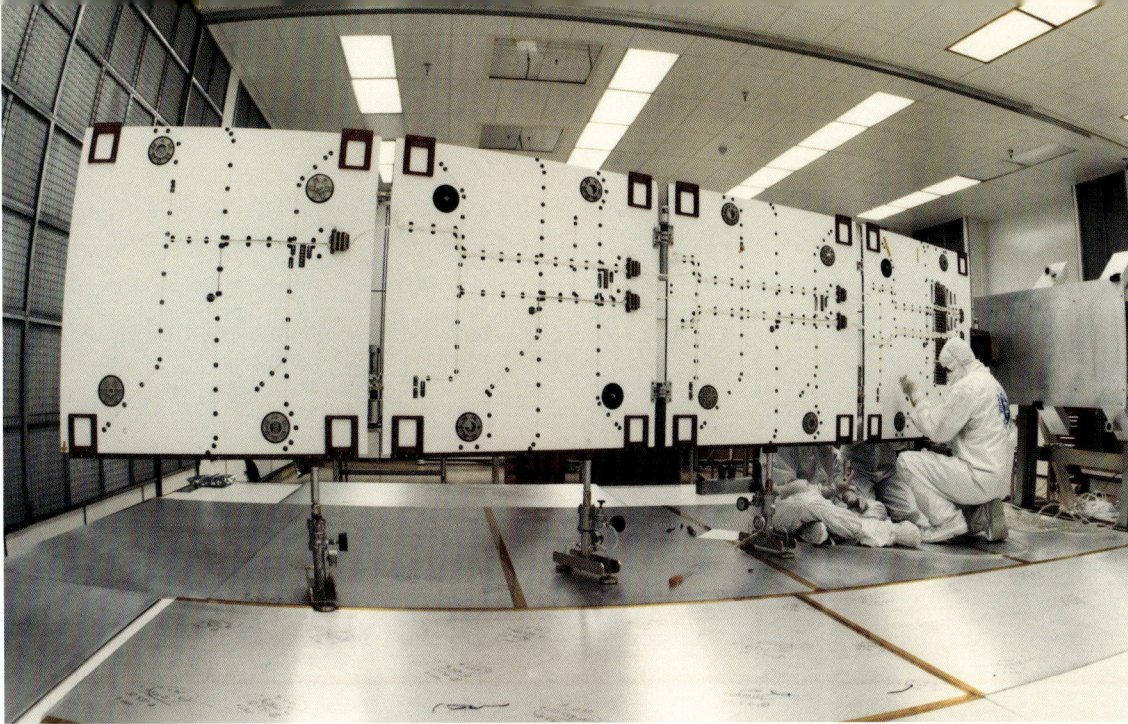

(Thermosphere, Ionosphere, Mesosphere Energetics and Dynamics), and MESSENGER (Mercury Surface, Space Environment, Geochemistry, and Ranging) missions, the Lab had leveraged its broad military and civilian space technical capabilities in a series of breathtaking projects.

Following the successful MSX and NEAR missions, NASA tasked the Lab's Space Department to design, develop, and build a series of next-generation spacecraft. Each one was predicated on finding answers to probing questions about our near-space environment, the solar system, and even beyond these planets. The Lab's vertically integrated work continually pushed through perceived scientific, engineering, and technical boundaries.

Back in 2001, APL's TIMED spacecraft had embarked on an odyssey to study the least explored and understood region of Earth's atmosphere, the mesosphere and lower thermosphere/ionosphere, 40 to 110 miles above the planet's surface. TIMED was the first comprehensive long-duration atmospheric study of these extremely variable forms of energy in the thermosphere.

For centuries, scientists were aware that the volume of solar energy in the thermosphere affected Earth's atmosphere, which responds uniquely to different types of solar storms. To determine why this was the case, instruments aboard TIMED measured the region's temperature, pressure, winds, chemical composition, density, and energy inputs and outputs. Other research focused on the effect of the thermosphere's variability on satellite communications and the role of human activities in the changing atmosphere, chiefly the release of gases like methane and carbon dioxide.

In 2015, 14 years after its launch, the mission celebrated 5,000 days of continuous data collection from more than 74,000 Earth orbits. Research results and discoveries have been documented in more than 1,700 scientific papers in national and international journals.

The APL-designed and -built MESSENGER spacecraft, designed to withstand the intense heat at Mercury, shown during testing at NASA Goddard Space Flight Center.

Several other spacecraft also were on the drawing board or set to launch in the early 2000s, each driven by a bold mission focused on daunting scientific challenges. In 2004, MESSENGER, the seventh in NASA's low-cost Discovery series, was launched to orbit the planet Mercury. Although the Mariner 10 space probe had made multiple flybys of Mercury in the 1970s, it had gathered information about less than half the planet's surface. Mercury's close proximity to the sun made it impossible for conventional telescopes to chance a closer glimpse. An orbiter mission could solve this problem, but the risks and costs were considered too high.

APL designed MESSENGER to overcome these impediments. Under NASA's Discovery program—which had been created thanks to the vision and leadership of the Lab's Tom Krimigis—the spacecraft was built to closely orbit the hot and rocky planet's surface to help scientists understand the forces that had shaped it. To undertake this intrepid quest, the planetary explorer would need to take advantage of clever orbital mechanics and mission design to save fuel. The spacecraft would travel a very long cosmic journey—nearly five billion miles over seven years, and six planetary flybys—before it could commence its yearlong study.

Once in orbit, it would confront tremendous temperature swings, from 850 degrees Fahrenheit to –350 degrees Fahrenheit. To withstand this stress, the spacecraft's structure needed to be tough and resilient, yet it also had to be compact and lightweight to lift off on a conventional rocket. Low weight was important for another reason: Most of MESSENGER's mass was needed for fuel to fire the thrusters that would move and then slow the spacecraft enough via the planetary flybys to permit Mercury's gravity to capture it.

To protect MESSENGER over the planet's hottest regions, APL staff members developed a cost-efficient ceramic-fabric sunshade. To address the weight considerations, they made the structure from a graphite-epoxy composition that was heat tolerant and strong. They even designed and developed a low-mass propulsion system that efficiently stored the spacecraft's propellant so it would make up only a little more than half the vehicle's weight.

"The United States had been trying for 30 years to do a Mercury orbiter," said Krimigis, who was head of the Space Department through much of MESSENGER's development. "We thought we could do it inexpensively with new materials, an ingenious mission design, and a comprehensive science payload. We look for things that really are at the frontier."

This is exactly what NASA had come to expect from the Lab, which had pioneered low-cost planetary exploration and, to that point, had designed, developed, and built 60 spacecraft. During MESSENGER's development, two other extraordinary space missions occupied the Lab's attention: the STEREO (Solar Terrestrial Relations Observatory) spacecraft, on a mission to provide a detailed three-dimensional look at the sun, and the New Horizons spacecraft, on a journey to Pluto and the outer reaches of the solar system.

The STEREO mission, consisting of two nearly identical spacecraft that were launched in 2006, was designed to provide insight into coronal mass ejections, powerful eruptions on the sun that can

cause severe magnetic storms when colliding with Earth's magnetosphere. The storms can damage satellites and cause power outages and are extremely dangerous to astronauts performing activities outside the space shuttle or space station. APL's interest in this field of study, known as space weather, would continue to grow in years to come.

By putting two spacecraft into an elliptical orbit around the sun, APL could enable stereoscopic imaging. Mission design engineers devised complex trajectories for the twin spacecraft—one ahead of Earth in its orbit around the sun and the other trailing behind—and used the moon's gravity to manipulate their orbits. Images sent to Earth provided the first glimpse of the structure and evolution of solar storms as they emerged from the sun and moved out through space.

New Horizons, the first mission in NASA's New Frontiers program, was designed to travel to the farthest reaches of the solar system on a mission to Pluto. Originally categorized as our solar system's ninth planet, Pluto came under increasing scrutiny and skepticism as other objects of similar size were discovered in the Kuiper Belt, the ring of celestial bodies beyond Neptune in which Pluto resides. Classification aside (Pluto was designated a "dwarf planet" not long after New Horizons launched), scientists hoped to unlock the mysteries of planetary evolution by studying the small icy world, only two-thirds the diameter of Earth's moon.

The 62nd spacecraft built by APL, New Horizons presented engineers with enormous design challenges. New Horizons would need to endure the hardships of a nearly 10-year journey, traveling 3.1 billion miles to the solar system's coldest, darkest frontiers. The design called for the fabrication of a compact half-ton spacecraft that could operate on limited power. The payload consisted of seven scientific instruments to study Pluto's unique geology, composition, and temperature and its dynamic atmospheric structure and composition. The instruments on New Horizons collectively drew less than 28 watts of power, representing a degree of miniaturization unprecedented in

RIGHT: *Following construction and intensive testing at APL, the New Horizons spacecraft—which would provide never-before-seen images of and data about Pluto—is prepared for shipment by Lab technicians and engineers and eventual launch by NASA.*

BELOW: *The New Horizons spacecraft roared into the afternoon sky aboard a powerful Atlas V rocket on January 19, 2006, achieving the fastest launch speed ever by a spacecraft (36,373 miles per hour).*

planetary exploration. Last, APL needed to develop an advanced communications system that could detect the faintest signals from Earth and with enough power for Earth to receive the large volume of data from the flyby.

APL's scientists and engineers—working closely with colleagues from Southwest Research Institute and a range of aerospace firms, NASA centers, and university partners—met each of these challenges. In the end, New Horizons looked a bit like a baby grand piano, due to the space probe's triangular shape and comparable mass. Its primary structural element was an aluminum central cylinder, which supported larger components like the propellant tank, the power source, and a series of internal and external panels on which the scientific instruments were mounted. To achieve the low weight goals, the panels were made of ultrathin sheets no thicker than two pieces of paper, with an aluminum honeycomb core. The spacecraft was also designed with unprecedented levels of autonomy, which allowed it to monitor and manage significant aspects of its operations during the long voyage.

Riding aboard an Atlas V rocket, New Horizons soared into the heavens on January 19, 2006, hurtling more than 36,000 miles per hour, the fastest launch speed of a human-made object in history. A mere nine months later, New Horizons captured its first faint images of Pluto during a test of the spacecraft's Long Range Reconnaissance Imager, also designed and built by APL. The images affirmed the ability of New Horizons to detect and track distant objects, a critical factor in navigating the spacecraft toward the Kuiper Belt.

The following year, New Horizons reached Jupiter, where it was given a gravity assist toward Pluto and the opportunity to exercise its instruments on Jupiter and its moons. Those working on this historic project breathed a sigh of relief. For the next eight years, they would track their cosmic voyager as it proceeded on its extraordinary journey.

Anthrax Terror

For several weeks in 2001, multiple news media outlets and the offices of two U.S. senators received mailed letters containing anthrax spores. Five people died and 17 others were infected by the fast-spreading bacteria.

In response, the Federal Bureau of Investigation launched one of its largest and most complex investigations in history. The specter of widespread casualties from other substances deployed by terrorists and adversaries compelled the Department of Homeland Security to reach out to APL with a crucial assignment—to apply the Lab's expertise in systems engineering and sensors to the rapid detection of potential threats in the U.S. mail system and other targets of potential contamination.

Since 1994, the Lab had been engaged in research to develop and support sensor systems countering the threat of chemical and biological attacks to U.S. military and civilian populations. To provide laboratory space for evaluating and quantifying experimental results, APL had built a Chemical and Biological Test and Evaluation Center at its main campus and used vegetative and spore-forming bacterial agents to simulate chemical warfare agents and toxic industrial compounds. Thanks to these successful experiments, great strides were made in the development of refined sensors better equipped to detect many physical, chemical, and biological agents.

APL plays a major role in all stages of counter-proliferation sensor development—from conceiving systems to prototyping, operationally testing, evaluating, adjusting for operational interoperability, and transitioning to manufacturing in the private sector. Technologies developed for these purposes include molecularly imprinted polymer chemical sensors, time-of-flight mass spectrometer biosensor systems, and the Electronic Surveillance System for the Early Notification of Community-based Epidemics (ESSENCE).

APL also has developed numerous sensors vital to surveillance and diagnostics in everyday medical and industrial settings.

APL led development of jamming techniques for two programs—one for the Marine Corps and one for the Navy—that provide ground forces with electronic systems, including jammers, to counter radio-controlled IEDs. (DoD)

Chapter 10

Responding to Unconventional Threats

In the years following September 11, the war against global terrorism arguably presented one of the most complex challenges to national defense in American history, due to the dispersed nature of extremist organizations, their adept use of open sources of technology, and their flouting of international rules of war. These new adversaries posed unique and growing challenges for the armed services, federal agencies, and intelligence-gathering organizations.

Given APL's distinctive competencies and its history of technological and process innovations, numerous sponsors solicited the Lab's assistance in an exceptionally diverse array of projects. Fighting terrorists on many fronts had proven to be a labyrinthine undertaking, involving widely dispersed insurgent groups whose unconventional maneuvers were decidedly different from those of a professional standing army. This asymmetric warfare was as much psychological and electronic as it was physical. Adversarial tactics included car bombings, cyber warfare, hidden improvised explosive devices (IEDs), and suicide bombings in densely populated urban areas.

To defend against such formidable challenges, the country had to rely in large part on the gathering and analysis of information signaling an emerging threat. APL's Applied Information Sciences Department and Homeland Protection Mission Area were tasked to respond to this need.

Among staff members' collaborative and expansive work was the development of a technology application that could process millions of data points recorded from airborne and ground-based devices. Using LIDAR (Light Detection and Ranging) surveying technology, the objective was to instantly transform the data into lifelike three-dimensional graphics. Such reconnaissance-quality images would be tremendously useful to the military in the real-time assessment of enemy fortifications. The challenge was in processing such massive amounts of information without overwhelming the computer system.

LIDAR principles are similar to those of radar: A laser light pulse is transmitted and its return signal is measured for time and range from the precise angles at which it is pointed. APL had been involved

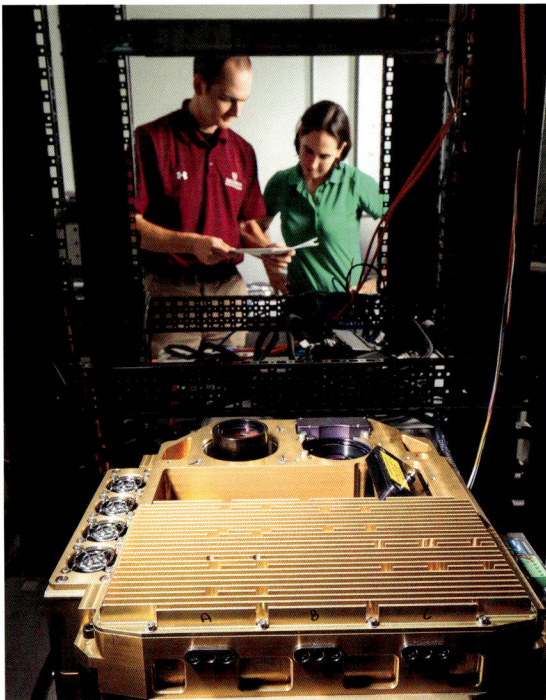

RIGHT: *APL's Jason Hunnell (left) and Kevin Murphy conduct operational flight testing of the precision gimbal LIDAR pointing instrument they and Lab colleagues built in 2005. The device is able to scan foliated targets multiple times in a single pass, revealing objects that might be hidden beneath the foliage. This capability provides improved geospatial intelligence capabilities to U.S. forces around the world.*

BELOW: *APL LIDAR researchers Austin Cox (left) and Rebecca Koslover, shown here with a LIDAR sensor undergoing testing and evaluation.*

in LIDAR imagery research since the 1990s, using it to generate contour maps of surface elevation for topography. The Lab's scientists and engineers now applied their expertise to solving the data overload problem. To manage the volume, they devised a series of algorithms based on a spatial indexing technique known as quad tree data storage and retrieval. The algorithms were embedded in a data analytics product called the QTQuad Tree Viewer, which processed and visualized the LIDAR data in real time. The software tool was spun off by APL as a start-up company called Applied Imagery in 2004 and marketed as Quick Terrain Modeler.

The spin-off did not preclude APL's continued research into other LIDAR applications. In the early 2000s, APL was tasked by various government agencies to assist with another surveillance and reconnaissance project. The objective this time was to develop and test a system that could peer through dense foliage to detect an adversary's vehicles, trails, troops, communications facilities, and other concealed objects of military significance.

The technology takes advantage of the tiny spaces in a dense forest canopy where light can penetrate. By pulsing photons of light at the canopy, some of it would fall through these gaps, researchers reasoned. By maneuvering the light back and forth at different angles, an even broader view of the topography below the canopy would emerge.

"We used LIDAR as a flashlight to see what otherwise could not be seen," said Jason Hunnell, physicist and supervisor of APL's Imaging Systems Group. Armed with this cutting-edge technology, in 2005 Hunnell and his colleagues built a precision pivoting platform or gimbal that could scan a foliated target multiple times in a single pass. "The more times you shine the flashlight at the target, the more likely you are to poke through the trees and see the details underneath," Hunnell explained.

Transferring Technologies

Over the years, some of APL's game-changing innovations have resulted in commercial products and technologies, including medical devices and software. In 1999, the Lab established a more formal path to help move technologies that are suitable for non-government uses into the marketplace. The aim of this effort has been both to protect the government's rights to its own technology investments and to see these innovations benefit society.

The program experienced a steady increase in activity as the Lab's work expanded into new areas, including advanced sensors and cyber defense technologies. Recent investments in innovation and collaboration have also spurred an increase in intellectual property and invention disclosures, the first steps in the process to claim ownership of and identify whether a technology might be suitable for transfer to the commercial market. Several have passed muster: Since 1999, APL has executed more than 550 licensing agreements for Lab-developed technologies and in some of those cases—nearly 40—created small companies to handle the commercial aspects of the transfer.

Today, APL collaborates with Johns Hopkins University as well as peer organizations, U.S. government contractors, entrepreneurs, and businesses to both operationalize and commercialize federally funded technologies. In some cases, APL cooperates with Johns Hopkins University's technology transfer program to avoid potential conflicts of interest that might arise as the technologies are transitioned to private industry.

In line with APL's mission of national service, the Lab's technology transfer program focuses on the public interest—broadening the impact of its many scientific and technical contributions for economic and societal benefit.

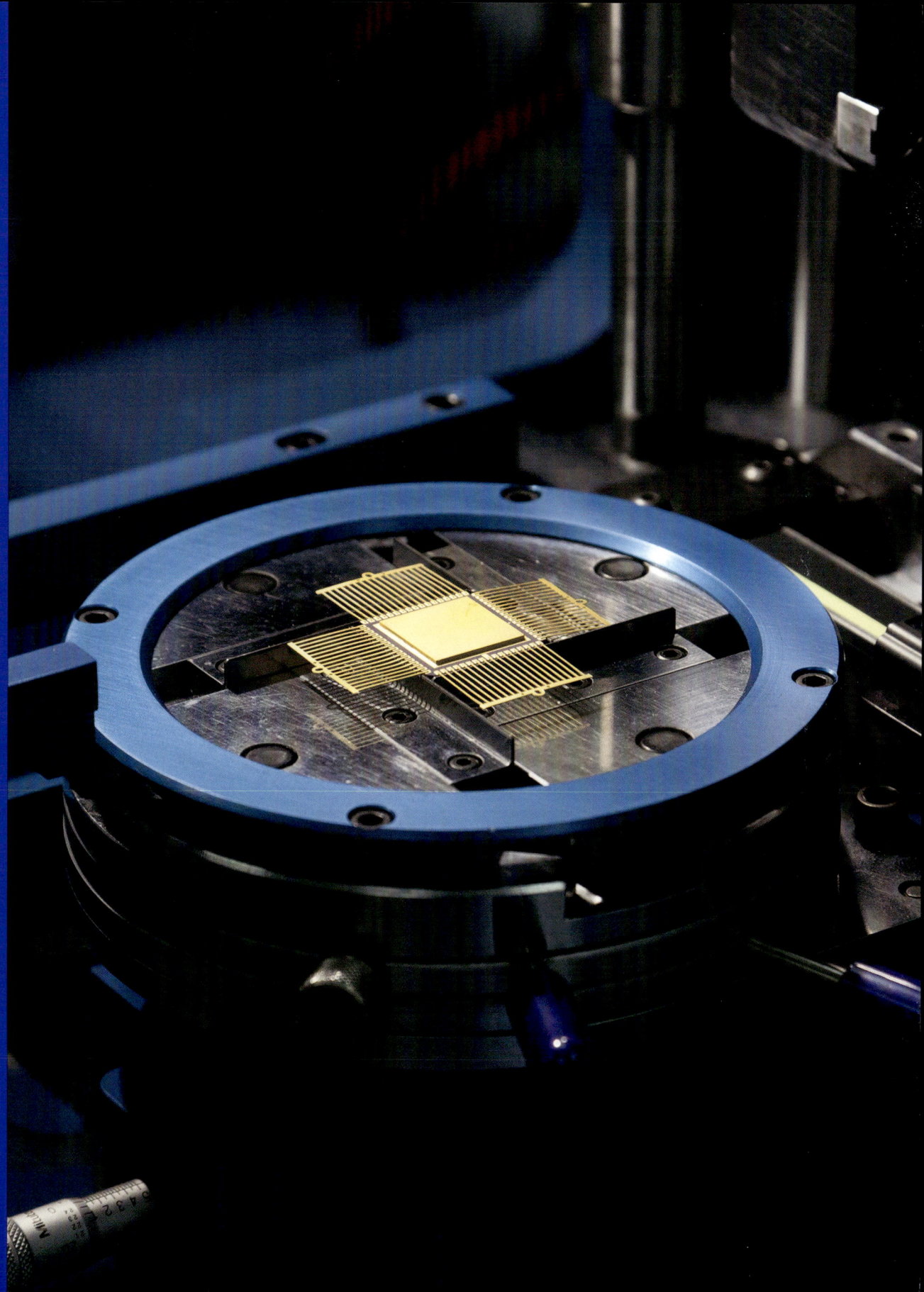

In response to the need for heightened airport security in the post–September 11 world, APL scientists and engineers developed testing methods and analyses for the TSA that are used in most airport full-body X-ray scanners. APL also designed and produced (using additive manufacturing) the body models used in TSA screener training.

The gimbal and the motor directing it were designed to fit into the existing airframes of surveillance and reconnaissance aircraft. The team also devised the software that calibrated the varied data sets produced by the cameras. Three years later, the software successfully passed developmental testing at a tropical test center, followed shortly thereafter by an equally productive operational test.

In 2010, the device was dispatched to assist operational forces, allowing U.S. forces to see vehicles, small buildings, trails, and other hidden assets, Hunnell said. "For instance, by erasing the trees, you realize that the wall of a hidden compound is actually 12 feet tall versus 6 feet tall. This is important information." He added, "I can confirm that on the very first mission where it was used, it helped save American lives." The Lab's research in LIDAR technology is bringing geospatial intelligence capabilities to U.S. troops around the world.

Other crucial defense projects were concurrently underway during the period. On behalf of the Department of Homeland Security, APL experts in biology, chemistry, physics, nuclear physics, and engineering were assembled to conduct research into aerosol, radiation, chemical, and micro-biological warfare tactics. The objective was to improve the detection of these agents through the development of more accurate and efficient test and evaluation methods.

The multidisciplinary team members leveraged their extensive and varied test and evaluation expertise to evaluate government-approved passenger, baggage, and cargo screening facilities, as well as the efficacy of biological, chemical, and radiological sensors. This work was critical to prevent explosives and other injurious agents from entering the mass transit, rail, and airport transportation systems. Such facilities were a frequent target of terrorist attacks because of their high concentrations of people and the attack's potential to cause large-scale disruption and fear.

Another counterterrorism-related APL project emerged after the so-called "underwear bomber," a self-proclaimed operative of the militant organization al-Qaida, failed to detonate the plastic explosives concealed in his undergarment while aboard a passenger aircraft. Rather than subject passengers to extended—and invasive—pat-downs by security personnel, the Homeland Security Department's Transportation Security Administration (TSA) developed scanners that could depict the full-body anatomy of a passenger. The precision of the scanners was very high, but it raised privacy concerns. The Lab was entrusted to puzzle out a solution.

"We advocated that the TSA develop an avatar resembling a chalk etching, instead of a person's actual anatomy, as an interface to illustrate possible threats, reducing the privacy concerns," said Jose Latimer, APL's Homeland Protection mission area executive. "TSA liked the concept and we were then requested to test and evaluate the system. It worked splendidly and is still in use today."

In areas where the U.S. military was active, concealed IEDs were a particularly grim threat. Such explosives accounted for more than two-thirds of all casualties endured by the United States and its coalition allies in Iraq and Afghanistan between 2003 and 2008. More than 80,000 IED attacks had occurred in Iraq alone, many of them triggered remotely using a radio frequency command link.

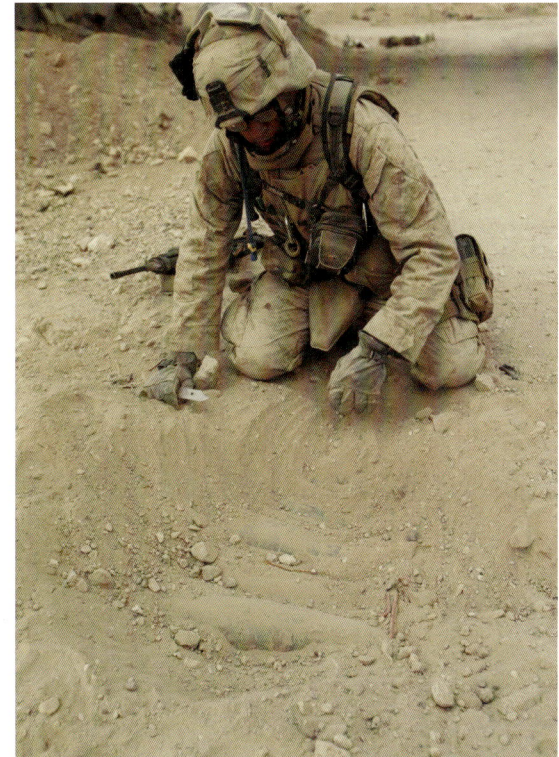

LEFT: *Devon Goforth (left) and Brian Melchler work in the Counter Radio Controlled-IED Electronic Warfare (CREW) Lab. APL research contributed to the creation of methods to thwart the use of radio-controlled IEDs in conflict zones across the world.*

BELOW: *Because concealed IEDs continue to pose a threat to the U.S. military, APL continually works to provide counter-measures and counter-countermeasures to DoD.* (DoD)

Based on APL's expertise in electronic warfare, the Navy and the Marine Corps tasked the Lab in 2008 to lead the development of electronic jamming techniques that could counter these radio-controlled IEDs. In subsequent years, APL provided these new capabilities to Navy and Marine Corps troops bound for the field. Because the enemy dynamically reacts to U.S. countermeasures, the Lab is now engaged in developing IED counter-countermeasures.

APL teams also are at work creating sensors that can better detect IEDs, applying their expertise to measuring radio frequencies, characterizing electronic devices, and building receiver systems. The challenges are manifold: Sensors to detect IEDs must operate in environments where there is a high amount of radio frequency interference. The sensors also must process information quickly enough to provide adequate warning. APL advanced the concept of a highly sensitive, unattended ground-based sensor that would provide tactical intelligence. The Lab also is developing data analytics solutions that can exploit the signatures produced by the materials and processes used in making an IED. These signatures range from the electronics manufacturer to the types of explosives used.

Revolutionizing Prosthetics

While staff members sought ways to ameliorate the threat of IEDs, they also put their energies toward the development of post-injury technologies to improve the lives of individuals affected by them. The increased use of IEDs in the ongoing conflicts in Iraq and Afghanistan—combined with superior lifesaving medical capabilities—resulted in a much higher number of wounded soldiers, soldiers who in past wars would not have survived their injuries.

Of the more than 50,000 U.S. troops wounded in action, approximately 2.6 percent suffered a major limb amputation, most of them because of an IED. A report issued by the Congressional Budget

RIGHT: *Vehicles such as this U.S. Army anti-tank guided missile Stryker—blown onto its side but still able to be repaired after an explosion in Iraq in 2007—were frequent targets for remote-detonated IEDs, which range in size from small anti-personnel devices to massive bombs capable of destroying tanks.* (U.S. ARMY)

BELOW: *APL researchers provided detailed studies of the various components used in IEDs and worked to better detect and defeat these explosives, which were the main cause of casualties suffered by U.S. and coalition forces in Iraq and Afghanistan from 2003 to 2008.*

Office in 2014 attributed the high amputation rate to new blood-clotting technology preventing death from a serious injury and to modern body armor that protected vital organs but not arms or legs.

Well before the report was issued, APL was researching the potential for revolutionary changes in the design and natural performance of prosthetic limbs. DARPA, which commissions "high-risk, high-reward" research addressing urgent challenges, was distressed by the high number of young men and women returning from war with missing limbs and had engaged and funded APL to take on this work in 2006. The agency asked the Lab to create a state-of-the-art robotic prosthetic limb with the physiological functions of the human arm that could be operated by a person's neural control mechanisms.

With funding provided by DARPA's Revolutionizing Prosthetics program, APL assembled a multi-national team of engineers, neural scientists, clinicians, technology developers, and academic and commercial partners across the United States, Canada, and Europe to pursue a highly aggressive research and engineering approach to developing a next-generation robotic arm. The team's objectives were twofold. The first was to create a prosthetic device that mimicked the natural function, control, appearance, and sensory perception of the human arm. The second was to develop methods to control and perceive sensation in a way that would mimic the natural arm.

Ultimately, the goal of this program was to enable a person to use a robotic arm and achieve a sense that the prosthetic was part of their body, not a robotic device. But first the Lab needed to develop the prosthetic prototype itself—to make a robotic arm with the same size, weight, and strength

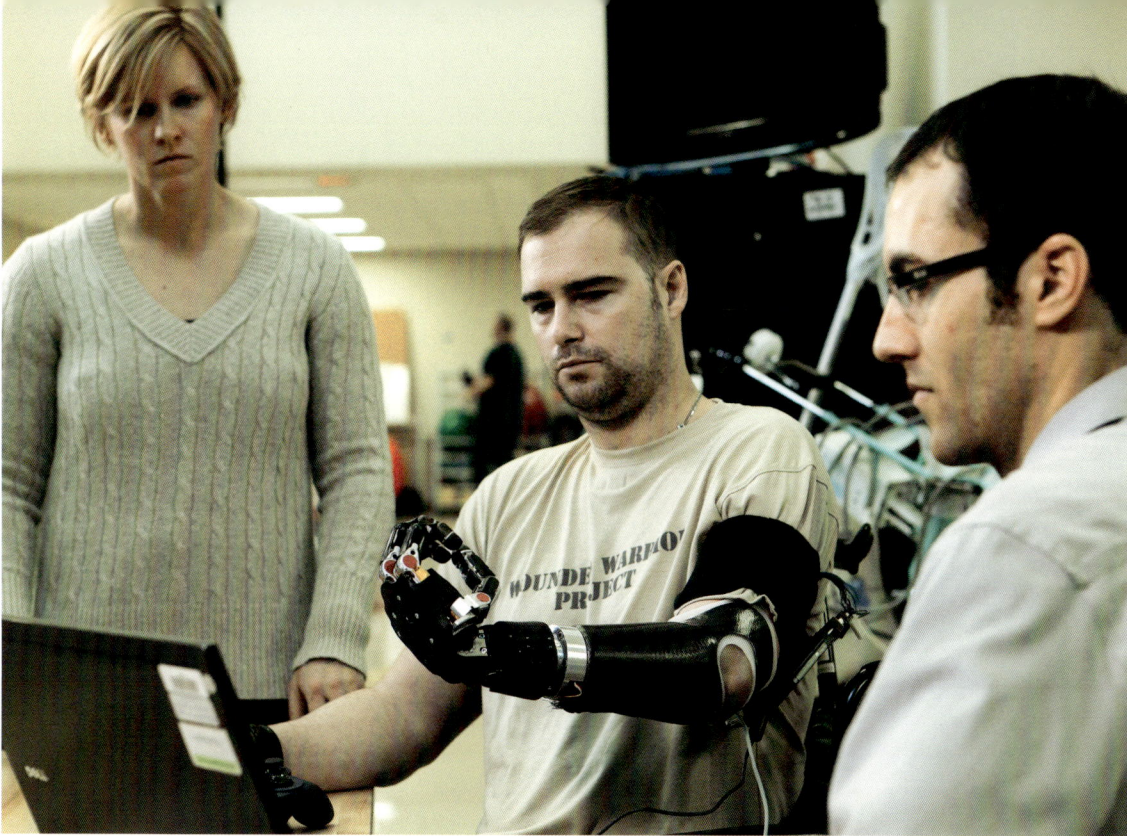

APL engineers Courtney Moran (left) and Bobby Armiger (far right) working with Technical Sergeant Joe Delauriers as he controls the MPL at Walter Reed National Medical Center. Delauriers lost both legs and his left arm in a September 2011 IED explosion in Afghanistan.

characteristics as a natural human arm. This initial phase was completed in 2007 and was demonstrated with amputees.

While this first prototype was limited to 8 degrees of freedom (versus the ultimate goal of 26 degrees of freedom), the team was able to interface the prosthetic device to peripheral nerves and demonstrate brain control of a high-dexterity prosthetic. They were also able to stimulate these same nerves to produce sensation that the patient perceived as coming from his lost hand. While these results were groundbreaking, the team was only just getting started. Feedback from these tests led to advancements that greatly increased the artificial limb's performance and sped up the development process in producing the next-generation prototype, the Modular Prosthetic Limb (MPL).

The MPL offered 26 degrees of freedom and had over 180 embedded sensors, making it the most sophisticated robotic arm in the world and enabling greater levels of control and dexterity than its predecessor, including individual finger movements resulting in a level of dexterity approaching that of the human hand. APL designed and developed major components of the prototype and demonstrated the fully integrated system in 2009. The next, and most challenging, phase of development entailed the goal of operating the prosthesis through neural commands directly from the brain.

To achieve this incredible brain-to-computer-to-limb interface, the team advanced a small implantable device with a hundred electrodes, each capable of measuring signals from individual neurons in the brain. To test the system concept, the devices were first surgically implanted in the cranium of a monkey to permit access to the animal's cortical signals. Brain signals were decoded to determine

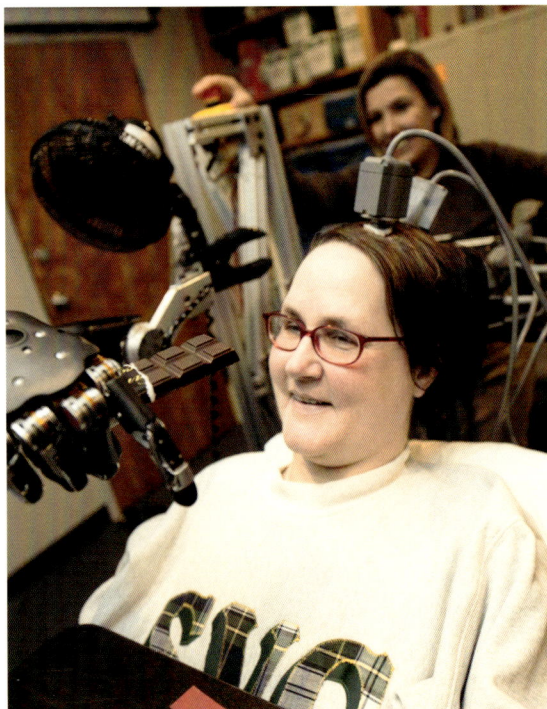

Jan Scheuermann, a quadriplegic who has worked with the MPL team at APL and the University of Pittsburgh Medical Center, has shown the ability to operate the prosthetic with her mind. Here, she brings a chocolate bar to her mouth. (University of Pittsburgh Medical Center)

the intended action and then translated into signals that would drive the robotic arm. Thus, when the monkey thought about moving its own arm, the robotic arm moved in the way the monkey's mind had dictated.

Eventually the monkey learned to move the robotic arm independently of its natural arm. The team was also able to re-create the sense of touch by using signals from the MPL's fingertips to stimulate the sensory area of the monkey's brain. The tests effectively proved the ability of the device to decode motor control signals and re-create natural sensation. A new era of neuroscience was born, and APL was ready to take it to the next level.

The success of the neural implant gave hope to the promise of similar tests in a human being. With additional DARPA funding, APL began to develop an advanced prototype arm, with the goal of having it ready for clinical trials. The promising work by the APL-led team was soon noticed by the media, and in January 2010, *National Geographic* published a cover story on the remarkable neural device, called "Merging Man and Machine: The Bionic Age."

The next year, Jan Scheuermann, a Pittsburgh mother of two, volunteered to have surgery to implant the neural transmitter in her brain. Scheuermann had a neurodegenerative disease that had paralyzed her from the neck down, disrupting the neural connection between her mind and limbs. A gifted writer who was studying to become a neuroscientist, she was the perfect candidate, and the procedure was successful. The implant sent impulses from neurons in her brain and the impulses were used to maneuver the MPL by interpreting her thoughts.

In June 2013, the *60 Minutes* television program aired the broadcast segment "Breakthrough." To illustrate the capabilities, CBS correspondent Scott Pelley asked Scheuermann to shake his hand. When the robotic arm did as Scheuermann's mind requested, he responded, "Oh my goodness." Scheuermann then asked if Pelley wanted to bump fists. To the newsman's utter amazement, they did.

"We had implanted electrodes on the right side of Jan's brain with the intention of having her control a single MPL, but we found out that she could do so much more," said Mike McLoughlin, chief engineer in APL's Research and Exploratory Development Department and the project's principal investigator. On November 28, 2014, Scheuermann achieved her personal goal: She fed herself a chocolate candy bar. Over the next several years, she went on to perform a number of other firsts, including flying a flight simulator! "Jan is a true pioneer—she showed us the possibility to move beyond the physical limitations of our own bodies," McLoughlin said. "Since working with Jan, the team has also demonstrated the ability to stimulate the sensory areas of the brain, re-creating sensation from the fingers." And on October 13, 2016, Nathan Copeland, the program's next paralyzed participant, shook President Obama's hand.

The team continued to push the limits of using the MPL with amputees. Johnny Matheny, who lost his arm due to cancer, underwent targeted muscle reinnervation (TMR) surgery at Johns Hopkins in late 2011. In 2013, he was featured on *60 Minutes*, demonstrating both sensation and control. In 2015, he became the first upper extremity amputee in the United States to be fitted with an osseointegrated

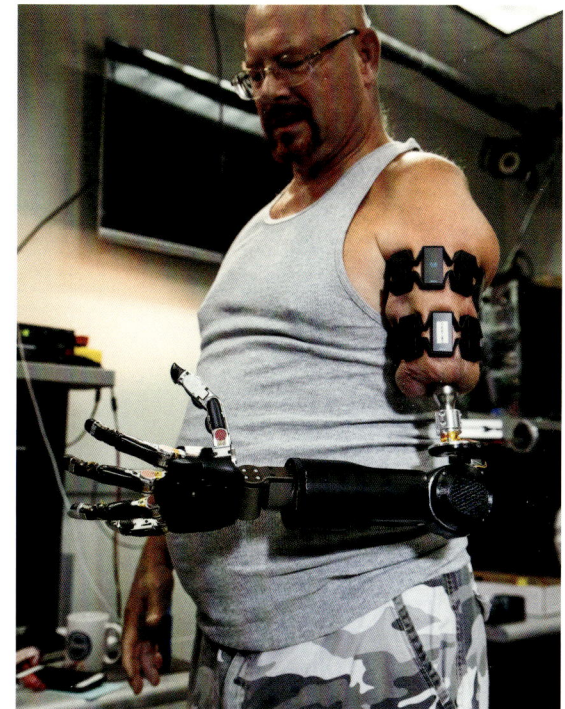

implant, which directly connects the prosthetic to remaining bone, and trying the MPL was the first thing he wanted to do. Matheny demonstrated a level of natural-like use of the MPL that was beyond anything the team had ever seen, and he was the first person to use the MPL out of the lab, always attracting a large following whenever he went out in public.

Another volunteer, Les Baugh, who as a teenager lost both arms after an electrical accident, stepped forward. In 2013, Johns Hopkins surgeons performed TMR to access nerves in Baugh's upper torso that would be used to control two advanced prosthetic limbs. Baugh was the first bilateral full-arm amputee to undergo this procedure. Afterward, he was able to simultaneously control two MPLs, recovering in minutes what had been lost for almost 40 years.

With training, Baugh learned to control the prosthetic simply by thinking about an action he wanted to perform. For instance, he was able to move several objects, including an empty cup, from a counter-height shelf to a higher shelf. To complete the task, Baugh's mind coordinated the control of eight separate motions. When a second prosthetic device was fitted to Baugh's other shoulder, he could control a combination of motions with both arms at the same time. One of the research program's most poignant moments came later during an APL board of managers meeting. Lab Director Ralph Semmel had just presented Baugh and other members of the Revolutionizing Prosthetics team with special coins honoring their achievements and tireless commitment to the project. As the board members broke into applause, Baugh dropped his coin. The room became uncomfortably silent for

The CRISM instrument is visible in this artist rendering as the large round tube on the bottom of NASA's Mars Reconnaissance Orbiter. Launched in 2006, it observed the presence of minerals that helped prove the existence of water on the surface of Mars. (NASA/JPL)

a few seconds, until Baugh sheepishly explained, "I thought about clapping, myself." Just thinking about applauding caused his hand to open and drop the coin. It was an amazing moment for the program and all associated with it.

Finding Water on Mars

Breathtaking advancements like the neural prosthetic arm make working at APL immensely rewarding for staff members. Another mind-blowing project delivering an equal dose of gratification was the quest to answer a question that had long baffled scientists—the existence of water on Mars.

In 2005, NASA launched the Mars Reconnaissance Orbiter spacecraft. On board was CRISM, which stands for Compact Reconnaissance Imaging Spectrometer for Mars. It was the most powerful spectrometer ever sent to the red planet, designed and built by APL to look for the residues of minerals that typically form in the presence of water, such as carbonates, clays, and salts. If water ever existed on Mars, these "fingerprints" would appear in evaporated hot springs, thermal vents, lakes, and ponds.

CRISM was just the latest in the more than 150 spacecraft instruments to APL's credit. The remote-sensing spectrometer could discern more than 500 different colors in reflected sunlight, indicating the presence of different surface minerals on the planet. This capacity was a huge leap in hyperspectral imaging. As the orbiter passed over Mars, the gimbal-mounted instrument followed the terrain, collecting detailed image data to determine its properties. In 2015, NASA announced that CRISM and its "partner" instruments aboard the orbiter had succeeded in their quest, providing strong chemical and visual evidence that liquid water flows today on the surface of Mars.

Operation Burnt Frost

For 40 members of the Lab's staff, another urgent, important mission presented itself in January 2008—the need to down an errant U.S. intelligence satellite carrying 1,000 pounds of frozen hydrazine fuel. In a scenario right out of the movies, the satellite was falling out of orbit and toward Earth. Were it to strike a heavily populated area, the highly toxic and flammable fuel could cause significant loss of life.

APL staff members joined a special project team composed of government, industry, and defense laboratory partners to determine how to address the perilous situation. One challenge was the satellite's tremendous orbital speed—17,000 miles per hour. Another was the high altitude. The Navy's ballistic missiles had never performed an intercept of an object at such fast speed and high altitude. A more vexing complication was that the Navy missile system had been intentionally designed to avoid hitting satellites.

The team needed to work quickly to find a way to intercept the satellite and, in particular, to rupture the hydrazine tank prior to its reentry. Normally a project of this scope would require a yearlong engineering effort and extensive crew training—but the satellite was predicted to come down within three months. Missile Defense Agency leadership determined that the Aegis Ballistic Missile Defense

LEFT: *During Operation Burnt Frost, U.S. Navy Petty Officer Second Class Andrew Jackson activates a modified tactical Standard Missile-3 from the Combat Information Center of the Aegis cruiser USS* Lake Erie *(CG 70), on station in the Pacific Ocean on February 20, 2008. The missile struck a nonfunctioning U.S. satellite as it traveled in space at more than 17,000 miles per hour over the Pacific Ocean. The nation called on APL, with its long experience with Aegis and Standard Missile, to make vital contributions to this critical operation.* (U.S. NAVY)

BELOW: *USS* Lake Erie *(CG 70) launches the Standard Missile-3, which intercepted the satellite during the Burnt Frost mission.* (U.S. NAVY)

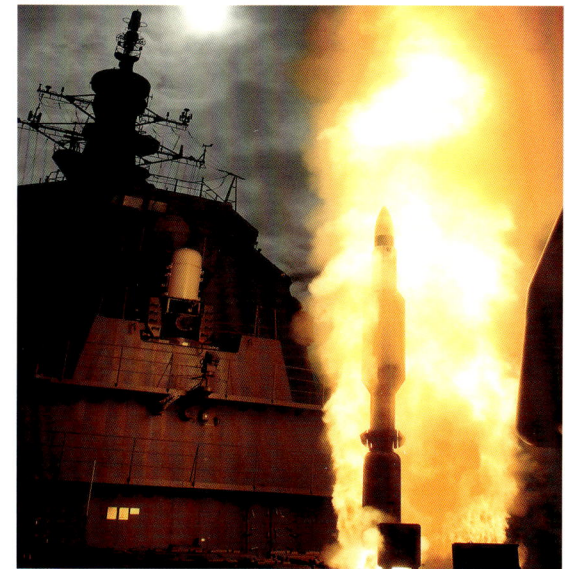

System offered the best chance of success based on the approach presented by the team. APL and its collaborators were given just over five weeks to accomplish the mission, a punishing timeline. After intensive round-the-clock studies of numerous potential alterations to the weapon system, as well as various concepts of conducting the mission, the team showed that the system offered an acceptable solution. In February 2008, President Bush approved the team's recommendations to destroy the satellite, tasking U.S. Strategic Command to execute the mission. The project was code-named Burnt Frost.

APL's participation was vital to the operation. As the technical direction agent for Aegis Ballistic Missile Defense, the Lab had deep experience with the key components that made up the missile defense system. This knowledge provided the staff with the end-to-end systems perspective needed to ensure the destruction of the satellite. Their objective was to rupture the satellite's fuel tank to dissipate the hydrazine before the satellite entered Earth's atmosphere.

One of the many challenges was the satellite's decaying orbit, which made it somewhat unpredictable. APL staff members, working with the Joint Space Operations Center, were able to characterize the target's movements sufficiently to determine the optimal position and time to shoot down the satellite. The staff worked closely with the design agents for the Aegis Weapon System (Lockheed Martin) and the missile (Raytheon Missile Systems) to propose and assess the modifications necessary to perform the mission. APL's analyses determined the ship's position for the engagement, and the team worked with Lockheed Martin to define the radar search sectors necessary to detect the satellite. APL employed its expertise, modeling, and facilities to provide confidence in the design changes.

On the bridge of USS Lake Erie *(CG 70) after the successful intercept of the satellite during Operation Burnt Frost are Captain Randall M. Hendrickson (now Rear Admiral, retired), commanding officer of USS* Lake Erie*; Rear Admiral Alan B. Hicks (now retired), program director of Aegis Ballistic Missile Defense; and APL Air and Missile Defense Department Head Conrad Grant, now APL Chief Engineer.*

On February 20, 2008, all Aegis systems were a go. At approximately 5:30 p.m. Eastern Standard Time, planning for the mission began in the basement of APL's Building 1. Data needed to execute the mission was passed from APL to Lockheed Martin in Moorestown, New Jersey, as well as to the Pacific Missile Range Facility in Kauai, before making its way to USS *Lake Erie* for the engagement.

At approximately 10:30 p.m. Eastern Standard Time, USS *Lake Erie* launched a single Standard Missile-3 at the satellite, which had been successfully tracked in the preceding days. A few minutes later, numerous sensors and radars detected the collision between the kinetic kill vehicle and the satellite. Videos released the next morning clearly showed that the hydrazine was completely neutralized. Over the next few weeks, the remnants of the wayward satellite safely burned during its reentry, crowning a "brilliantly successful mission with a satisfyingly quiet finale," the U.S. Naval Institute reported.

Throughout the mission planning phase, APL team members were in daily contact with Missile Defense Agency leadership and served as the conduit between the Missile Defense Agency and the analytical efforts. During the mission execution, APL staff members were present in field locations across the country assisting key military leaders.

Securing the Border

The Secure Border Initiative launched by the Department of Homeland Security was conceived in 2005 as a way to protect the nation's borders and coastlines from smuggling and illegal immigration. The technology focus of this program proposed a comprehensive system of cameras and sensors. However, after years of development, the department reached a technology impasse and temporarily halted development.

APL was called in to apply its systems engineering expertise to see what could be done. "The problem, as we saw it, was the need for a systems engineering approach to the solutions they were developing," said Jose Latimer, APL's Homeland Protection mission area executive. "They really needed an independent technology perspective."

The Lab sought to help the U.S. Border Patrol understand the technology integration that would be required and help it articulate its needs to justify the acquisition program decisions. "Our staff members sat down with border patrol agents in places like Nogales, Arizona, asking about their real requirements, finding out where there were 'gaps,' and discussing actual scenarios of how people jump the border," Latimer said. "This helped us document what they needed in their specific environment, which shaped what needed to be built."

APL had applied such a capability gap analysis process many times before. Since the border patrol agents represented a diverse set of expertise and experience levels, their self-evaluation was a solid foundation for insightful analysis. As a result, APL experts developed a suite of analytical tools to help the agents visualize and analyze their operational capability and performance. This Total Station View, as the system is called, displays and quantifies various environments, including tactical and technical elements of each patrol's operations, strengthening overall border security.

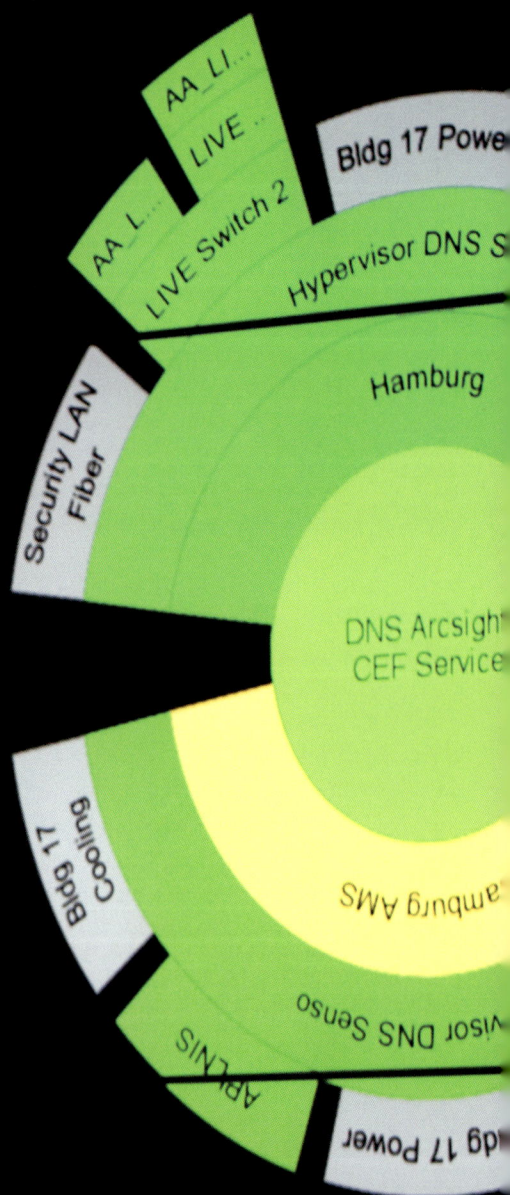

Elisha Peterson in APL's LIVE Lab, a unique facility that helps researchers develop solutions to continually evolving cyber threats.

Chapter 11

Thriving in an Age of Uncertainty

As the war on terror escalated, cyberattacks on the country's information systems became a growing concern. In less than a decade's time, cybersecurity had emerged to become one of the most serious challenges confronting the United States.

The number of cyberattacks by well-funded terrorist groups and hackers acting on behalf of other nations increased alarmingly in the early 2000s. In 2007, more than 80,000 attacks on just Defense Department networks were recorded. To thwart these invaders, several government sponsors turned to APL for crucial assistance.

"Our goal is to help the government meet critical national security needs," said Ray Yuan, who joined APL in 1985 and is today mission area executive for Cyber Operations. "Consequently, we've been called on to design, develop, and test capabilities that protect government networks and key mission systems."

Multiple sponsors, including the Navy, NSA, DARPA, DoD, and the Department of Homeland Security, reached out to APL's Applied Information Sciences Department to develop critical technologies enhancing the security of the nation. As a result, this relatively new APL technical capability grew swiftly in personnel, projects, and expertise. By 2010, the staff was engaged in a multitude of cyber defense projects to protect information and services connected to the internet as well as national security systems.

These efforts were extremely wide-ranging. Depending on the project, the Lab sought ways to prevent an adversary from getting into the nation's systems or ways to gather intelligence to stop an attack that was already in progress. Staff members also created more objective ways of measuring the effectiveness of cyber detection and the nation's cyber defense preparedness. They evaluated new information technology architectures to identify and defeat malicious cyberattacks. And they developed an effective systems approach that allowed cybersecurity analysts in government and industry to collect, analyze, and, most important, share cyber threat information.

LIVE Lab allows cyber experts—like Kim Glasgow—to detect and monitor intrusion attempts on APL's network in real time. To assess new cyber defense techniques for the government, APL uses LIVE Lab to mirror its real-time network as a testing ground.

The Lab experienced a major cyber intrusion in 2009, bringing home the vulnerability of its own systems. Fortuitously, APL had just recruited a new chief information officer (CIO), Michael Misumi, who had created the cybersecurity strategy for the nonprofit research institution RAND Corporation. In his first days on the job, Misumi assembled a team of cyber research personnel from across the Lab to begin a comprehensive sweep of APL's network. In time, using advanced software, they were able to ascertain that the Lab had been hacked.

The new CIO made the difficult decision to observe the hackers' progression through APL's network to discern the intent and progress. "Unfortunately, these were pretty sophisticated intruders who caught on to what we were doing, and they started extracting as much information as they could, none of it classified," Misumi said. "As soon as we saw data flowing out of one part of the network, we shut that part off. Then we would see data leakage elsewhere and shut that down. Finally, we pulled the plug on the whole thing, disconnecting our main website from the internet."

With backing from APL's director Rich Roca, Misumi instructed that every system across the Lab be scanned and purged of malware. Once clean, the system was upgraded with new cyber defense features. Altogether, the team was able to upgrade 8,000 systems in just three days. Although cyber-attacks continue to hit APL's network on a daily basis, thanks to the Lab's ongoing and leading-edge efforts, these intrusions are quickly identified and obstructed.

The hacking attack changed APL's approach to its own cyber situational awareness. Previously, those at the Lab conducting cyber research on behalf of government sponsors had little connection with Misumi's teams. They now work much more closely to discuss emerging cyber threats facing both the nation and the Lab, experimenting with developmental cyber defense features on APL's own network. This partnership gave rise to the development of a boldly innovative APL research facility, called LIVE (Live data, Integration, Validation, and Experimentation) Lab. In a large, darkened facility that looks like a near-future situation room, staff members map a duplicate of APL's internal network on banks of giant television screens to detect cyber intrusions. They then implement different cyber monitoring and security technologies to observe their impact on the flow of information as the intruder moves from one system to another. APL also uses this data and network visualization capability to support sponsor cyber training and exercises.

"We're rare among organizations that provide the government with technical insights into cyber capabilities by using our own network as a testing ground," said Tim Galpin, who joined APL in 2004 after a career as a Navy officer and is currently the Lab's assistant director for programs and strategy. APL's mandate today is to broaden its cyber efforts beyond point solutions toward mission resilience for key sponsor systems and full-spectrum cyber operations. Drawing from its disciplined systems engineering expertise, ongoing research efforts, and facilities such as LIVE Lab, APL creates agile systems engineering methodologies to address continually evolving cyber threats.

With Roca's tenure as director coming to a close, the APL board of managers began a national search for a successor. Unlike the previous search, which resulted in an external candidate being selected,

BELOW: *In 2014, APL hosted an Office of the Secretary of Defense project designed to improve the skills of our nation's cyber warriors, working hands-on with military service personnel.*

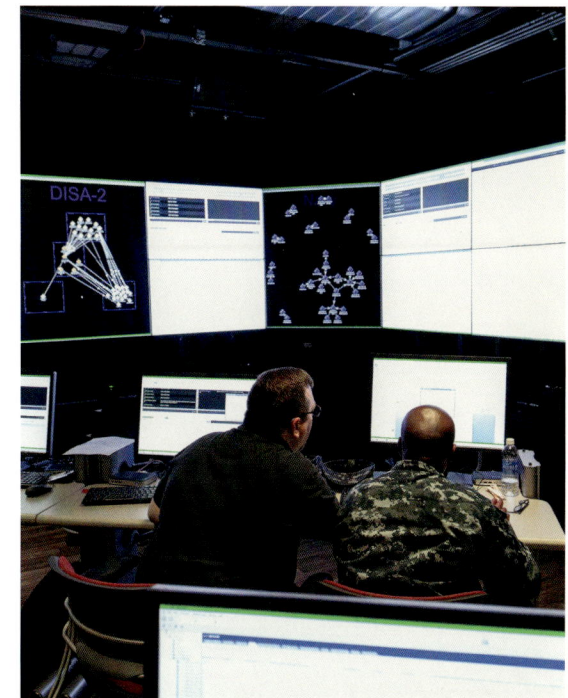

this time, the board would find the right person for the job within the Lab's ranks. During his tenure as Lab director, Roca is credited with increasing the Lab's focus and alignment on sponsor needs and is known for his efforts to expand the Lab's sponsor base and his willingness to take on risks associated with several major NASA-funded missions that would cement the Lab's scientific legacy in the years ahead. Roca served as emeritus director after his retirement in 2010.

New Leader Takes the Helm

Ralph Semmel, who at the time led the Lab's Applied Information Sciences Department, was selected to succeed Roca as the director in 2010. An engineer and computer scientist by training, Semmel joined APL in 1986 after serving in multiple leadership positions in private industry and the U.S. Army.

Having worked at the Lab for more than 25 years at the time, Semmel had served successfully in a variety of technical and executive leadership roles at all levels across the organization. His experience and knowledge of the Lab were essential in how he would approach his new role, as APL confronted increasing austerity in government research funding. One of the reasons the board members had selected Semmel was their confidence in his ability to clearly articulate the value of the Lab to government officials in Washington.

Against this backdrop, Semmel initially focused on two major issues—lowering the cost to deliver APL's sponsored work and spurring innovation and collaboration across the Lab. His strategy was to treat these two challenges in tandem. If the Lab could lower its cost to deliver, some of the savings could be used to invest in innovation and collaboration initiatives.

"The Lab has always done great technical work, but the changing environment demanded that we become even more agile than we had been and bring forward more innovative concepts to our sponsors," Semmel said. "To successfully respond to rapidly evolving sponsor needs and compete

More Than Meets the Eye

In 2013, APL scientists partnered with the Johns Hopkins University School of Medicine and the Wilmer Eye Institute for the Eye PATCH (Protection and Treatment for Combat Healing) project, an effort to find effective solutions for soldiers' eye injuries. The team—including Xiomara Calderon-Colon (left), Morgana Trexler, and Marcia Patchan—created three materials that could help repair eye injuries and be easily applied in the field: a cellulose bandage, made to protect the affected eye and release antibiotics to prevent infection; a collagen reconstructive membrane, a gel-like substance designed to repair more serious injuries; and an eye adhesive that is strong, portable, and easy to apply to penetrating eye wounds. The effort was sponsored by the U.S. Army.

effectively for the nation's top talent, we also needed to be more broadly recognized as the innovative organization we are." To gain broad acceptance, Semmel was cognizant that he and the executive team needed to carefully and thoughtfully widen the Lab's emphasis on innovation and collaboration. Following extensive planning, engagement, and communication with numerous leaders and groups throughout the Lab, he gained buy-in on the new strategy and approach, which included one of the most sweeping reorganizations in the Lab's history. The resulting organization realigned APL's mission areas into four sectors and two enterprise technical departments, supported by four enterprise service departments. This grouping consolidated the Lab's sponsor-facing capabilities in air and missile defense, force projection, asymmetric operations, space exploration and security, research and exploratory development, and national security analysis.

In addition, APL leaders introduced a succession of innovation and collaboration initiatives, including a series of internally funded grant programs to encourage staff members to bring forward innovative ideas and concepts outside traditional channels to solve sponsor challenges. The first of these were Ignition Grants, which were intended to empower the staff and provide a high degree of freedom to explore new ideas. To receive such grants, individual staff members, or teams of collaborators, propose ideas or research areas, from which the entire staff is invited to vote to select the best ones. Ignition Grants were followed in subsequent years by Combustion and Propulsion Grants, which provided substantially more resources to focus on high-risk research for the Lab's sponsors that had the potential for game-changing impact and might even lead to new defining innovations. Another initiative was a series of short, sometimes even edgy, videos promoting innovative work being done across the Lab; these videos familiarize staff members with Lab projects that might be relevant to their own work. Called Tech Splash, they number more than 100 as this book goes to press. Semmel has remained a visible and vocal champion of innovation initiatives, emphasizing creativity, diversity of thought, agility, and teamwork.

As APL's leadership continued to implement the initial phases of Semmel's plan, the Lab confronted a significant operational challenge. The government planned to reduce the ballooning federal deficit by placing limits on annual defense budget appropriations. The federal funding caps would decrease each successive year, a process called sequestration, taking an ax to the budgets of many sponsors' programs.

The prescient efforts already underway to control costs, spur innovation, and ensure that APL was working at the leading edge in all of its programs had positioned the Lab well as it braced for what was expected to be a reduction in sponsored research program funding. As a result, the expected reductions never materialized, due largely to APL's placing the right bets and focusing on critical challenges that truly were enduring priorities of the government.

Space Exploration Accelerates

Despite the looming challenges of sequestration, the time for major scientific discoveries had arrived, as several of APL's NASA-sponsored space exploration missions were reaching their destinations

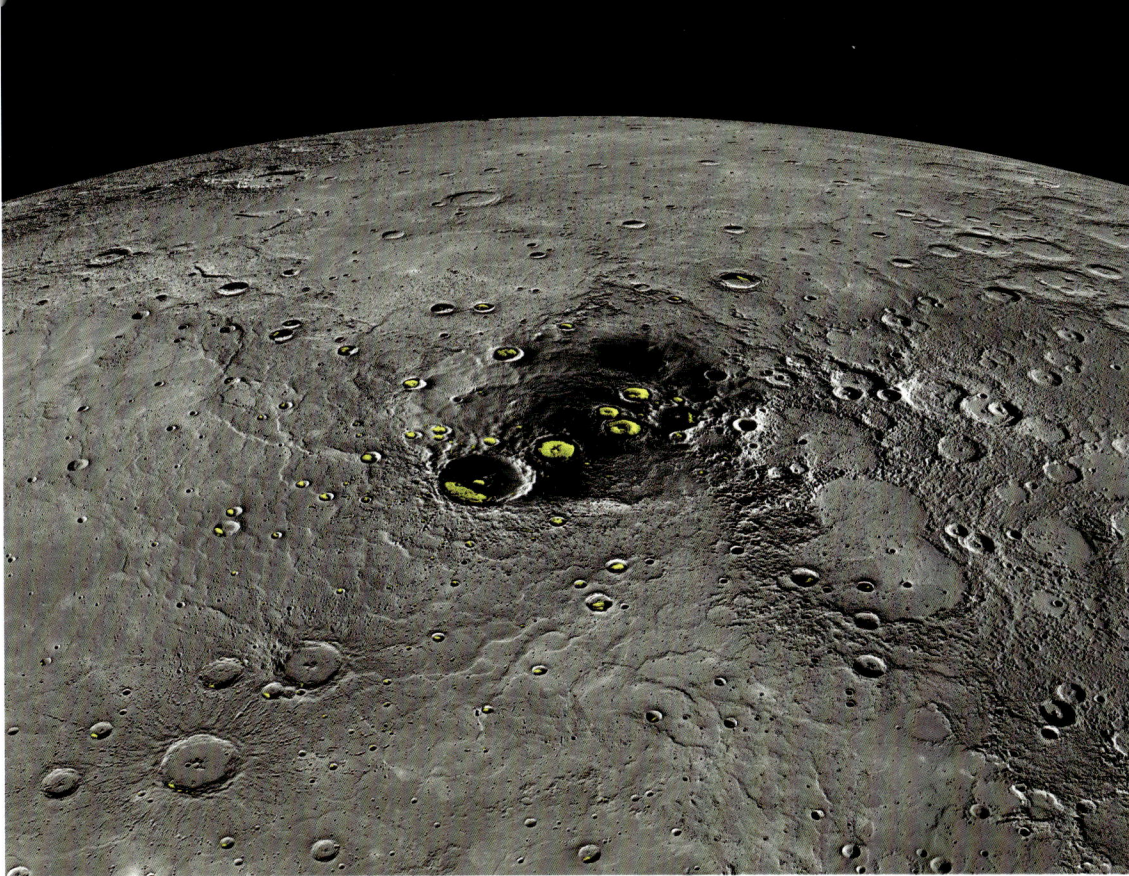

The MESSENGER spacecraft, built by APL, has collected compelling evidence that water ice exists on Mercury. In this view of the planet's north polar region, the yellow regions in many of the craters mark locations that show evidence for water ice. (NASA/APL/CARNEGIE INSTITUTION OF WASHINGTON)

after years of flight or preparing for launch. The MESSENGER spacecraft, launched in 2004, began orbiting Mercury in 2011. The low-cost mission defied the conventional wisdom that a scientific mission to study the planet closest to the sun would cost billions of dollars because of the blistering temperatures. Fortunately, the Lab's ceramic-fabric sunshade and other heat-deflection and mitigation technologies performed in perfect balance. The solar arrays rotated off the sun when it was at its hottest, while simultaneous adjustments in the spacecraft's position shielded its more sensitive parts from experiencing Mercury's scorching temperatures.

MESSENGER's observations dramatically changed how scientists understood the planet. Its chemical composition was more similar to that of Venus, Mars, and Earth than had been expected, and MESSENGER confirmed the presence of ice at the planet's poles. The spacecraft captured images and data on a huge expanse of volcanic plains and a series of mammoth vents measuring up to 16 miles across. These openings appear to be the source of hot lava flowing across the planet's surface.

Meanwhile, another APL spacecraft—actually two of them—was in the process of exploring the two donut-shaped rings of highly charged particles surrounding the Earth, discovered by former APL physicist James Van Allen in 1958. Subsequently named the Van Allen Belts, they are a byproduct of our planet's protective magnetosphere. Within the belts are fast-moving electrons and ions that can damage space-based technologies, such as the communications and GPS satellites that operate within the rings. They also pose a threat to humans in spaceflight.

Predicting the Progress of Viruses

Understanding how a virus propagates is important to preventing viral outbreaks and curing disease. In nature, viruses compete with one another for dominance within the human body. The body's immune system responds and begins to attack viruses once they are detected. But there are variants in the viral population that can escape these evolutionary pressures to eventually dominate the group.

To understand which classes of viruses will emerge and when, APL and Harvard University developed a prototype capability that rapidly mimics the natural evolution of a virus in the lab. This can potentially improve the nation's ability to detect emerging diseases, while addressing such other challenges as bacterial drug resistance, food safety, and biological weapons defense.

By applying APL's expertise in systems biology, optics, and biological assay development and Harvard's prowess in microfluidics (a technology characterized by the engineered manipulation of fluids at the submillimeter scale), scientists applied droplet-based microfluidics to segregate and propagate a viral population as individual viral lineages. This allows researchers to perform millions of in vitro evolutionary experiments simultaneously. The genomes of the evolving viral populations in each segregated lineage could be sequenced individually to determine mutations that enable viruses to evade evolutionary stresses, drugs, and antibodies.

The game-changing tool, dubbed the Rapid Acceleration of Laboratory Evolution (oRACLE) Chip, effectively imitates Mother Nature, reducing a process that takes years to complete to just a few days, with material costs of $2.50. By isolating and characterizing, for example, a new influenza virus strain faster and earlier in the flu season, researchers—like APL's Joshua Wolfe (left), Peter Thielen, and Audrey Fischer Hesselbrock—can quickly develop a vaccine that matches the strain emerging as the dominant virus.

While scientists understood that the radiation belts swelled and shrank over time, they were unsure how space weather—the source of the aurora that shimmers in the night sky—contributed to this phenomenon. To better understand these mechanisms, APL designed and built twin Van Allen Probes, launched in 2012, to study this hazardous region of space, putting the satellites into an area that other spacecraft avoid. The mission is on behalf of NASA's Living With a Star program, which is predicated on improving the scientific community's understanding of the sun's impact on the solar system.

Solving National Security Challenges

While APL's space missions received substantial media attention and public acclaim, other efforts, such as the Lab's historic warfare analysis contributions, progressed more quietly but with the same determination. APL's Assessment Division from the early 1950s had evolved through the decades into the Naval Warfare Analysis Department in the 1980s and the Joint Warfare Analysis Department in the 1990s. Now chartered as the National Security Analysis Department, its staff members were conducting multi-mission assessments concerning a wide range of evolving national security issues.

From this work, APL's contributions to the crucial National Command Program emerged in 2006. The program is responsible for conducting strategic analyses of mission-critical nuclear, continuity, and senior leader command and control systems that support the National Leadership Command Capability (NLCC). APL has been successful in spearheading a broad operational and technology modernization effort, in collaboration with the Defense Department's NLCC Management Office.

"In today's dynamic asymmetric threat environment, you need the ability for multiple decision-makers to collaborate instantly," said John Forte, who led this effort for the National Security Analysis

Engineers (from left) Esther Showalter, Akinwale Akinpelu, Warren Kim, and Tony DeSimone in the APL Secure Communications Assessment Network (SeCAN) Laboratory evaluate technology to support nuclear command, control, and communications decision-making. This provides senior government officials with the capability to communicate securely during national emergencies.

Mission Area and is now deputy mission area executive for Homeland Protection. "Multiple leaders must be in on the call to support the decision that is determined. To provide these vastly enhanced secure communications and collaboration capabilities, we realized we needed to modernize the NLCC from the core. To do it, we leveraged every skill set we had."

Advances in Integrating Air and Missile Defense

Although the Mountain Top exercise conducted in the 1990s had proven that an Aegis ship could engage a target missile beyond the horizon, Navy surface missiles continued to use a semi-active sensor for terminal homing, which required the ship to illuminate a target with a large microwave dish antenna for the missile to home in on the target reflection for the actual intercept. The Standard Missile-6, the Navy's new premier extended-range anti-air warfare missile, deployed an active seeker in addition to the semi-active sensor, which provided its own illumination of the target.

The active seeker mode and the now-miniaturized advanced airborne radar whose prototype was tested during Mountain Top were the final spokes in the wheel necessary to intercept targets beyond the firing ship's horizon. As the technical direction agent for the Navy's Cooperative Engagement Capability (CEC), Aegis, and the Standard Missile, the Lab took on the task of pulling together these and other critical pieces to further improve the capability of the Navy fleet to counter air and missile threats at significantly greater distances.

The ambitious goal of the Naval Integrated Fire Control – Counter Air (NIFC-CA), as the project was called, was for Aegis warships to be able to use remote radar sensor data to execute anti-air warfare engagements over the horizon of the shooting platform against an adversary's distant anti-ship

LEFT: *In 2010, APL engineers (from left) Jon Lindberg, Wirak Lim, Emily Hebeler, Jin Zhang, Bryan Gorman, and Nigel Tzeng test a prototype element of the Lab-developed NIFC-CA capability known as the integrated multi-warfare planning tool.*

BELOW: *APL's Ashley Llorens (right), an internationally acclaimed rap artist, celebrates APL's 70th anniversary with a special "APL Rap" performed with some "help" from Director Ralph Semmel at the spring 2012 All-Hands State-of-the-Laboratory presentation.*

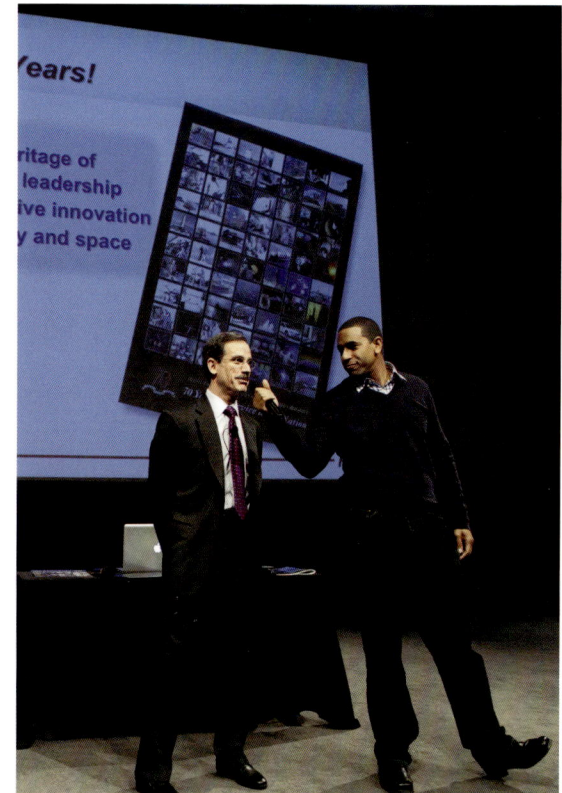

long-range cruise missiles. In 2014, all the pieces—Navy ships and aircraft—came together as a single network for testing by the Navy at sea.

In one early test, prior to the airborne sensor, the Aegis destroyer USS *Sampson* served as the remote sensor, gathering data about two incoming cruise missiles that were built to act and look like actual threat cruise missiles. *Sampson* supplied this radar measurement information to the Aegis warship *Chancellorsville* via CEC. That ship subsequently launched two Standard Missile-6s with active seekers that guided them directly to intercept the targets beyond *Chancellorsville*'s horizon. This capability, long sought by the Navy, marked another crucial step toward the development of a joint integrated air defense.

Major progress was also made in defending the United States and its allies against the growing threat of ballistic missile attacks. The U.S. Navy long believed its Aegis Combat System could play a vital role in defending the United States and forward-deployed forces against ballistic missile attack. In the years since, five *Ticonderoga*-class cruisers and 25 *Arleigh Burke*-class destroyers, armed with a combination of the Aegis system, AN/SPY-1 radar, and Standard Missile-2s, have been modified, with the introduction of Standard Missile-3s, to serve as ballistic missile defense platforms. These ships, currently serving in the Pacific and European theaters, provide the nation with an important component of national missile defense—intercepting short- and intermediate-range ballistic missiles before they reenter the atmosphere.

In 2009, APL led a study for the Missile Defense Agency that, in turn, led to the development of a land-based Aegis Ballistic Missile Defense capability known as Aegis Ashore. Aegis became the cornerstone of President Barack Obama's Phased Adaptive Approach to the defense of Europe against

Engineers and researchers from APL played a key role in the first Aegis Ashore intercept flight test on December 9, 2015. During the first-of-its-kind test, conducted at the Aegis Ashore Missile Defense Test Complex at the Pacific Missile Range Facility, Kauai, Hawaii, a Standard Missile-3 Block IB Threat Upgrade guided missile successfully intercepted an air-launched medium-range ballistic missile target. (MDA)

ballistic missiles. The first phase would consist of Aegis ships deployed in the Mediterranean Sea, the second phase would bring in an Aegis Ashore facility featuring the Standard Missile-3 Block IB in Romania, and the third phase would include the Standard Missile-3 Block IIA being developed cooperatively with Japan.

In 2014, in collaboration with Lockheed Martin and Raytheon, APL engineers were central to Aegis/Missile Defense Agency efforts to successfully flight-test this land-based ballistic missile defense capability known as Aegis Ashore. The Lab later played a key role in the first intercept test of the Aegis Ashore system, which used remote tracks from the Army AN/TPY-2 radar to launch the Standard Missile-3 and cue the Aegis Ashore SPY-1B, with data from both radars guiding the Standard Missile-3 to destroy an incoming target at the Pacific Missile Range Facility in Hawaii. APL experts worked closely with the Missile Defense Agency and industry partners to plan the complex test scenario and analyze system performance. The successful operational test was a critical milestone for Aegis Ashore, which is now in operation in Romania.

As this book goes to print, APL staff members are working closely with the Missile Defense Agency, the Navy, Lockheed Martin, and Raytheon to perform a test with the newest missile and weapons system to enter the ballistic missile defense inventory, the Standard Missile-3 Block IIA. This missile and its associated weapons system will increase the variety of threats that can be intercepted, while also significantly increasing the area a ship can defend. When deployed in Aegis Ashore, it will complete the president's 2009 Phased Adaptive Approach for the defense of Europe against ballistic missiles.

As the Missile Defense Agency's technical direction agent for the Aegis Ballistic Missile Defense and the Standard Missile-3 programs, APL has long been a vital contributor to the development and validation of these ballistic missile defense capabilities, directly engaged in more than 30 test flights over the past 15 years.

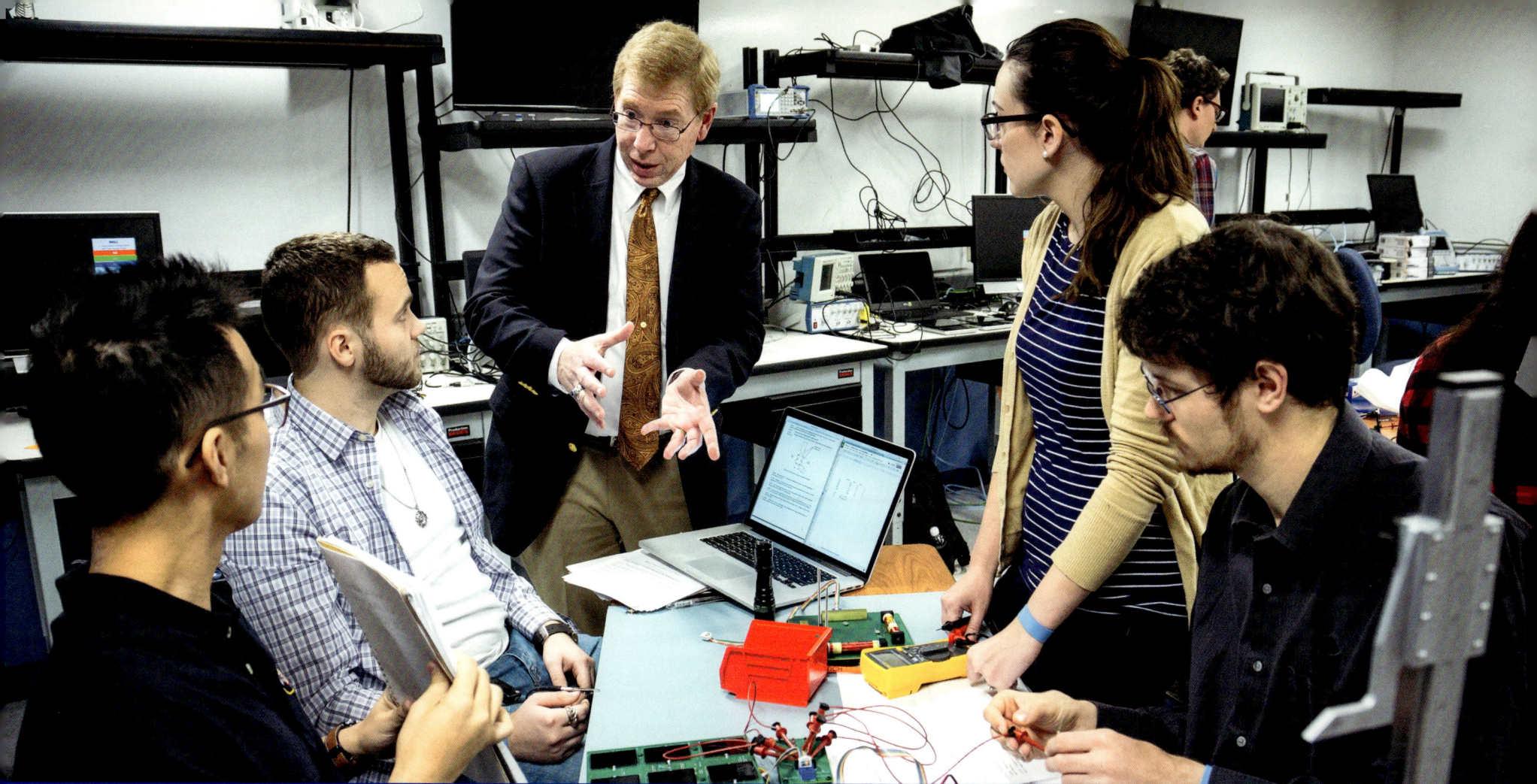

Continuing Education

Keeping its staff members on the cutting edge of technology has been a goal since APL's beginning. After the end of World War II, APL leadership took many steps to ensure that the Lab would not become obsolete. One step was to offer informal education and training programs.

By the late 1950s, APL recognized the need for a more formal in-depth education program. In 1958, the JHU Evening College began sponsoring courses on the campus exclusively for APL staff. These courses, taught by APL senior scientists and engineers, were not part of a degree program.

Recognizing that a formal degree was necessary for career advancement, APL created the JHU Evening College Center (APL Education Center) in 1964, offering a master's degree in electrical engineering. Other scientific and technical degree programs soon followed, and the program was offered to the public.

Today the APL Education Center partners with the Johns Hopkins Whiting School of Engineering and its Engineering for Professionals (EP) program, the largest professional engineering graduate program in the nation. Its more than 2,500 students and nearly 600 master's degree graduates each year come from APL and the Whiting School, as well as from government and regional technology companies. More than 90 percent of students come from outside APL.

Nearly 200 APL staff members (like Paul Ostdiek of the Space Exploration Sector, center) teach EP courses, and 11 of the 19 offered programs are chaired by Lab staff. One of the larger programs, systems engineering, leverages APL's expertise in developing complex prototype systems.

Since 1964, more than 18,000 students have earned master's degrees through EP programs. Several of the APL-based programs partner with commercial companies to develop tailored courses to meet their changing professional needs.

To accommodate full-time working professionals, classes are offered mainly on weekday evenings at campus facilities and asynchronously online. Currently, more than 80 percent of degree program courses are offered online.

Shown together for dramatic effect, these high-resolution, color-enhanced images of Pluto (right) and its nearest moon Charon were captured by the New Horizons spacecraft, which was designed, built, and operated by APL for NASA. It made the historic flyby of Pluto on July 14, 2015. (NASA/JHUAPL/SwRI)

Chapter 12

Beyond New Horizons

As APL neared its 75th anniversary, the campus in Laurel, Maryland, buzzed with anticipation. Nine years after its launch to the outer reaches of the solar system, the New Horizons spacecraft was set to make the first-ever flyby of Pluto on July 14, 2015. The excitement grew palpably in the months leading up to the historic event.

All NASA missions originate with the purpose of exploration and discovery, but few stirred the public's imagination like the New Horizons mission. Since American astronomer Clyde Tombaugh's discovery of Pluto in 1930, the dwarf planet had earned a unique place in the hearts and minds of many. Pluto was the underdog, the little planet at the outer edge of the solar system. When it was downgraded to "dwarf planet" status in late 2006, Pluto took on the guise of the antihero.

"As the solar system's last unexplored planet and the only one discovered by an American, Pluto's initial exploration would be a unique celebration of scientific achievement," said APL Director Ralph Semmel. "And it is a credit to the New Horizons team that the spacecraft actually carried some of Clyde Tombaugh's ashes, a fitting tribute to this pioneering astronomer."

As the mission to Pluto progressed, APL was also engaged in multiple diverse projects. These endeavors included wide-ranging work to assist numerous sponsors with their ongoing efforts in the Iraq and Afghanistan wars and against the constant, deadly tide of terrorist activities, including cyber and biological threats. At the same time, established missions on behalf of the Navy continued to evolve.

The transfer of knowledge from one area of research at the Lab to another became more common, due in part to the growing emphasis on collaboration and the cross-pollination of skill sets. For example, scientists and engineers involved in the revolutionary work on brain–computer interface technology were collaborating with experts in data analytics to explore cross-disciplinary approaches to long-standing problems of detection and classification. This capability was direly needed by DoD, which was fielding data about the actions of possible adversaries from an ever-increasing array of

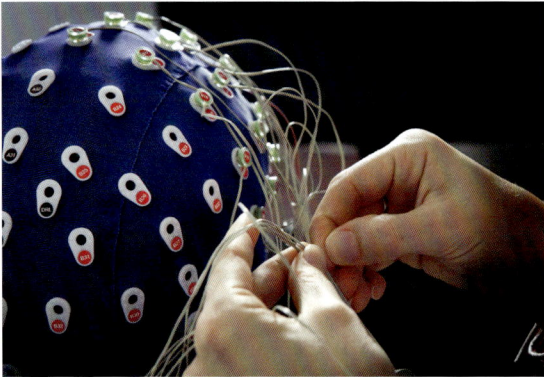

APL researchers used EEG to learn how people find precise information when presented with a high volume of images. This research could help defense analysts sort through vast amounts of data when looking for threats hidden among reams of benign information.

sensors in the air, at sea, and on land. This river of data flowed much faster than the rate of human interpretation that could provide analysis.

The Lab responded to the problem with its characteristic outside-the-box thinking, exploring the application of rapid serial visual presentation (RSVP) techniques to quickly expose a human operator to many visual images. By pairing these techniques with electroencephalography (EEG)—the measurement of electrical activity in different parts of the brain—the researchers could use machine learning techniques to collapse the spatial information from multiple EEG sensors (and multiple time points from each sensor) to generate a single rating score for each stimuli/image.

Because the human brain can perceive the gist of an image in a fraction of a second and still pull useful impressions from a cluttered scene, the combination of EEG and RSVP could speed up the rate of human interpretation of images. The resulting system offered the electronic equivalent of riffling through a book to get a general impression of what it contains, the mind rapidly picking out aspects of the images and text. The technique is one of several methods of directly accessing the mind and brain the Lab is exploring to transform how intelligence analysts sort through information.

"Right now, the system is fairly rudimentary; the fidelity is not where we would like it, given the billions of neurons that transmit nerve signals to and from the brain at around 180 miles per hour," said Jim Schatz, a mathematician by training who joined the Lab in 2009 and today is head of the Research and Exploratory Development Department, more commonly known as REDD. "But we are working hard to get there."

REDD was formed in 2011 through a merger of APL's Research Center, Science and Technology area, Biomedicine area, and the Advanced Fabrication Branch of the Technical Services Department. The philosophy of this new organization was to apply the advanced fabrication capabilities for early prototyping to bridge the traditional "valley of death" between research and applications; in other words, the capability for exploratory development was added to research.

Starting in the 1990s, APL sought to apply its biomedical capabilities to counterproliferation, and eventually to homeland protection, by developing a capability for fusing information that might give evidence of emerging diseases or biological attacks. This effort gained more urgency after September 11. An initial area of focus was global health surveillance, which aimed to improve or defend the overall health of specific populations through the application of information technology. The Lab developed systems to collect, analyze, model, and report public health data to discern evidence of disease outbreaks at the earliest stages. By more closely scrutinizing the progression of a disease, down to the level of a single person spreading a deadly virus or bacterial infection to another person, researchers were convinced they could make better projections on susceptibility across people and regions.

With experience gained from 15 years of working on DoD-sponsored electronic disease surveillance systems, APL software engineers, analysts, and epidemiologists now put their skills, intellects, and imaginations together with those of their colleagues at the university to collectively develop more advanced electronic disease surveillance technologies, while also making these open-source tools

freely available for distribution and user modifications. The Global Health Surveillance team's ongoing work explores a range of algorithms for use in predictive analytics tools that forecast possible future events in real time, such as when a localized disease is likely to flare up and become an outbreak. Such information can help public health officials in their mitigation and resource allocation strategies.

From Government Shutdown to a New Era of Innovation

As these vital projects commenced or continued, the Lab confronted a significant operational challenge. Due to the failure of the U.S. Congress to pass legislation in time to appropriate federal funds, the government partially shut down on October 1, 2013, suspending routine government operations. At the time, it was unclear how long the impasse would last and how significant its impact would be on the Lab and its staff members. With an All-Hands Strategy Update planned for the following week, Semmel called together the senior executives to discuss the situation.

"Although most of our sponsored programs had a funded backlog of work, many federal employees had been furloughed and we were at risk of literally running out of money if the government could not pay for work performed," Semmel said. "Unless the situation could be resolved relatively soon, we would face a situation where we would not be able to pay our staff and would have to consider furloughs or eventually even more drastic measures."

The impact was already being felt elsewhere across the federally funded research and development community, and the concern was growing by the day among APL staff members. The Lab did not want to risk losing even one talented person during the shutdown or suspend work due to a funding shortfall. To ensure staff members would continue their vital work and have assurance of near-term financial stability for themselves and their families, the Lab decided to withdraw its $100 million line of credit and secure additional financial backing from officials at Johns Hopkins University. This capital would be further augmented by the development fund that APL had accumulated for contingencies and opportunities.

To stay engaged with a growing and diverse staff, Director Semmel regularly meets with constituencies from around the Lab, including staff members and students participating in APL's many Science, Technology, Engineering, and Mathematics (STEM) programs.

At the all-hands meeting, Semmel calmly laid out a detailed explanation of the current situation along with the Lab's plan to weather a federal government shutdown of undetermined length. Speaking to a standing-room-only crowd at the Kossiakoff Center and to other packed venues across the campus via video streaming, Semmel spoke plainly about possible outcomes. He explained that nothing could be assured long term but described how APL was managing the situation as well as what staff members could do together to enable the Lab to prolong the money it now had on hand. He also pledged to keep everyone informed as the events unfolded.

Fortunately, the situation abated within two weeks, and the federal government reopened for business October 16. "As difficult as this situation was, we managed as a team to work through the shutdown with minimal disruption to our sponsors' critical programs," Semmel said. "Equally important, we were able to fully support and tangibly demonstrate our commitment to our staff members."

As the newest in a venerable lineage of APL directors, Semmel proved to be an adept CEO. His focus on strategy and execution coincided with an emphasis on cost control and innovation. "Ralph also has a great sense of humor, which is needed when people are working so hard," said Michael D. Hankin, chair of APL's board of managers and the CEO for Brown Advisory Incorporated in Baltimore. "And he has very smart people running each of the different sectors and mission areas—not just some of the best scientists and engineers in the world but also individuals who have spent time in government and know how to execute."

With the crisis resolved, the Lab quickly returned to normal operations. Despite forecasted reductions in defense research funding, the Lab's sponsors continued to rely on APL's responsiveness. Bolstered by the sponsors' confidence in APL and what looked to be stable funding ahead, Semmel and the executive team decided the time was right to articulate an even bolder vision and strategy to lead the Lab and its staff members forward into the future.

PGSS: Funny Name, Huge Impact

As the wars in Iraq and Afghanistan entered their ninth year in 2010, the newly appointed commander of NATO and American forces in Afghanistan, General Stanley McChrystal, planned an ambitious campaign to push forces forward to small operating bases. The aim was to extend influence over broader areas and better protect civilians. To do so, he urgently needed ways for these forces to maintain situational awareness near the bases, as a number of them had previously been overrun by insurgents.

APL, in conjunction with Naval Air Warfare Center, responded with an intrepid idea: a portable, low-cost aerostat, essentially a moored balloon loaded with sensors that could keep a continuous watch over these forward positions. Flight equipment and sensors were tucked in a gondola below the blimp-shaped airship. "NAVAIR named this creation the Persistent Ground Surveillance System, or PGSS (pronounced 'pigs')," said Neal Brower, APL program manager for the effort. "The real story is that this rapid-prototyping effort was successfully developed and fielded in a scant seven months, just in time to support soldiers and Marines deployed as part of the surge." Shown here are staff members (from left) Craig Hughes, Jonathan Hijuelos, and Jim Velky, who supported PGSS testing and fielding.

The sensor-produced data is transmitted through a fiber optic cable extending from the gondola to a ground station. In case of a malfunction, a backup wireless link also transmits the data. The aerostat fills quickly with helium at launch and ascends rapidly to a high altitude, making it difficult for adversaries to shoot it down. APL built the first two gondolas and then transitioned further production to industry, while supporting system integration for each of the 60 units deployed to Afghanistan.

Lieutenant Colonel Seth Folsom, who commanded 3rd Battalion, 7th Marines, based in Helmand Province, Afghanistan, relied heavily on PGSS to provide an "eye in the sky" over his forward operating base. "The enemy hated and feared this system, but they could not stop it," Folsom said. "It was really a game-changer for our operations."

Minotaur: Remote Surveillance

The Minotaur Mission Management System, developed by APL, integrates and displays data and information from multiple airborne surveillance platforms to provide real-time situational awareness and tracking of surface contacts at sea or on land. Minotaur's automated, real-time features include geographic registration of disparate sensors, tracking of objects using all sensor modalities (radar, full-motion video, and signal intelligence), automatic length estimation of vessels, and precision cross-cueing of sensors. This groundbreaking capability has been fielded for proof-of-concept validation on more than 10 different manned and unmanned airborne platforms and ground stations. Technical advancements continue, and existing capability is now being transitioned to government-designated activities. Pictured here are (from left) Don Henderson, Emeka Ezekwe, and Kellie Rich.

APL's culture had always been one in which people made critical contributions to critical challenges. But this vital culture alone would not be enough to maintain pace with rapid technology developments and the evolving threats confronting the nation. The new strategy encouraged staff members to look beyond critical contributions to pursue defining innovations that resulted in truly revolutionary advances. Such innovations are evident throughout the Lab's history—the radio proximity fuze, satellite-based navigation, surface-to-air guided missiles, and advanced sonar systems, among others. In each case, the Lab's contribution produced a game-changing advantage for the nation.

Building on its multitude of program achievements as well as the many innovation and collaboration initiatives that had gained traction in recent years, the Lab launched several new investments in facilities and internally funded research and development to explore technology developments outside APL's traditional research areas. One of the more significant among these was a program designed to fund a pipeline of game-changing ideas, called Project Catalyst. In its final state, close to $6 million per year would be added to the Lab's investment pool for inclusive teams to develop and pursue high-risk concepts that could lead to defining innovations in response to major challenges facing the nation.

In 2015, APL also created a new Intelligent Systems Center to serve as a hub for the Lab's growing work in robotics, autonomous systems, neuroscience, and artificial intelligence. The intent was to provide collaboration space for experts in these diverse technical disciplines to explore some of the greatest challenges of our time. The center actually traces its roots to another recent pilot innovation center called Central Spark that continues to serve as a nexus of creativity for staff members, composed of "neighborhoods" in which staff members can collaborate on a variety of activities.

The various successes that emerged from these and other innovation endeavors led to a strategic decision in 2015 to establish a National Health Mission Area in partnership with Johns Hopkins Medicine. The initiative sought to combine Johns Hopkins' world-renowned expertise in medicine with APL's deep experience in complex systems engineering. By integrating these capabilities, a new standard for health care across the nation would be established.

Among the collaborative venture's initial goals was to reduce the risk of unintentional medical errors caused by faulty hospital data. Such mistakes result in hundreds of thousands of deaths each year in the United States. The partners believed many errors could be prevented through improved information management and coordination of care. In effect, they would address the issue as a systems engineering problem. For example, if a ventilator system could share data and functionality with other medical devices across the health care enterprise, like an infusion pump, defibrillator, and electrocardiogram analyzer, it would reduce the possibility of incorrect data resulting in a medical error.

"Health care technology is grossly under-engineered," said Peter Pronovost, M.D., director of the Armstrong Institute for Patient Safety and Quality at Johns Hopkins Medicine. "By combining our clinical health care systems knowledge and APL's systems engineering expertise, we are developing systems and practices that have the potential to revolutionize health care—from detection of disease and diagnosis to therapeutics and coordination of care."

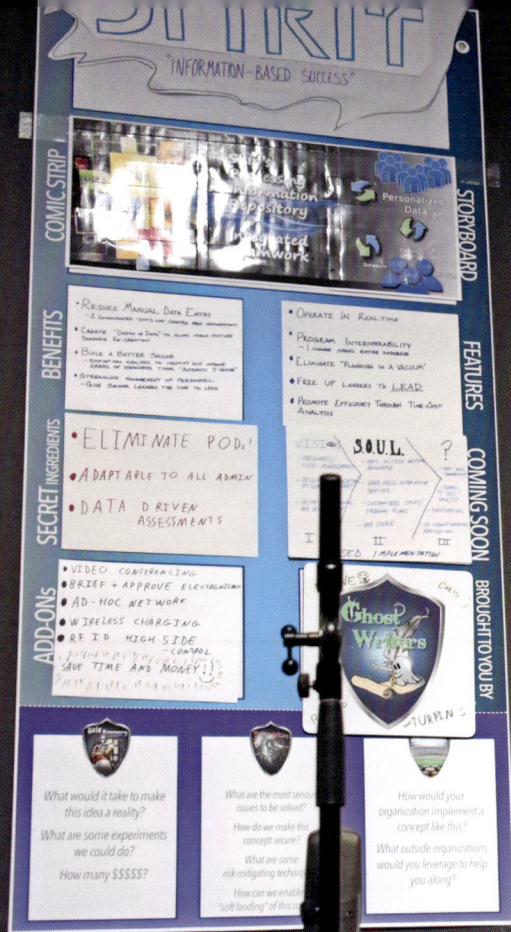

TANG: Engaging Digital Natives

Tactical Advancements for the Next Generation, or TANG, began with an important challenge—to determine how to make U.S. submarine systems more intuitive. This was the burning interest of Admiral John M. Richardson, who headed the Navy's submarine force in 2011 and today is chief of naval operations.

"Admiral Richardson came to us and presented a challenge," recalled Lisa Blodgett, head of APL's Force Projection Sector. "He said, 'Look, I'm frustrated that we have these systems on our submarines, some of them built 30 years ago, with these green displays that look archaic. Meanwhile, we've got these young sailors using their smartphones and tablets for all sorts of things. Shouldn't we be leveraging the innate capabilities of these digital natives?'"

To answer the challenge, a small team at APL partnered with government sponsors to create and lead an innovative, organizationally diverse team that brought together industry-leading technologists, commercial design practitioners, key stakeholders, and junior sailors such as Navy Lieutenant Tyler Turpin, shown above. The team used a radical human-centered approach to deliver user-inspired concepts to the fleet—and to deliver them fast.

To do this, the team used design thinking—a divergent/convergent process that reframes the challenge space through immersive research and analogous insight. With each structured brainstorming and rapid prototyping cycle, feedback collected from the participants enabled quick iteration of innovative warfighter-designed concepts that supported the mission.

From a foam core prototyping mock-up generated at the first TANG event, junior submarine sailors designed a concept that replaced a $128,000 joystick control system with a $28 Microsoft Xbox controller for the photonics mast of *Virginia*-class submarines. Senior Navy officials were so impressed that they fast-tracked prototyping and installation of the concept onto the Navy's most formidable subsurface platform. This is just one example of the TANG team igniting creativity to deliver solutions to the fleet.

The APL-led TANG team has been activated to tackle other challenges—from integrated air and missile defense to surface ship maintenance to aviation mission support—with prototyping efforts currently underway to field a bevy of unique solutions that truly meet warfighters' needs.

Alan Ravitz, chief engineer of APL's National Health Mission Area, and Johns Hopkins Medicine ICU nurse Rhonda Wyskiel, show a clock she drew to illustrate her idea for a timer that would indicate when a patient should receive a particular therapy. Her design was incorporated into the tablet-based Project Emerge system, shown in front of Ravitz. (Johns Hopkins Medicine)

The partners are applying APL's mastery of systems engineering principles and practices to the patient care competencies of Johns Hopkins Medicine, ensuring that patients receive treatments producing positive medical outcomes. "Our goal is to create a health care system that continuously 'learns' in order to improve," said Alan Ravitz, chief engineer of the National Health Mission Area.

Pluto Explored

As the Lab ushered in a renewed era of innovation, one of its most remarkable inventions, the New Horizons spacecraft, continued on its voyage to Pluto, three billion miles away. APL designed, built, and—since its launch in 2006—has operated New Horizons from a mission control center on campus. En route, the spacecraft took a close-up look at Jupiter and its four largest moons, using its remote sensing instruments to probe the solar system's largest planet. Images depicted diverse clouds formed from ammonia and welling up from the lower Jovian atmosphere. The first lightning ever seen beyond Earth was observed, and on Io, one of the planet's largest moons, the cameras detected a volcanic eruption in progress. In all, New Horizons made more than 700 observations of Jupiter and also conducted a dry run for the Pluto flyby.

The point of the flyby was to use Jupiter's gravity to boost the spacecraft toward Pluto. From there it faced an eight-year cruise toward the Pluto system, during which it would spend about two-thirds of its time in a hibernation mode designed to preserve the onboard systems—a first for a NASA spacecraft, and just one of the APL innovations that made the mission possible. New Horizons came out of hibernation for the last time on December 6, 2014.

As the planned Pluto flyby date of July 14, 2015, neared, the spacecraft was the talk of the world, with the event covered by the global media on a daily basis. Then, on the Fourth of July, just as the tiny

planet was coming into view, New Horizons went silent. The cause appeared to be an overload of the main computer, which had been instructed to do two things at once—process commands sent from mission operations and compress an array of stored science data. To avoid further damage, the spacecraft automatically switched back into safe mode. APL's staff at mission control, quickly recognizing the situation from rehearsals, deliberated their next move.

Over the next 48 hours, APL's New Horizons Mission Operations Manager Alice Bowman and her team worked around the clock, taking only intermittent naps, to bring the spacecraft back online. With hours to spare, they were able to solve the problem, and the planned nine-day sequence to guide New Horizons to Pluto recommenced. The computer was cleared and successfully uploaded. Bowman attributed the solution to "the awesome power of a team that is so much more than the sum of its members."

In the days prior to the flyby, the Kossiakoff Center hosted nearly 2,000 scientists, members of the global media, and APL staff members. The guests attended panel discussions and press conferences and watched live shows on a giant television set built by NASA especially for the occasion. Each day, a variety of images and news reports were broadcast and webcast from APL to the rest of the world.

On the morning of July 14, during a raucous countdown, the New Horizons team and APL's many visitors, most of them waving U.S. flags handed out for the occasion, ticked down the seconds—"five, four, three, two, one, Pluto!" Hugging and cheers ensued around the room.

That evening, a burst of telemetry reached mission control, affirming that New Horizons was healthy and doing what it was intended to do. "We have carrier lock," Bowman announced, meaning that NASA's Deep Space Network had linked up to New Horizons. "We have collected all the data, and we are outbound from Pluto." The mission operations personnel erupted in another round of cheers,

Free-Space Optical Communication

For more than 40 years, researchers have sought to develop free-space optics (FSO)—laser-based communication technologies—as an alternative to conventional radio frequency and microwave communications. FSO has the potential to be a real game-changer, offering long-range, high-capacity data-transmission rates that are highly resistant to detection and interception. In just the past decade, technological advances have allowed research to move forward, and APL began work on FSO in 2005. The following year, APL and its research partner established a 91-mile FSO link between Maui and the Big Island in Hawaii. Following a successful DARPA-sponsored and APL-led demonstration of a hybrid laser/radio frequency system in 2012, the Lab has focused on this promising new research that offers a robust, high-volume, low-detection communications capability.

TOP LEFT: *Alice Bowman (right), mission operations manager for the New Horizons mission, Karl Whittenburg (center), and Nick Pinkine (left) await word from the spacecraft during the historic Pluto flyby on July 14, 2015.*

BELOW: *During the New Horizons Pluto flyby, APL played host to hundreds of scientists, members of the news media, and other visitors. In this photo taken during a NASA news briefing held in the Kossiakoff Center auditorium, New Horizons science team members discuss some of their initial thoughts based on images captured during the spacecraft's flyby of the Pluto system.*

chanting "U-S-A! U-S-A!" Bowman then led the team into the Kossiakoff Center auditorium for a press conference, where they were greeted with a standing ovation.

The following day, the first close-up pictures of Pluto arrived, revealing the dwarf planet's surface and some of its moons in incredible detail. The stunning, instantly iconic image of Pluto clearly depicted the shape of a heart across one-third of its face, confirming the dwarf planet's romantic aura for all time. Over the next year and a half, other images and data were transmitted to mission central. By then, New Horizons was already speeding farther into the Kuiper Belt on a journey that would take it beyond the solar system.

Focus on the Future

The extraordinary satisfaction provided by New Horizons is just one of many remarkable experiences captivating the more than 15,000 people who have found their life's calling at APL throughout its history. Since its modest beginnings in an old auto dealership, entrusted with the development of a viable proximity fuze during World War II, APL has continually pushed the envelope of technical possibility. The sheer volume and breadth of the Lab's critical contributions over the decades are astonishing.

"The culture is not just about building things to specifications but wanting to know what the problems are," said Aili Kujawa, who joined APL in 1989 and is the director of human resources today. "People here focus on the real need, not just what the sponsor perceives to be the need. Sometimes this requires going beyond what the sponsors are telling you to do."

Coupled with APL's commitment to constantly striving for the best solutions is unquestionable integrity, something that is at the heart of the Lab's work. "Truthfulness and professionalism have been the hallmarks of APL since the beginning," said former director Carl Bostrom, reflecting recently

Twenty-two of America's most senior national security leaders, including the deputy national security advisor, the deputy secretary of defense, and the secretary of the Air Force, gathered at APL on September 10, 2016, to take part in a war game that explored potential responses to scenarios that threatened U.S. space-based assets. The exercise, which was based on rigorous analysis of capabilities, took place in APL's Collaborative Analysis Center (or CAC), formerly known as the WAL.

on the Lab's approaching anniversary. "That has always been the key to what we do. It was then and remains so today."

For current and past members of APL's staff, their work to make the nation safer, solve the puzzles of the universe, and contribute to the health of everyone, everywhere, is uniquely fulfilling. Staff members not only pursue their passions for service and discovery but also work with brilliant colleagues who are equally impassioned and eager to collaborate.

"What I think makes APL special is our culture," said Donna Gregg, who has worked at APL for more than 30 years and now leads the Asymmetric Operations Sector. "APL is full of very smart, dedicated staff members who have tremendous respect for one another. They are proud of what they do individually, but they are also part of a much greater team where lifelong friendships are made."

Christine Fox, who had served as acting deputy secretary of defense and joined the Lab in 2013 as assistant director for policy and analysis, sees her role as building an even stronger bridge between the government's critical future needs and the Lab's competencies, world-class expertise, culture of innovation, and intellectual assets.

"At the Pentagon, I had the privilege to see firsthand the value of APL to solving our country's most dire challenges," Fox said. "Technology and world events are becoming dramatically more complex. With this change, APL's role as a trusted technical advisor will be more important than ever."

Over the past 75 years, each APL generation has contributed to extraordinary advancements in science and technology, setting an example of meritorious work that is replicated by the scientists and engineers that follow. This cycle of constant creativity bodes as well for the future of the Lab as it does for the security, competitiveness, and prosperity of all Americans.

Acknowledgments

Rarely in my many years as an author and journalist have I encountered an organization as technically complex and intriguing as the Johns Hopkins University Applied Physics Laboratory, or a group of people so dedicated to national service. Given the sensitive nature of APL's work, this book is necessarily an incomplete story of the generations of scientists, engineers, and other professionals who quietly have played a vital role in the security of our nation and the advancement of science and engineering.

Though it is beyond my means to do so personally, I want to thank the many people within the Laboratory who reviewed or contributed to this book in some way. In my research and writing, I had the opportunity to meet and speak with many impressive and enthusiastic leaders and technical experts, each eager to share what they could about this noble enterprise and its work. I would, however, be remiss if I did not acknowledge the contributions of a small team of people who actually helped produce this book.

This book would not have been possible without the efforts of Margaret Brown, Geoff Brown, Martha Stum, and Gerry Bennett, whose detailed archival sleuthing uncovered the photos that helped tell the Lab's story; Jerry Krill, Dan Tyler, Russ Gingras, Gary Sullins, Harry Charles, Doug Hudson, Dan Wilt, Mike Buckley, and the many other fact checkers, whose early reviews contributed to the book's accuracy; Tony Rodriguez at NAVSEA, whose thoughtful review is appreciated; and Magda Saina, Erin Richardson, and Don Vislay, whose design, editing, and production supervision resulted in the book you are holding. Finally, I would like to thank my editorial assistant, Kristin Mehus-Roe, who so ably helped shape the manuscript.

About the Author

PHOTO BY JAKE GRAVBROT

RUSS BANHAM has chronicled the history of more than 25 companies. His award-winning books include *Higher*, a history of aerospace giant Boeing, *The Ford Century*, the international best-selling history of Ford Motor Company, and *Rocky Mountain Legend*, the national best-selling chronicle of the Coors brewing dynasty. He also wrote *Wanderlust*, profiling the historic design and cultural impact of the iconic Airstream travel trailer, and *The Fight for Fairfax*, detailing the contentious economic growth of northern Virginia in the aftermath of World War II.

On the Cover: 75 Years

Key

March 10, 1942
The Applied Physics Laboratory begins operations to address the critical challenge of defending Navy ships from enemy air attacks.

1943
The proximity fuze achieves its first combat success as USS *Helena* shoots down two enemy aircraft in the Pacific.

1944
APL develops the Mk 57 gun director and fire control system to increase effectiveness of the fuze, which is used in Europe at the Battle of the Bulge.

1945
APL's pioneering "Bumblebee" guided-missile program demonstrates the first successful ramjet flight and first acceleration of a ramjet vehicle to supersonic speed in free flight.

1946
APL begins a high-altitude research program using captured German V-2 rockets and APL's own Aerobee rocket.

1947
APL demonstrates roll stabilization at supersonic speeds during a supersonic test vehicle (STV)-2 launch at a Navy test site.

1948
An APL camera, carried on a V-2 rocket, captures the first photo of the curvature of the Earth from space (which was printed in *National Geographic* magazine in October 1950).

1949
To answer the Navy's urgent need for a tactical missile while ramjet research continued, the STV-3 was rapidly converted to a Terrier missile.

1950
APL uses wind tunnel testing and early computers to develop simulated missile flight trajectories and data reduction.

1951
The first successful flight of a ramjet guided missile and the first target kill lead to a prototype design of the Talos missile.

1952
APL leads the Terrier improvement program, applying a systems engineering approach and proving how sectionalization increases production efficiency.

1953
APL researchers design a modulated molecular beam mass spectrometer to study chemical reactions, used for the first detection of the H_2O free radical.

1954
APL develops a homing guidance system for Terrier.

1955
APL begins development of Tartar, a semi-active homing missile for small ships.

1956
Terrier becomes operational aboard USS *Boston*, the world's first guided-missile ship.

1957
The Navy assigns APL a major role in the Polaris system evaluation, with the Lab performing the first flight test analysis.

1958
APL begins development of the world's first Doppler-based, all-weather, satellite navigation system: Transit.

1959
APL develops the Air Battle Analyzer for naval anti-air warfare issues, the first computer-supported air defense planning tool.

1960
The first APL-developed Transit satellites are launched into orbit.

1961
APL significantly advances space technology by developing and launching the first satellites to carry solid-state particle detectors, electronic memory, and radioisotope power.

1962
The Navy expands APL's test and evaluation role for the Polaris missile system.

1963
APL's Battle Simulator Facility tests decision-making in combat situations.

1964
APL develops the Beacon Explorer satellite for NASA.

1965
APL begins its biomedical collaboration with Johns Hopkins medical institutions.

1966
APL begins test and evaluation of the Pershing land-based strategic ballistic missile system.

1967
APL designs and builds the Department of Defense Gravity Experiment (DODGE) spacecraft for defense research.

1968
APL expands its civilian research programs into fields including transportation, fire prevention, prosthetics, and energy.

1969
APL is named the principal technical direction agent for the new SSBN Security Technology Program to ensure the survivability of the strategic submarine fleet.

1970
APL demonstrates the experimental Automatic Detection and Tracking System, the precursor to modern air defense tracking systems.

1971
APL guidance experiments for the Tomahawk cruise missile program improve the accuracy of TERCOM, a terrain-contour matching system.

1972
APL's civilian research program develops an "accelerating walkway" and a harbor traffic control system.

1973
AN/SYS-1 is successfully tested aboard USS *Somers* and installed aboard Navy guided-missile destroyers.

1974
APL successfully tests its engineering development model of the AN/SPY-1 computerized radar system for Aegis aboard USS *Norton Sound*.

1975
APL's Geodynamics Experimental Ocean Satellite C (GEOS C) spacecraft demonstrates the first successful satellite-to-satellite tracking.

1976
APL microprocessor applications include a mechanical arm for quadriplegics, submarine data processing, and a radar altimeter.

1977
The APL-built Low Energy Charged Particle instrument launches aboard Voyager to explore the outer planets.

1978
APL's air defense work expands to include the coordination of multiple ships, as the Lab is named the technical direction agent for the Navy Battle Group Anti-Air Warfare Coordination (BGAAWC) program.

1979
APL builds the Sonar Program Analyzer (SPAN), a programmable acoustic signal processor.

1980
The first use of a satellite link in the Standard Aries oceanography experiment includes the launch of 1,000 Airborne Expendable Bathythermograph (AXBT) ocean sensors.

1981
The first Aegis ship, the cruiser USS *Ticonderoga*, launches, with APL serving as the technical advisor for Aegis.

1982
The Navy appoints APL as the Tomahawk technical direction agent for engineering support.

Key

1983
USS *Kennedy* hosts a demonstration of the APL Digital Data Converter (DDC) auto-gridlock system, which becomes the basis for the Cooperative Engagement Capability (CEC).

1984
The Active Magnetospheric Particle Tracer Explorer (AMPTE) creates the first ever artificial comet by releasing barium clouds into space to study how charged particles from the solar wind travel through Earth's magnetosphere.

1985
APL demonstrates distributing sensor and weapons data, the first stage of CEC.

1986
Delta 180 launches. The following year, President Ronald Reagan awards APL a Presidential Commendation for the success of the mission's first missile intercept in space.

1987
APL is appointed the lead laboratory for the Critical Sea Test, beginning a 10-year active acoustic test program to improve the performance and stealth of submarines.

1988
The APL-developed ingestible temperature capsule, which remotely monitors body temperature, is made commercially available.

1989
APL accuracy evaluations aid development of the new Trident II (D5) missile.

1990
APL activities during Operation Desert Shield include a "Gulf Crisis Room" in the Warfare Analysis Laboratory (WAL), as well as Transit, Aegis, and Tomahawk systems support.

1991
USS *Arleigh Burke*, the first Aegis destroyer, enters the fleet with upgrades from APL's Combat Systems Evaluation Lab.

1992
APL and Johns Hopkins University develop pattern-recognition algorithms to automate mammogram analysis.

1993
APL develops an Army Tactical Control System for the Defense Satellite Communications System.

1994
The Treasury Department establishes the Securities Technology Institute (STI) at APL to protect U.S. currency.

1995
APL hosts a virtual operating environment for Kernel Blitz, a major exercise combining live action with a pioneering test of computer technology.

1996
APL has two milestone space launches: Midcourse Space Experiment (MSX), APL's largest spacecraft, and Near Earth Asteroid Rendezvous (NEAR), the first NASA Discovery mission.

1997
A Standard Missile with a prototype infrared seeker intercepts a target in a missile defense flight test.

1998
APL collaborates with the Johns Hopkins medical institutions and the University of Maryland to develop miniature mass spectrometers for counterproliferation and biomedical applications.

1999
APL's innovative Advanced Natural Gas Vehicle begins field tests.

2000
The success of APL's Area Air Defense Commander (AADC) capability in a large naval exercise leads the Navy to recommend expedited development.

2001
NEAR completes its extraordinary science mission with a "bonus" soft landing on the surface of asteroid Eros.

2002
APL develops the Electronic Surveillance System for the Early Notification of Community-based Epidemics (ESSENCE) disease surveillance system.

2003
APL provides new electronic jamming technology for overseas combat operations.

2004
The APL-built MESSENGER spacecraft, the first Mercury orbiter, launches.

2005
APL evaluates the first sea-launched ballistic missile test of the Trident II in the Pacific Ocean.

2006
The APL-built Solar Terrestrial Relations Observatory (STEREO) spacecraft launch on a mission to image the sun in 3-D.

2007
APL evaluates the Tactical Trident SSGN submarine for operational readiness.

2008
The Burnt Frost mission brings down an errant Earth-bound satellite with a Standard Missile-3.

2009
APL leads the team that develops the first 26-degree-of-freedom prosthetic arm.

2010
Foliage-penetrating LIDAR technology becomes operational.

2011
The APL-developed Persistent Ground Surveillance System (PGSS) deploys overseas.

2012
In Flight Test Maritime-18, the Aegis Ballistic Missile Defense system intercepts a separating ballistic missile target in a complex debris environment.

2013
APL introduces a new generation of small satellites with the launch of two experimental cubesats designed for a range of national security and space science operations; the image shows one of these cubesats.

2014
A Colorado man becomes the first bilateral shoulder-level amputee to wear and simultaneously control two of APL's Modular Prosthetic Limbs.

2015
The APL-designed, -built, and -operated New Horizons spacecraft makes its historic Pluto flyby in July, completing humankind's initial reconnaissance of the solar system.

2016
Researchers using APL's Live data, Integration, Validation, and Experimentation (LIVE) Lab develop new tools and methodologies to combat cyber threats and challenges for the Lab and its sponsors.

Index

C

CAC **135**. *See also* Collaborative Analysis Center; *See also* WAL; *See also* Warfare Analysis Laboratory

Calderon-Colon, Xiomara **116**

California **21, 27, 28, 51**

Canada **63, 104**

Cannonball (missile) **19**

Cape **78**

Cape Canaveral, Florida **30, 33, 61, 69**

Cape Henlopen State Park, Delaware **17**

Carnegie Institution of Washington **5, 7, 8, 117**

CDC **127**

CEC **54, 55, 64, 65, 66, 78, 79, 80, 120, 121, 140**. *See also* Cooperative Engagement Capability

Central Green **34, 84**

Central Intelligence Agency **87**

Central Laboratory Assessment **38**

Central Spark **83, 130**

Chambers, Helen **57**

Charbonneau, William **60**

Charles, Harry **84**

Charon **124**

Chemical and Biological Test and Evaluation Center **97**

Chesapeake Bay **78**

Cheston, Theodore **43**

Chi, Albert **107**

Chief of Naval Operations **81, 131**

China Lake, California **28, 51**

Chubbuck, John **35**

Civil Space Mission Area **1**

CIWS **66**. *See also* Phalanx Close-In Weapon System

Clark, Vernon **81**

Clayton, Brooke **77**

Cobra (ramjet missile) **14, 16, 17**

Cold War **25, 37, 53, 59, 65, 66, 67, 68, 80, 89**

Cole, Raymond **60**

Collaborative Analysis Center **135**. *See also* CAC; *See also* WAL; *See also* Warfare Analysis Laboratory

Colorado **140**

Combat Systems Evaluation Lab **140**

Combustion Grants **116**

Compact Reconnaissance Imaging Spectrometer for Mars **108**. *See also* CRISM

Computing Center (APL) **32**

Congressional Budget Office **103**

Contracts and Budgets Group **34**

Convair **25, 26**

Cooperative Engagement Capability **54, 64, 65, 78, 120, 140**. *See also* CEC

Copeland, Nathan **106**

Counter Radio Controlled-IED Electronic Warfare Lab **103**. *See also* CREW Lab

Cove **78**

Cox, Austin **100**

Craven, John **56**

Crete **16**

CREW Lab **103**. *See also* Counter Radio Controlled-IED Electronic Warfare Lab

CRISM **108**. *See also* Compact Reconnaissance Imaging Spectrometer for Mars

Critical Sea Test **140**

Crosley Corporation **10**

Currie, Malcolm R. **50**

Cyber Operations Mission Area **1, 82, 113**

Cybersecurity **3, 82, 83, 87, 88, 101, 113, 114**

D

Daingerfield, Texas **20, 26**

Dam Neck, Virginia **65**

Daniels, Ronald J. **iv**

DARPA **30, 79, 104, 106, 113, 133**. *See also* Defense Advanced Research Projects Agency

Dassoulas, John **61**

DDC **54, 140**. *See also* Digital Data Converter

The Deadly Fuze: The Secret Weapon of World War II **6**

Deep Space Network **133**

Defense Advanced Research Projects Agency **30**. *See also* DARPA

Defense Communications Business Area **88**

Defense Satellite Communications System **140**

Defining innovations **vi, 13, 28, 33, 43, 45, 55, 70, 76, 116, 130**

Delauriers, Joe **105**

Delaware **14, 16, 17**

Delaware Bay **17**

Delta 180 **58, 61, 140**

Delta 181 **59, 61**

Delta 183 **59, 61, 69**

Demo 90 **65, 66**

Denmark **57**

Department of Defense Gravity Experiment **29, 139**. *See also* DODGE

Deputy National Security Advisor **135**

Deputy Secretary of Defense **135**

Desert Shield **61, 63, 140**

Desert Storm **61, 62, 63**

DeSimone, Tony **120**

D-40 Cannonball **19**. *See also* Cannonball (missile)

Digital Data Converter **54, 140**. *See also* DDC

Digital Scene Matching Area Correlator **48**. *See also* DSMAC

Director of Defense for Research and Engineering **51**

Director of the Office of Scientific Research and Development **16**

Discovery program **69, 70, 94, 140**

DoD **42, 45, 49, 50, 67, 68, 86, 98, 103, 113, 125, 126, 127**. *See also* U.S. Department of Defense

DODGE **29, 139**. *See also* Department of Defense Gravity Experiment

Dragon Drone **60**

Drone **10, 60, 79, 80**. *See also* UAV; *See also* Unmanned aerial vehicle

DSMAC **48**. *See also* Digital Scene Matching Area Correlator

Dynamic Time-Critical Warfighting Capability (DTCWC) **89**

E

EA-6B Prowler **51**

EA-18 Growler **51**

Early prosthetic limb **56, 139**

Earth **5, 10, 21, 29, 30, 32, 33, 40, 41, 61, 69, 70, 93, 95, 96, 108, 109, 117, 132, 139, 140**

East Coast **76**

East Germany **66**

Eaton, Alvin **26, 41, 42, 80**

Echo Range **51**

EF-111A **51**

Egypt **42**

8621 Georgia Avenue **9, 10, 11, 20, 33**

Eilat **42, 44**

Eisenhower, Dwight **19**

Eisenhower, Milton **47**

Electronic Surveillance System for the Early Notification of Community-based Epidemics **97, 140**. *See also* ESSENCE

Engineered Materials Lab **85**

Engineering Facilities Division **84**

Engineering for Professionals **123**. *See also* EP

Environmental Test Laboratory (APL) **41**

EP **123**. *See also* Engineering for Professionals

E Pluribus Oscillator **9**

Eros **69, 70, 140**

ESSENCE **97, 127, 140**. *See also* Electronic Surveillance System for the Early Notification of Community-based Epidemics

ESSM **66**. *See also* Evolved Sea Sparrow Missile

Europe **5, 20, 87, 104, 121, 122, 139**

European theater **121**

Evolved Sea Sparrow Missile **66**. *See also* ESSM

2001 • JASON A. ABRAHAMSON • NISHA AGRAWAL • JULIA ANDRUSENKO • MARTIN S. ANNETT • JAVIER G. ARMENDARIZ • EDWARD C. ARON • MARK A. ATHEY • JORGE A. AVILES • VINCENT L. BAILEY • FRANCIS E. BAKER JR. • JOSEPH B. BAKER • KEVIN G. BALON • ROWLAND J. BARKER JR. • RODNEY S. BARNES JR. • SHAWN W. BARNETT • LAUREN I. BARON • MASON M. BARON • NICHOLAS A. BARRESI •
CHRISTOPHER J. BATTLES • KATHRYN E. BECHTOLD • MAX A. BECK JR. • LUKE A. BECKER • DAVID A. BENIGNI • YURI C. BERNSTEIN • PRISCILLA A. BERRY • WAYNE L. BETHEA • ROBERT F. BEZELIK • JONATHAN C. BIERCE • RICARDO C. BLACKETT • JACQUELINE A. BLIZZARD • MICHELLE L. BLOOR • THOMAS J. BLUM • PAUL N. BOIE • DUANE E. BONIFACE • BRUCE A. BOWMAN • JOANNA BOYETTE • CHERYL A. BRENNEN
• MICHAEL M. BRIDGES • SIDNEY L. BRUCE • THOMAS H. BUCHANAN • ANDREW R. BUCK • STEVEN A. BURKE • REBECCA M. BURNETT • REGINA BUSACCO • WALTER L. BUSBEE • MICHAEL F. BUSCHMAN • MICHAEL W. BUTLER • MARK E. BYRKIT • KIANA D. CAMPBELL • DAVID I. CARL • CRAIG J. CARMEN • CARL L. CARPENTER • STEPHEN S. CARR • JOSEPH P. CARRIER • CATHERINE E. CARROLL • DANIEL M. CHALK
• HELEN R. CHAMBERS • JEREMY M. CHARFAUROS • PETER M. CHEN • KEVIN C. CHENG • CHRISTOPHER P. CHIU • WILLIAM CHUNG • CAROLYN D. CHURA • BRIAN P. CLIFFORD • LAWRENCE F. COAR • JAMES G. COCHRAN • MORRIS B. COHEN • MICHAEL J. COLBY • RYAN M. COLLINS • APRIL H. COMMODORE • JESSICA COMPTON • JON C. CORNICK • NATHAN P. CRAMER • ADAM S. CROCK • JOHN E. CROSSLEY •
DAMIAN D. CUNNINGHAM SR. • OMAR S. CUSTODIO • BOHDAN Z. CYBYK • SHAWN C. DANCIK • JAMES A. DEBARDELABEN • MICHAEL A. DELANEY • PLAMEN A. DEMIREV • CAROL A. DICKSON • SAMUEL M. DIEDRICH • CHRISTOPHER P. DIEHL • JERROLD E. DIETZ • ATHANASSIOS DIMAS • JEFFERY S. DIXON • SVEN H. DOERSAM • MICHELLE M. DONEGAN • JAMES P. DONOVAN JR. • GILBERT K. DORSEY •
ELIZABETH A. DOWNS • DAVID G. DREWRY JR. • PAUL D. DRONEBURG • OWEN E. DUDLEY • DREW A. DUNN • TENEQUA DUPUY-FRANCIS • ARTHUR L. EDWARDS • CLINTON L. EDWARDS • JANICE M. EGBAIYELO • JULIENNE S. ELENCWEIG • ELAINE A. ERAMO • TRACEY A. ESTEP • ADELE M. EVANS • CHRISTOPHER L. EVANS • ALAN S. FABER • BRIAN E. FARRELL • YVONNE M. FEILINGER • DAVID J. FELDMAN •
JANINE M. FIELD • ROBERT W. FINCHAM • GUNTER FINKENAUER • JEREMIAH V. FINNIGAN • JACOB FIRER • MICHAEL J. FITCH • JAMES R. FITZGERALD • SAMUEL G. FIX • BLOSSOM D. FLASH-WINFREE • JOHNNY L. FOGLE • MICHAEL P. FORD • MICHAEL L. FOREHAND • STEVE O. FORTNEY • MICHAEL G. FRANK • LISA M. FREEBURG • TRI M. FREED • ANDREW S. FREEMAN • SUSAN M. FURNEY • ROBERT J. GALLAGHER JR.
• DIANA F. GARRETT • JAMES F. GARTEN • CAROLYN B. GASARCH • TIMOTHY M. GEIPE • CHRISTOPHER G. GOODWIN • THERESA S. GORAY • ERIC D. GRAHAM • TREVOR J. GRAVES • ELIZABETH B. GRGURICH • GABRIELLE A. GRIFFITH • REID S. GURNEE • WESLEY F. HABERT • DANIEL V. HAHN • JAMES S. HANSEN • SHERYL L. HAPPEL LEWIS • RONALD E. HARDESTY JR. • JONAS M. HARMAN • LINDA K. HARRELL
• WILLIAM J. HARRIS • JOHN J. HASLUP • ROBERT C. HAWTHORNE • MICHAEL B. HEALY • LESLIE A. HEDDERLY • GARY M. HEILIGMAN • SCOTT D. HEITKAMP • CARL C. HERRMANN • DAVID J. HICKINBOTHAM • VOGEL M. HILL • DANIELLE P. HILLIARD • KURT V. HILSMEIER • SCOTT A. HILTERBRICK • JOHN E. HINRICHSEN • PHILLIPS S. HOEPER • DOUGLAS H. HOFFMAN • ARTHUR W. HOOPER • TOMOAKI HORI •
GERALD E. HOWARD • CHRISTIAN A. HRESKO • SYAU-YUN W. HSIEH • ERIC B. HU • PATRICK J. HUDSON • ROBERT C. HUFFMAN • BENJAMIN A. HUGUENIN • MARY S. HUNT • JENNIFER L. HURD • TIMOTHY J. HURLBURT SR. • MELISSA E. JANSEN • THOMAS B. JENNINGS • ANDREW H. JOHNSON • CAROL A. JOHNSON • LORNA M. JOHNSON • RODNEY M. JOKERST • MELISSA A. JONES • ANDREA A. KAGEL •
MICHAEL KALANDROS • RAVINDER KAPOOR • MICHAEL A. KARLS • BRIAN T. KEANE • KARA S. KEENER • MICHAEL A. KELLY • ROBERT J. KENDALL-KUPPE • MICHAEL KENNEDY • NADER A. KHATIB • BRIAN H. KIM • ALFRED J. KING III • ANIL K. KOCHHAR • KYLE B. KOEPPEN • HAJE KORTH • JEFFREY A. KOUL • JOSEPH G. KOVALCHIK • CHARLES T. KOWAL • JOHN G. KUCHINSKI JR. • HOWARD W. KULP JR. •
KRISTY P. KULSKI • ELIZABETH M. KYLE-BOWLSBEY • BARRY J. LABONTE • BRENDA L. LAFON • DAVID J. LANE • CARLTON J. LEUSCHEN • JEFFREY S. LEVIN • ANDREW W. LEWIN • WILLIAM G. LIGGETT • ASHLEY J. LLORENS • NORBERTO R. LOPEZ • ARETHA N. LOVELL • FRANK P. MACKOWICK • JENNIFER D. MACNEIL • STEVEN J. MARSHALL • IAN X. MARTINS • EDDIE L. MCDONALD • WILLIAM G. MCGRAW JR. •
JOANNA D. MELLERT • HUI MEN • SANDOR S. MESTER • MEGAN K. MEYER • CHRISTOPHER H. MICHAELIS • IAIN A. MILLER • LAURIE F. MILLER • TIMOTHY C. MILLER • MARY A. MIRANTES • PATRICK D. MOON • TERRI D. MORRISON • DAVID A. MOWATT • JACK R. MURPHY JR. • FRANCIS W. MURRAY • DAVID A. MYERS • KENNETH E. NELSON • JOE D. NOBLES JR. • LAURA A. NOLAN • BRENDA J. ORLIN • PAUL H. OSTDIEK
• WILLIAM D. OWINGS • CHRISTOPHER W. PALOW • KEYUR J. PANCHOLI • ANTHONY PARKER • ALLEN L. PARRISH • MICHAEL V. PAUL • DANIEL A. PELETIER • ALLISON L. PELTIER • LINDA A. PEREGRINO • MARK E. PERRY • CLARK E. PERSON • DEBORAH L. PETERS • JOHN H. PIERSE • SKYLONN L. PINKETT-LACCORE • NICKALAUS T. PINKINE • JESSICA L. PISTOLE • MARK E. PITTELKAU • TODD W. PLUNKETT •
WALTER O. PREISSLER • STANLEY H. PRINCE • DANIEL K. PROFFEN • BRIAN T. PUMPHREY • JIMMI L. PUTMAN • RALPH E. RALSTON III • RICHARD D. RECTOR • CHRISTOPHER L. REDMOND • ALYSEN L. REGIEC • MICHAEL R. REID • KENNETH S. REINHARDT • EDWARD P. RHYNE • CHARLES C. RIALL • DONALD L. RICHARDSON • JOHN M. RILLING • CHARBEL G. RIZK • KEVIN J. RODRIGUES • EGIDIO ROSSANO •
THOMAS V. ROSSBERG • AMY E. ROUECHE • DARRYL W. ROYSTER • SUSAN L. ROYSTER • DONALD A. RUFFLE • KIMBERLY M. RUNKLES • JENNIFER L. SAMPLE • CHARLES L. SARGENT JR. • RANDY SAUNDERS • BRUCE J. SAVADKIN • VALENTINO D. SAVAGE • CHERYL S. SCHEIN • JANICE M. SCHOFIELD • STEPHEN M. SCORPIO • HERMANN B. SEQUEIRA • ROBERT S. SEVICK • KALPESH B. SHAH • JOSEPH M. SHEA •
HELEN E. SHECKLER • JOSHUA E. SHIPP • RICHARD R. SHULTZ • DEANE E. SIBOL • MARGARET SIMON • RICHARD SKALLOS • JOSEPH F. SKORA • EDWARD G. SNYDER • GLEN SOUTHARD • WILLIAM E. SPARROW JR. • MARIA R. SPEZIO • KEVIN L. STEWART • MARK T. STEWART • ROBERT E. STEWART • EMILY E. STOLL • WILLIAM C. STRATTON • JANET M. STRONG • SALVADOR H. TALISA • JENNIFER R. TANZMAN
• ALVIN D. TARVER • HOWARD W. TAYLOR • JOLYNN B. THAGARD • DANIEL J. THOMAS • MICHAEL W. TOLEDANO • GRANT M. TREGRE • GERARD V. TRUNK • DARYL I. TUCK • JOHN C. TUCKER • REGINA G. TURNER • DAVID B. UNDERHILL • JON D. VANDEGRIFF • BIENVENIDO B. VENERACION III • JAMES L. VENEZIANO • CAROL A. VERMILYE • ROBERT K. VERNOT • TRACY L. WACLAWSKI • LYNDA E. WAGNER •
VIRGINIA V. WALKER • DARLENE L. WALL • RANDI S. WALTERS • D. T. WARFIELD • DOUGLAS W. WEAVER • RICHARD W. WEBBERT • VICTORIA L. WEISKOPF • EVELYN L. WELLMAN • ELIZABETH F. WESNER • BRIAN M. WHIPPLE • CARL WHITE • THOMAS WIENKE • ROBB C. WILCOX • CRAIG B. WILLIAMS • PERRY W. WILSON • CHARLES L. WINSTEAD JR. • JEAN K. WITTER • BRIAN C. WOLVEN • WILLIAM C. WOOD
• SUSAN B. WOOLRIDGE • JEFFREY A. WRIGHT • JOANNE J. WRIGHT • **2002** • LUIS J. ALVAREZ • LINDA A. ANDERSON • DAVID M. ASHWORTH • NEAL D. BACHTELL • RONALD E. BACHTELL • THOMAS J. BARLEY • ELIZABETH D. BARNES • VIRGIE E. BASKERVILLE • MARTIN A. BAUMAN • MARGARET E. BEECHER • MARK G. BERNACIK • SUNITA K. BHATIA • BALLARD J. BLAIR • CHRISTINA M. BONEBREAK •
AARON S. BOTELER • CHARLES W. BOWERS • JOHN R. BRACY • WALTER S. BRADLEY • BENJAMIN M. BRAWLEY • RICHARD T. BROCKMEYER • GINGER M. BRONKE • NICHOLAS T. BRONN • VELMA M. BROOKS • JATARA C. BROWN • THOMAS A. BROWN • EUGENE R. BRUCE • LYNNE D. BRUNSON • DAVID B. BUSSEY • ANDREW B. CALLOWAY • GEORGE J. CANCRO • MICHAEL L. CARULLO • AMY K. CASTNER •
BENJAMIN J. CATHCART • JOANN K. CHAMBERS • KIMBERLY A. CHINERY • KEVIN L. CLEMENTS • KELLY E. COLEMAN • CECILIA S. COLLAT • BEVERLY A. COLLETT • STEVEN J. CONARD • JESSICA A. CRAVEN • ADRIENNE E. CRISS • JENNIFER P. CROTHERS • JOHN J. CYRUS • KWASI A. DABI • NICHOLAS M. DALESIO • SUSANNE M. DANIELS • JANET E. DEERY • MICHAEL D. DIROSSI • CHRISTIAN W. DRABENSTADT •
PAUL V. DUDEK • ADAM M. DUFFEK • MICHAEL R. ELLERY • CARL S. ENGELBRECHT • EDITH L. ENGLEHART • BRITTANY C. EVANS WARD • MARK F. FACEMIRE • WILLIE C. FAIR • SHARON A. FELDE • BIRGITT J. FIELDS • ROBERT K. FINLAYSON III • DANIEL M. FISCHER • TRACY D. FISHER • YECHEZKIA FISHER • BRITTANY C. FLEMING • JOHN A. FLETCHER • ELAINE N. FLORIO • ANDREW T. FORD • JAMES B. FORTIER
• VIRGINIA B. FOSTER • STEVEN L. GETTMANN • RICHARD G. GIBBS • MICHAEL W. GIBSON • TONI L. GLEASON • ELIZABETH L. GRECO • PETER W. GREEN • TERESA F. GREEN • MELISSA S. GREENE • DONNA L. GRIFFITH • SALVATORE A. GUARNIERI • ANNE T. GUGEL • TERRY M. GUILER • SARAH A. HAMILTON • CHARLES B. HARGIS • WALLACE E. HARRIS • JESUS J. HERNANDEZ-FLORES • EDGAR E. HICKMAN •
PATRICK A. HILL • DONALD L. HOFIUS • JUDITH A. HOLLER • TIMOTHY G. HORNER • JIA-NING HUANG • JAMES F. HUDSON • JASON C. HUNNELL • SCOTT F. JACKSON • KENNETH M. JENKINS • LUCAS D. KAGEL • DON E. KING • THOMAS L. KING • BARBARA J. KLINEFELTER • JOHN E. KNAUFF • CULLEN D. KREISEL • CHRISTINE M. KRIDER • DAVID L. KUBIK • ROBERT S. LANGE • BRETT D. LAPIN • ERIC J. LAZUR • DIEM H. LE
• DANIEL J. LEA • MATTHEW S. LEESE • ROBERT D. LEIBLER • CHAO-KANG J. LIANG • PHILIP W. LINDBERG • JOHN S. LINDERMAN • STANLEY E. LINGLE • THOMAS A. LOGUE JR. • FRANCIS A. LOPATA • DENNIS G. LUCARELLI • GERALD T. LYNOTT JR. • WILLIAM R. MACNEIL • JOSEPH B. MADDOX • DAVID J. MALICK • MICHAEL A. MANGAN • STEPHEN A. MARCHETTI • JEFFREY K. MARQUART • ANTHONY M. MARTHALER
• MICHAEL W. MATHERS • CHRISTOPHER M. MCCORMICK • DANIEL J. MCGOWN JR. • JENNIFER A. MCKNEELY • DEBORAH P. MENDAT • TROY E. MILLIKEN • JAMES G. MILNE • JAMES E. MITCHELL • JULIE K. MODLIN • DONALD P. MONAHAN • TERENCE J. MOORE • MICHAEL J. MORRISON • ERIN P. MOYER • JOHN D. MUHITCH • ANTONIO MUNOZ • DAVID H. NAPOLILLO • HADI NAVID • REGINALDO C. NERA •
NICHOLAS D. NEWHOUSE • CHRISTOPHER P. NOWICKI • PAUL R. OBER • TERRY W. O'BRIEN • DOMINIC O. OFFER • ADERINTO J. OGUNNIYI • GREGGORY L. O'MARR • GEFFREY K. OTTMAN • JASON R. OXENRIDER • DAVID J. PACIFICO • MICHAEL H. PAK • THOMAS E. PALMATIER • SUZANNE M. PALMER • BRIAN T. PARKER • ROLAND A. PARKER • DAVID M. PATTERSON • ROBERT M. PATTERSON • KELLIE PERRY •
CHERYL A. PETERS • NANCY L. PHILLIPS • ELAINE V. PICKETT • ANITA L. PIERCE • FOREST E. PLATT • CHARLES E. PLIS • TRACY L. PRICE • CHARLENE M. PURCELL • SARAH R. PURWIN • HARLAN RAY III • DAPHNE L. REED • PATTI K. RESTIVO • ELI A. RICHARDS • SEAN C. RIDEOUT • FRANZ J. RIGGIERI • BENJAMIN Y. ROCA • STEPHANIE M. ROGERS • ERIC R. ROSENLOF • SAMUEL T. SANDER • WILLIAM J. SCANLON III
• JENNY R. SCHAEFER • VERNETTA D. SCOTT • GORDON G. SEAGRAVE • THOMAS G. SEILER • RONALD F. SENIOR • KAREN R. SHANDERA • UDAY J. SHANKAR • VINCENT P. SHAY • JOE M. SHEHAN • SCOTT D. SIMPKINS • REGINA M. SKIPPER • MATTHEW H. SLATER • MICHAEL F. SMITH JR. • ANDRE' S. SMITH • TAKITA L. SMITH • PAUL D. SPUDIS • ANN M. STAHL • JAMES E. STANSBURY • ROBERT J. STEELE •
LANCE STEWART • LESLIE R. STOUT • KEVIN D. STUM • STEPHEN D. SUDKAMP • BRIAN D. SWAYNE SR. • CHRISTOPHER R. TAYLOR • ANDRE J. TEAGUE • JOHN O. TEEHAN • PETER D. TENNYSON • MELLISA L. THEODORE • MICHAEL J. THIBODEAU • TERIA G. THOMAS • JOHN R. TROLL • LORRAINE TROPF • WILLIAM J. TURGEON • FRANKLIN S. TURNER JR. • JOHN I. UPSHUR • CYNTHIA A. UTTERBACK •
MATTHEW C. VALENCIA • KIRI L. WAGSTAFF • JOSEPH D. WARFIELD JR. • BRIAN N. WASHINGTON • ELISHA V. WATKINS • MONTE M. WATKINS • HAROLD A. WEAVER JR. • BETTY JANE S. WHITNEY • GEORGE S. WILLIE • LINWOOD F. WILLIS • MELISSA J. WIRZBURGER • JOHN M. WYATT • THOMAS R. YOUNG • JOSEPH A. YUREK • URSULA S. ZIMMER • **2003** • CYRUS ABDOLLAHI • KAROLYN A. ABRAM • ALAN ADAMS
• PAUL B. ADAMSEN II • MARC B. AIROLA • DEBRA R. ALEXANDER • WARD P. ALLISON • CLINT T. APLAND • RANDALL M. ARVIZU • RAJ J. ASHAR • ROBERT L. ATKINS • JOHN T. BAER • NEAL A. BAKER • GARY D. BALLARD • CHERRY A. BARRETT • PRINCE BASNYAT • JEFFREY C. BATIS • ROBERT F. BEHLER • BRUK T. BERHANE • MERCEDES N. BIGGS • EDWARD J. BIRRANE III • DAVID J. BLACK • VACHE N. BLAGMON
• MARTIN E. BOEGNER JR. • NATHAN T. BOGGS • JACOB E. BOON • ROBERT A. BOURDELAISE • JESSICA N. BOWLES-MARTINEZ • MATTHEW W. BREINER • DENISE A. BRENEMAN • LOUIS H. BUELL JR. • CALVIN W. BUHRMAN • ELLA D. CAMERON • OSBALDO CANTU JR. • ALISON K. CARR • MARVIN D. CARR • JERRY L. CARSON • JEFFREY S. CHAVIS • ARTHUR J. CIAMPA • THOMAS R. CLARK JR. • CARL G. CLAYTON •
MICHAEL G. CLINCH • DAVID S. COHEN • CATHERINE M. COLANGELO • ROBERT G. COLE • CURTIS COLEMAN • GEORGE L. COLES JR. • VALEREE A. COMBS • GLENN R. COOK • LAURA B. COOK • MARKUS E. DALE • TRACEY L. DEAR • SANDRA M. DERRICOTT • SHARDUL S. DESAI • MICHAEL J. DESYLVA • REBECCA C. DIBARI • RANDY M. DICOSTANTINO • KIRK B. DILLON • ROBERT M. DOBYNS • MICHAEL J. DOLAN •
ANNETTE M. DOLBOW • ERIK T. DONALD • BHARAT T. DOSHI • PATRICIA J. DRAPER • DAVID A. DRZEWIECKI • JEFFREY A. DUNNE • DIANNE L. DUNTON • TERRY O. DUPONT • JENNIFER P. EARWOOD • DERON L. ELMOND • GERALDINE S. EPSTEIN • OSAMA I. FARRAG • BASSAM S. FARROHA • ALBERT J. FASULO II • HEYWARD H. FELLOWS • SUSAN M. FINGERMAN • SHEILA EILEEN O. FITZGERALD • GEORGIA L. FLANAGAN
• MARK A. FLEISCHER • WAYNE W. FLETCHER • EDWARD E. FONTES • LESLIE M. FRALEY • DAVID P. FRANKFORD • CHARLES K. FRICK JR. • MATTHEW E. GARR • KIMBERLEY A. GARRETT • CHERYL A. GELLER • JOHN H. GEYER • SANJOY GHOSH • WILLIAM S. GIBSON • JESPER W. GJERLOEV • ROSE M. GLASSER • RAYMOND H. GODIN • LINO A. GONZALEZ • BRYAN M. GORMAN • BRIAN G. GRAHAM • CHRISANTHE P. GREEN
• DOUGLAS S. GREEN • LEILA M. GREEN • ARIEL M. GREENBERG • CHARLES C. HALL • ARTHUR R. HAMMONS JR. • ROBERT R. HARTER • NOAH J. HAYWARD • JENNIFER A. HEIMBERG • KATHERINE A. HENSHAW • JONATHAN C. HIJUELOS • WESLEY A. HILDEBRANDT • LATOSHA N. HILL • LASHONDA D. HINDS • NGOCDUNG T. HOANG • ELIZABETH M. HOOKS • ANDREW R. HOOVER • JAMES A. HORRIS • GERAD D. HOUSE
• FRANK W. HSU • RAY T. HUDDLESTON JR. • CANDI M. HUDSON • LEONARD L. HUDSON • WILLIAM C. HUGHES • JUDY E. HURLEY • GREGORY C. HUSTEAD • RONALD M. JACOB • DANIEL A. JACQUES • EVAN N. JALBERT • TAO JEN • ERIC R. JOHNS • ALAN L. JOHNSON • DESHAWN J. JOHNSON • SUSAN M. JOHNSON • DAVID J. JONES • KELLY L. JUDGE • ERIK D. JUSTEN • VIJAY S. KAILAS • ANCHAL KAUSHIVA • CAROLYN C. KEGLEY
• BARBARA A. KLEINKNECHT • MATTHEW V. KOZLOWSKI • TIMOTHY O. KRUEGER • MICHAEL D. KUTZER • JONATHAN W. LABIN • KATHERINE A. LAFLEUR • GARY J. LETSCH • BRIAN D. LEVIN • BESSIE Y. LEWIS • KRISTINA L. LEWIS • GEORGE B. LINK • TIMOTHY P. LIPPA • THOMAS H. LLANSO • MELINDA P. LOCKE • KEVIN T. LUDDY • SANTOS LUGO JR. • CARL J. LUMPKIN • BETH G. MAGEN • STEPHEN J. MAIN •
MICHAEL T. MARLEY • MEKISHA Z. MARSHALL • MICHAEL J. MASHNER • JASON L. MASSEY • DANIEL C. MASTERS • MARION F. MCALISTER III • KEVIN M. MCCARTY • VICTOR R. MCCRARY JR. • KIM MCELIGOT • DAVID R. MCKINSTRY • PHILIP E. MECKEL • BRUCE D. MILLER JR. • MIHRAN MIRANIAN • JEFFREY C. MITCHELL • LAWERENCE E. MIZE JR. • GREGORY A. MOLVIK • MICHAEL A. MONGILIO • JAIME MONTEMAYOR
• JUSTIN S. MORRISON • TYRELL D. MOYD • VICTORIA W. MURRAY • SUBHASH C. NAGPAL • PAUL G. NAPOLI • ASHISH NEDUNGADI • KIRBY L. NELL • SHANELL R. NERO • ANDREW J. NEWMAN • BARBARA J. NICHOLSON • DAVID M. NORTON • CHRISTOPHER D. OBREMSKI • BRIAN P. O'CONNOR • LAURIE K. O'CONNOR • MARK M. O'CONNOR • JOHN D. OETTING • CYNTHIA C. OWCA • JOHN F. PALASIK JR. •
JASON T. PAPADEMETRIOU • DELORES PARHAM • RUDOLPH V. PARK • TERESA I. PETERSON • CHI H. PHAM • ERIC N. PIAZZA • CHRISTINA K. PIKAS • MICHAEL J. POBAT • KELLY L. POLICH • MATTHEW J. POTTER • MARILYN A. POUNDS • CHRISTOPHER L. POWERS • MELISSA L. PUGH • JILL R. PUMPHREY • REX H. RAMBO • JOSEPH T. RAMSBURG • DARWEN RAU • KEITH J. REBELLO • MICHEL A. REECE • DAVID N. RESHEF
• CATHARINE M. RHINE • THOMAS W. RICHARDSON • MARIA C. RIGLING • TINA L. ROBERTS • ROBERT M. ROBINSON • TIFFANY M. ROEBUCK • KARLA M. RONCAL • AUSTIN G. ROTTIER • JOACHIM S. SAUR • ROSHAWNNA N. SCALES • VAL J. SCHAEFER • BRIAN M. SCHAFFER • JOHN F. SCHLOMAN • JOHN A. SCIRICA • JAMES R. SHELBY • LYNETTE C. SHELTON • MARY A. SHUPACK • MARC A. SIEDBAND •
RANDALL A. SLAGLE • JOSEPH E. SLUZ • CLAYTON A. SMITH • WAYNE A. SMITH • MIRIAM P. SMYLES • KEITH A. SOLDAVIN • MICHELLE M. STEVENS • JOSE M. SUAREZ • DANIELLE L. SUTTON • STACEY A. SWIERZBINSKI • ERIN M. SYMONDS • NATHANIEL R. TABERNERO JR. • WANDA M. THOMPSON • GREGORY B. TODD • DAWN M. TOLLE • THOMAS TURCO • NICKOLAS M. TYRIS • NIGEL H. TZENG •
ALEKSANDR Y. UKHORSKIY • ERIC J. VAN GIESON • FRED R. VECERA III • MICHAEL A. VINCENT • DAVID S. WACHTER • RONALD G. WARHOLIC • JOSEPH WASHINGTON • CHRISTOPHER R. WATKINS • GREGORY L. WEAVER • ANDREW T. WEBB • RONALD L. WEBER • KARL W. WICK • JAMES P. WILEY • KRISTIN A. WILHELM • JOHN P. WILKINSON • JEANNINE K. WILLIAMS • SCOTT M. WILSON • JOSEPH A. WOLFROM
• YANYI L. WONG • DENNIS W. YARBROUGH • CAROL D. YATES • ELIZABETH R. ZIEGLER • HOLLY A. ZIEGLER • M. WEIDAW • TIMOTHY S. WESCOTT • ELIZABETH A. WHITE • KARL E. WHITTENBURG • RICHIE A. WILLIAMS • THOMAS J. WILLIAMS • FRANCIS T. WILLIAMSON • JON W. WILLIG • PUCK-FAI YAN • CHRIS YUNKER • **2004** • KAREEM A. AARON • GEORGE P. ABITANTE • ROHITH C. ADAVIKOLANU •
SHANELL J. ADDISON • DAVID A. ADVERSARIO • HENRY ANDERSON JR. • ERIC W. ANDERSON • RYAN K. ANDREWS • MATTHEW P. ANGERT • JOHN M. ARKOIAN • ANGELA C. ATKINS • KURT A. BAHNSEN • DAVID N. BARSIC • MICHAEL J. BATTLE • MARCUS P. BAUER • CHERYL A. BEARD • NEIL P. BEAUCHAMP • SHARON E. BEHUM • MIGUEL A. BENITEZ • JOSEPH A. BENNETT • DEBBIE L. BERG • ELLEN A. BICKEL •
TREMAYNE M. BLAIR • SCOTT B. BLOOM • JOHN H. BOCKIUS III • DAVID S. BOGDAN • CHANANN V. BOYD • NORMAN R. BRISCOE • JORGE E. BRITO • NICHOLAS A. BROWN • KELLY A. BRUNS • JOSEPH P. BRUSSEAU • VICTORIA R. BUDA • PAUL F. BUNUAN • PHILIPPE M. BURLINA • ELIZABETH P. BURNS • LARRY BUTLER • EBRIMA M. CAMARAH • PAULETTE W. CAMPBELL • JOHN D. CANTU • BARBARA H. CAPLAN •
STEPHANIE L. CARLSON • RAMIRO CARRASQUILLO JR. • CHRISTOPHER C. CARTER • JAMES E. CARTER • JAMES P. CAVANAUGH • PETER J. CAVENDER • ROBERT J. CEPEK • TIMOTHY G. CHAMBERS • THOMAS CHAMPITTO • CHRISTOPHER J. CHESMAR • PHILIP F. CHIMENTO JR. • MARY BETH A. CHIPKEVICH • JOHN P. CLANCY • JESSE C. CLARKE • JACQUELINE S. COBERLY • GLENN E. CONRAD JR. • STEVEN R. CORLEY
• LAURA COSENTINO • RICHARD S. COST • DAVID A. CRAWFORD • CHARLES B. CRIST JR. • KAREN N. CRIST • RICHARD T. CROOM • CHARLES E. CROSS • DAVID M. CULVER III • THOMAS H. CURTIS • SARAH M. DAMIANI • MICHAEL J. DEANE • MARY W. DEMANSS • MICHAEL L. DENNIS • JEFFREY L. DERRETH • ANTONIO DESIMONE • MICHAEL N. DESMARAIS • OREST I. DIACHOK • CHRISSY M. DOLBIN • NICHOLAS B. DOLBIN
• GEORGE E. DONOGHUE JR. • TAMAR A. DONOVAN • ERIN H. DORI • WILLIAM R. DRUCE • MARY R. DUCKHORN • DONALD P. DUNCAN • DANIEL A. DUTROW • ANURAG DWIVEDI • CRAWFORD A. EASTERLING III • JENNIFER L. EDWARDS • BRUCE L. ELLIOTT • KINGSLEY C. EROWELE • KATHERINE L. EVANS • SEAN M. FAHEY • JULIE L. FARMER • CHARLES L. FARTHING • EDWARD E. FAUST • BRIAN H. FEIGHNER •
PAUL T. FERNAN • ERIC J. FINNEGAN • RICHARD J. FINNEGAN • WILLIAM B. FITZPATRICK • CHRISTOPHER B. FOLEY • OLGA L. FONTANEZ • WALTER M. FONTZ • STEVEN L. FORSYTHE • MATTHEW M. FRIEL • CAROLYN L. FRITTER • TIMOTHY J. GALPIN • TIA GAO • SANFORD S. GARDNER • BRIAN J. GAROFALO • TRACY K. GAUTHIER • MATTHEW E. GERWELL • KAREN GIAMMALVO • DAVID M. GIBSON •
BRITTANY R. GOODENOW • RALPH L. GOOTEE III • SHERRI R. GRAHAM • DONALD D. GRANTHAM • ELWOOD GREEN III • JOSE J. GUZMAN • ANDREA M. GWINN • BRIAN K. HABERMAN • JESKO M. HAGEE • MEAGAN L. HAHN • MARK T. HAIRFIELD • ROBERT J. HANNON • SHARON R. HARMON • SUSAN T. HARRISON • JOHN C. HARRITY • KRISTINE L. HARSHAW • FELICIA HASTINGS • THOMAS A. HAWKINS •
SPENCER S. HAYCOCK • DANIEL A. HEDGECOCK • THOMAS A. HEFFNER JR. • ROBERT M. HEITSENRETHER • JAMES E. HENDERSON JR. • LAMONT D. HENDERSON • MELISSA D. HENDERSON • LAURA E. HENNESSEE • LYDIA N. HENRY • KENNETH E. HIBBARD • DAVID J. HILL • MARY E. HILL • EVA M. HINDS • RICHARD L. HOFF • AMY A. HOFSTRA • PATRICK G. HOGUE • MARY R. HOLLIDAY • CARL W. HOLTJE •
REKHA S. HOLTRY • JENNIFER E. HOPES • PATRICK C. HOPFINGER • BARRY P. HUANG • PHILIP M. HUANG • JOHN C. HUMPHREYS • SHAUN T. HUTTON • MARQUEZ L. JACKSON • MIA Z. JACKSON • XI JIANG • ANIL JOHN • JEFFREY J. JOHNSON • WALTER A. JOHNSTON JR. • BERNADETTE T. JONES • SUZANNE E. JONES • LOUIS L. JUDGE III • TARA L. KAHLER • JAMES T. KAIDY SR. • KENNETH M. KALUMUCK • NDEGWA R. KAMAU
• SUBRAMANIAM KANDASWAMY • CHI-FENG KAO • ERIC R. KEE • WILLIAM K. KELLER JR. • JUDY T. KELLY • JULIA A. KENNEDY • BENJAMIN D. KERMAN • MARY C. KERN • ELIZABETH A. KESLER • TODD J. KIGHT • CINDY K. KIM • CRYSTAL S. KIM • ESTHER J. KIM • PAUL Y. KIM • BRIAN W. KIND • NAN KING • VINCENT B. KNOX • MARK J. KOPYC • NATHAN T. KOTERBA • JAMES K. KRESGE • MELANIE W. KUNAPRAYOON
• MARCUS B. KWOK • JOHN S. KWON • KWEEDAY T. LAMADINE • JOEL B. LAND • STEPHEN F. LANGE • KEVIN M. LANGONE • MATTHEW H. LEAR • MICHAEL P. LEDLEY • TEAHO LEE • DAVID A. LENNOX • ROBERT R. LEONHARD • ANGELA W. LI • SHANNON R. LIEBERG • KEVIN M. LIGOZIO • CAREY M. LISSE • JUSTIN M. LLOYD • JANIS E. LONG • CORY R. LORENZ • CHUCK L. LOUIE • PAUL A. LOWE • CHANTAL S. LOYER
• STEVEN D. LUTZ • DONALD P. MACKEY • LORI A. MAGRUDER • MICHAEL C. MALCHIODI • JAMES K. MANZUK • STEPHANIE A. MARTIN • LESLIE A. MARTINELLI • ROBERT P. MASCOE JR. • JACQUELINE A. MATTERN • STEPHEN M. MCCARTHY • RICHARD B. MCCLURE • LESA A. MCCOMAS • JEFFREY S. MCDONALD • JOSEPH M. MCDONOUGH • KEVIN D. MCGEE • CATHERINE A. MCGEEHAN • JAMES A. MCGOVERN •
KENNETH H. MCKNEELY JR. • MARTHA W. MCNEIL • PETRONILO MEDRANO • THOMAS S. MEHOKE • NISHANT L. MEHTA • BRIAN T. MELLO • MARGARET E. MELLO • JULIE L. MERRITT • MATTHEW B. METLIS • MICHAEL MICCIOLO JR. • FREDERICK MILLER III • JAMES D. MILLER • MARGARET M. MITCHELL • ROBERT J. MITCHELL • JEFFREY MOGELINSKI • ELIZABETH M. MONTANTE • KEVIN L. MOORE • BRIAN A. MUNOZ
• JULIE A. NAPP • ROBERT T. NARH • MANDY L. NATTER • LINDA A. NEWTON • CHRISTOPHER B. NOLAN • JONATHAN E. NORMAN • JORDAN S. NOVGROD • EDMUND H. NOWICKI • THOMAS R. NUTTER • JENNIFER J. OCKERMAN • DAVID J. OLIVARES • STEPHANIE S. ONG • GREGORY A. ORNDORFF • DANIEL J. PANNULLO • STERGIOS J. PAPADAKIS • MATTHEW P. PARA • TAMMY L. PARSONS • CATHERINE L. PAYNE
• DALLAS L. PEARSON III • STEVEN D. PEDUTO • LATONYA M. PENDERGRASS • JAMES R. PENDOCK II • FRANCES R. PERRINE • LAUREN L. PERSKIE • MICHAEL E. PESCI • CAMERON K. PETERSON • STEVEN D. PETERSON • DAVID M. PIERSON • LESLY A. PINOL • JEFFREY B. PLESCIA • RUSSELL I. POPKIN • JOE A. PRESLEY JR. • JACK L. PRINCE JR. • KATHLEEN A. RAETZ • JAMES W. RAISTRICK II • JESSICA C. RAMELLA-
ROMAN • MICHAEL A. RANDOLPH SR. • MATTHEW L. RANKIN • BRIAN R. RAPIDS • DAVID M. REED • JOHN H. REHMERT • JASON I. REID • TERRELL D. REID • JANNELLE M. RICHARDSON • KEVIN A. RICHARDSON • CHRISTIAN J. RIESER • STEVEN G. ROBINSON • WILLIAM S. RODNEY • PEDRO A. RODRIGUEZ JR. • DOUGLAS K. ROLDAN • ANNE-MARIE ROSENTHAL • THOMAS P. ROY • DEREK V. RUSH • HASSAN M. SAFFARIAN
• NICHOLAS S. SANIDAS • ROBERT L. SCHARRINGHAUSEN III • JOHN G. SCHUSTER • JENNIFER B. SELLERS • REBECCA L. SEPAN • CEDRIC S. SHANNON • KIRK A. SHAWHAN • THAI J. SHERIDAN • STEVE W. SHERMAN • NICHOLAS J. SICALIDES • BRADLEY M. SIEGLER • ROBERT V. SIGILLITO • MARVIN L. SIKES JR. • AARON R. SILVERMAN • JEANNE D. SINGMAN • TIMOTHY P. SINNOTT • SCOTT A. SKEEN •
CHRISTOPHER S. SKURSKY • RANDALL T. SLEIGHT • DANIEL C. SMITH • JENNIFER L. SMITH • MATTHEW T. SMITH • WENDY D. SMITH • MATTHEW R. SMOUSE • PETER L. SNYDER • ROBERT L. SOUDER JR. • SCOTT F. SPECK • DOROTHY R. SPENCER • MICHAEL C. SPRINKLE • MARIO D. STALKER • MATTHEW C. STAMM • MARCELLA P. STEERMAN • MARK S. STEPHENS • JESSIQUE A. STEWART • GARY R. STONEBURNER
• ROBERT D. STRAIN JR. • ROBIN D. STRAUSS • TERENCE M. STUCKART • JOSHUA D. SUERETH • DARRYL M. SULLENS • GREGORY D. SUTTON • ROBERT L. SWEENEY III • LEON V. THEISEN • JEFFREY E. THELEN • JANE M. THOMAS • BRYCE A. THOMPSON • MICHAEL W. THOMPSON • JEFFREY A. TOBER • ERIC J. TOLLEFSON • JANET L. TOLLEFSON • JOHN S. TOPPER • AUDREY C. TRAPP • ROSE E. TREPKOWSKI •
RUSSELL J. TURNER • WILLIAM S. TWIGG • JASON G. TWILLEY • KEVIN R. UTZ • STEVEN J. VANDERWALKER • DAVID W. VIEL • WILLIAM J. WAILGUM JR. • SCOTT E. WEATHERWAX • CARLYN H. WEAVER • NANCY E. WEBB • GLENN R. WEHAR • DAVID R. WEIR • DANIEL D. WEISS • JACQUELINE E. WELLS • LINDA K. WHITSITT • ELLEN O. WILKINSON • CHARLES A. WILLIAMS • JEREDINE B. WILLIAMS • BRUCE L. WRIGHT
• CHRISTOPHER G. WRIGHT • MARK A. WRISLEY • ALBERT K. WU • SCOTT E. WUNSCH • MICHAEL C. YEAGER • JOSHUA B. ZADER • DAVID R. ZARET • DAVID R. ZEITZER • JOSEPH W. ZULAUF • SHEILA H. ZURVALEC • **2005** • NATHAN J. ABRAHAM • MARITES S. ABSALON • JOSEPH D. ADAMS • LAN D. AFRAM • ABIMBOLA A. AKINKUOWO • JOSEPH A. AKINYELE • COURTNEY R. ALEXANDER • AMY J. ALLEN •
ALEXANDER M. ALM • ALLAN B. ANDERSON • CHARLES T. ANDERSON • JOANN ANDERSON • JUSTIN R. ARNOLD • TIMOTHY R. ASHFORD • RAPHAEL T. AUSTIN • THOMAS R. BALDWIN • DANIEL J. BANKMAN • GAVIN T. BAYLEY • JAMES D. BEATY • ALAN F. BECKNELL • JOHN S. BEECHER-DEIGHAN • AARON BEJARANO JR. • DIANE J. BELL • DWARAKESHWAR R. BELLAMKONDA • KENNETH C. BENNETT • JOANNE L. BERG
• PAMELA L. BERMUDEZ • JOHN D. BIGELOW • ALLYSON M. BISSING-GIBSON • GEORGE A. BORLASE • TERESA R. BOSSOM • JOSEPH D. BOSTIC JR. • PAUL W. BOUDRA JR. • ALEXANDER BOULE • BLAIR S. BOWMAN • TRACY E. BRADLEY • ERICA B. BRAWLEY • SARA BRETHAUER • MARGARET BROWN • ROBERT C. BROWN • JOHN M. BRUPBACHER • DEBRA L. BUCZKOWSKI • LAWRENCE S. BULANDA • JAMES M. BURCK
• JOHN W. BURKE • STEWART S. BUSHMAN • HUGH R. CAMERON • MARK R. CAMPBELL • DOROTHY A. CANTER • JONATHAN C. CASTELLI • NANCY L. CHABOT • PRASHANTH S. CHALLA • PHILIP CHAN • ALHAD M. CHANDE • WEILUN CHENG • SHERRI L. CHESMAR • DOUGLAS L. CLARK • TIMOTHY J. COLLINS • CHARLES R. COOK • JOHN T. COOPER • LEWIS J. COOPER • CATHERINE M. CORRIGAN • ROBERT P. COTTRELL
• TINA M. CRAIG • FRANCIS X. CRISTE • MARY K. CUDDY-MIERZWA • ENRIQUE G. CUEVAS • CAMILLE R. DANIEL • BETH E. DAVIS • STEVEN L. DEAL SR. • DUANE W. DEAL • RUSSELL R. DEHART • CARLOS E. DEL CASTILLO • NEIL DELLO RUSSO • JEFFREY J. DEMERCHANT • NICKOLAS M. DEMIDOVICH III • JULIE L. DIMINO • PETER T. DINSMORE • THERESA M. DOHERTY • ANDREW J. DOMBARD • OTIS W. DOSS •
JOHN G. DUMLER • DAVID M. DUROSE • ORVILLE A. EARL JR. • SEAN C. ELLICOTT • ELLEN J. ELLIOTT • JEROLD W. EMHOFF II • TIMOTHY A. ERICKSON • MARK A. ERIKSON • JOSEPH A. FALISE • REBECCA E. FARMER • JAMES W. FAULCONER • DEBORAH K. FONTAINE • JASON C. FORD • FREDRIC D. FORNEY JR. • KISHA J. FOSTER • SONIA R. FRANCKEL • DAVID S. FRANKLIN • PAUL A. FRIHAUF • ANITA C. FUNK •
BRIAN P. GADDIS • JAMES W. GALANIE • ANDREW P. GALLERSTEIN • JUSTIN F. GALLOWAY • ANITA L. GANESAN • DAVID A. GARBER • JOHN GFELLER VI • NATASHA L. GIBSON • MEGAN L. GOFORTH • ARNOLD C. GOLDBERG • A. R. GOLSHAN • RAVI P. GOONASEKERAM • ANDREW C. GRAYBEAL • MICHAEL C. GROSS • JENNIFER L. HADRY • MICHAEL A. HAINES • JEROME J. HAMILL • JEFFREY P. HAMMAN • TIMOTHY S. HAN
• MICHAEL J. HANNA • SHERI L. HANSEN • RONALD K. HARRISON II • PARAMASIVIAH HARSHAVARDHANA • HELEN M. HART • LOGAN K. HAUENSTEIN • PURNELL A. HAWKINS • JAMES M. HAYES • JEFFREY W. HEATH • MISTY R. HECHINGER • JENNIFER D. HEIDTMAN • SCOTT M. HENDRICKSON • ARTEMAS P. [illegible] • CHARLES A. HIBBITTS • KAREN D. HIGGINS • MATTHEW E. HILL • ANGELA M. [illegible] •
STEPHANIE D. HOHMAN • JENNIFER S. HOLLENBECK • DENNIS S. HOLLOWAY • NATHANIEL C. HORNER • TANYA Y. HORSEY • JAMES V. HUGHES JR. • HOWARD J. HUNTER • DEBORAH A. HURMAN • NADIA M. HUSSAIN • KYLER M. HUTZ • OLUSESAN A. IWARERE • ANTHONY H. JACKSON • GAIL D. JACKSON • ARTHUR D. JACQUES • ROBERT R. JAILALL • CHRISTOPHER J. JAMES • ROBERT J. JAMISON JR. • MARK A. JENSENIUS
• JONATHAN C. JIANG • AMANPREET S. JOHAL • MARTHA A. JOHNSON • KENNETH B. JONES • SHERRY L. JONES • TALISA M. JOSEPH • MICHAEL T. JOZKOWSKI • RADFORD R. JUANG • COLLEEN E. JUAREZ • JUAN C. JUAREZ • ELIZABETH M. JUSTICE • ROBERT KARMAZIN • ANGELA C. KELLY • RAHENA R. KHONDOKAR • SITARAM KOWTHA • KRISTY L. KRONMEYER • CIDAMBI K. KUMAR • MELANIE I. LAMBERT •
DARRYL J. LANCASTER • RONALD K. LANCASTER • WARREN C. LATHE JR. • KEIR C. LAURITZEN • RYAN M. LAYER • TONY G. LE • JENNIFER A. LEAR • PATRICK M. LEISTER • JACK D. LETZER • LEAH C. LEWIS • BRYAN E. LINKOUS • NANCY T. LINTON • MARY KAE LOCKWOOD • PATRICK V. LOFTUS • DANIELLE P. LUCAS • JACK L. LUM • COREY M. MALLORY • JENNIFER L. MANN • ROYCE C. MARSINGILL III • SEAN R. MARTIN
• GLENN M. MASON • MARCIA L. MCADOO • JESSEE R. MCCLELLAND • MICHAEL P. MCCOY • JENNIFER H. MCDONALD • CHARLES D. MCDONELL III • FRANCESCA R. MCFADDEN • THOMAS E. MCILROY JR. • THOMAS F. MCLAUGHLIN • MONIQUE P. MCWHITE • GREGORY K. MELCHER • ADAM M. MENSH • HAROLD F. MEYERS • ANJALI K. MILANO • CHRISTOPHER T. MILLER • GREGORY J. MILLER • MARY K. MILLER •
JAY G. MOORE • NYOKA M. MOREY • GLENN C. MORTENSEN • SUSAN M. MORTENSEN • ERICH H. MUELLER • MELINDA L. MYERS • KERRIN S. NEACE • KENNETH S. NELSON • MARLA R. NEUBAUER • TRANG T. NGUYEN • TUAN K. NGUYEN-VIET • MATTHEW W. NOBLE • MICHAEL NORKUS • JOSEPH A. NORMAN • KEVIN G. NORMAN • DONALD A. NOYES • KJELLMAR OKSAVIK • JAMES F. O'NEIL • JUSTIN D. OSBORN
• KWAME OSEI-WUSU • EDWARD W. OTT JR. • LINDA L. PAUL-HICKS • JASON C. PAULSEN • GREGORY D. PAYTAS • CHRISTOPHER T. PEARRE • JAMES A. PENDERGRASS • RYAN T. PETERSON • STEPHEN P. PHILLIPS • BRENDAN S. PICCOLO • PAMELA A. PITTMON • KORY J. POSTMA • JAMES D. POWELL • AMELIA R. PREHN • XAVIER D. PRESTON • GEORGE S. PYRYT • RACHEL S. QUIZON • JENNIFER A. RAINEY •
GAIL S. RAYBURN • WILLIAM M. REID • GEORGE C. REILLY III • NATHAN S. RELLER • ROGER W. REMINGTON • STEPHEN B. REMINGTON • CARLOS A. RENJIFO • STEVEN L. RICHTER • STACEY M. RIDENOUR • DEBORAH A. RIDINGS • ANDREW S. RIVKIN • MELVIN C. ROBERTS • WILLIAM K. ROBERTS • AMANDA G. RODGERS • DONNA M. RODNEY • LAURA M. RODRIGUEZ • LEWIS M. ROUFBERG • DAVID M. ROUSE •
NEIL A. RUBENSTEIN • DENNIS L. RYAN III • ABIGAIL M. RYMER • ERIC W. SAARI • ERIC R. SANGER • ERNEST J. SATTERFIELD • ADAM C. SAWYER • ROBERT K. SCHAEFER • JEFFREY S. SCHEIB • DANIEL C. SCHEINERMAN • DOUGLAS C. SCHMIDT • TIBOR J. SCHONFELD • CHARLES F. SCHUMAN • MARSHA R. SCHWINGER • FRANK P. SEELOS IV • SHAWN E. SEMAN • DAVID M. SEPAN • STEPHEN S. SHAW •
STEPHEN A. SHINN • SHERYL P. SHRECKENGOST • NAMRATA R. SHRESTHA • RINA SHRESTHA • ZIPORA SIDEL • JEFFREY H. SIMMONS • LEROY D. SIMMONS • CASSIUS K. SIMS • BARBARA J. SIPES • ANNA S. SLOWIKOWSKI • ANGIE P. SMALLS • RUTHE R. SNYDER • REUBEN T. SORENSEN • DANIEL A. SPRECHMAN • CELENA L. SPRY • STEPHEN J. STAFFORD • MONICA A. STARNES • JODI K. STEAGALL •
JEFFREY E. STEINBERG • MARVIN N. STEINGART • MARIAN R. STOKES • CHRISTIAN A. STONEBURNER • VALORIE J. STOUGH • LAURA R. STRAUCH • LARRY D. STRAWSER • RHONDA L. STRIANESE • ADAM P. SUMEY • LAURA J. SUMMERS • CAROL L. SYLVIS • MICHAEL R. TABERNERO • THOMAS P. TAKACS • NARUHISA TAKASHIMA • DIANE L. TANG • ZHUANGBO TANG • SALLY W. TARQUINIO • ROBERT E. TENCH
• WILLIAM D. TENCKHOFF • TIMOTHY N. TERLAJE • MEAZA TESHOME • CHRISTOPHER M. THELEN • DAVID E. THOMAS • MICHAEL D. TRELA • LARRY J. TRENT • ROSE M. TRINGALI • SONIA K. TSUI • SUSAN M. URS • GEOFFREY S. UY • KELLY A. VAN HOUTEN • JOEL H. VAN SICKEL • LAURA A. VANDERBERG • JONATHAN P. VAN'T HOF • GLENN J. WADSWORTH • MICHAEL L. WAGNER • JON R. WARD • MILDRED R. WEARS
• ASHLEY K. WEAVER • VIJITHA WEERACKODY • BRENDA K. WETZEL • BRENDA Z. WHEATLEY • MALCOLM J. WHITE • AMY L. WILLIAMS • DANIEL P. WILLIAMS • PAMELA L. WILLIAMS • DANIEL P. WILT • JESSICA R. WILT • JAYNE M. WINES • RAYMOND C. WINES • JAMES H. WISE • CLARENCE WONG • MELISSA K. WONG • CHRISTOPHER C. WRIGHT • DAVID E. WRIGHT • MAUREEN E. WYNN • DAVID Z. XIA • JAY YOO
• DAVID W. YOUNG • VALERIE J. YOUNG • JOSEPH D. ZANETTI • DAVID P. ZEPF • JIN F. ZHANG • HAI ZHENG • YIHUA ZHENG • YANG ZHOU • **2006** • AKINWALE A. AKINPELU • JACQUELINE AKINPELU • RICHARD R. ALFINI • CARLOS E. ALFONSO • AIMEE M. ALUZZO • LORNA I. ALVAREZ • OLIVIA C. ANDERSON • ROBERT S. ARMIGER • ERIC T. ARNOLD • DAVID G. ASBURY JR. • KATHLEEN A. ASHER • GREGORY S. AVICOLA
• FREDERICK M. AVOLIO • SANDRA D. BAILEY • LANCE M. BAIRD • RICHARD B. BAKER • DALE L. BALDWIN • CHRISTOPHER A. BARE • KEVIN T. BARRETT • LAURA R. BATEMAN • BRIAN A. BAUER • LEIGH A. BAUMGART • DAVID BAZELL • SCOTT A. BEATON • LENORA A. BEDFORD • JUSTINE F. BENKOWSKI • MICHAEL E. BENSO • ANA LETICIA F. BENTO • ALICE F. BERMAN • SIMMIE F. BERMAN • CRAIG A. BERNAS
• WILLIAM E. BISHOP • DAVID R. BISSON • RICHARD W. BLANK • LAWRENCE R. BLEAU • MARK O. BLOECHL • KENT E. BODURTHA • TAMMY L. BOND • AMANDA E. BOOZE • NATHAN D. BOS • TIMOTHY A. BOWSER • JONATHAN W. BOYD • CYNTHIA D. BRAXTON • JENNIFER L. BREIDENICH • KELLY M. BRINKLEY • DANIEL G. BROSIUS • ANGELA S. BROWN • DANIEL C. BROWN • KENNETH D. BROWN • VERONICA T. BROWN
• ENRIQUE R. BRUGUERA • HEATHER M. BRUNDAGE • JEFFREY S. BRUSH • DANIEL B. BRYANT • ROBERT B. BURGIO • JOHN S. BURKS • DONNA M. BUSH • JEFFREY A. BUSH • FLORETTA C. CABINESS • JOHN R. CALLAHAN • MICHAEL T. CARR • FRANCISCO CASANOVA • IBOLJA CERNAK • LEE J. CERRETA • BRYAN B. CHA • AMY S. CHALMERS • RYAN J. CHERNIAK • DANIELLE S. CHOU • ILYA A. CHUKHMAN •

BRIAN S. CHWIEROTH • BENJAMIN R. CLARE • BROOKE H. CLAYTON • JOHN G. COLE • TERESA-ANNE D. COLELLA • KEVIN A. COLIN • NICOLE M. COLLEY • BRYAN R. COLLINS • CARLOS A. COMPERATORE • JOSEPH A. CONSUGAR • PETER D. COOK • RABON E. COOKE • REBECCA L. CORDER • TIMOTHY L. CORNETT • COURTENAY V. COTTON • THOMAS W. CRAIG • WILLIAM B. CROWNOVER • MANUEL A. CRUZ •
JEFFREY P. CULLINA • DILLAN J. CUNNINGHAM • ANDREW A. DANTZLER • DARYL C. DAVIS • JUDITH M. DAVIS • KIMBERLY D. DAVIS • MARGARET E. DEAN • KUNAL A. DESAI • GEORGE J. DESHESKY • AMY L. DODSON • ELDWIN L. DODSON • BRIAN H. DONOHUE • CHAD J. DORAN • CRYSTAL J. DORSEY • JEAN M. DOUGHERTY • LINDA J. DRAKE • BRIAN P. DUNCAN • KELLEY D. EASTER • EHREN M. EHMANN •
LAUREL A. EIERMAN • KEISHA M. ENGLISH • RYAN M. FARRELL • ONORIO FELICIANO JR. • LOUIS J. FETTER JR. • DENNIS H. FIKE JR. • RUSSELL A. FINK • JUAN E. FISHER • ROBERT G. FITZGIBBONS • CHRISTIANE I. FLEURANT • ROTUNDA L. FLOYD-COOPER • PAYTON A. FLYNN SR. • LISA L. FLYNN • SUMMER C. FOWLER • WADE F. FREEMAN • TOREY B. FROST • KIMBERLY A. FUNK • BRYANT S. GARCIA • ELSIE GARCIA
• TODD M. GERECKE • JENNIFER L. GFELLER • SUHAS GHANTE • PAUL W. GOLDEN • JOSEPH N. GOMES • CHRISTOPHER M. GOODSELL • MATTHEW D. GORDON • GREGG B. GOYETTE • DANIEL J. GRADY • LEMONTE GREEN • DAWN M. GREENMAN • MICHELLE L. GREY • JULIAN B. GRIZZARD • DAVID A. GRUNSCHEL • JEFFREY R. GUY • THOMAS M. HAARD • NATHAN A. HAGAN • SHERRI A. HAINES COSBY • JOHN M. HALL
• THERESA L. HAMM • SEAN T. HAPPEL • ROBERT T. HARRIS JR. • GENEVIEVE C. HART • JAHNA M. HARTWIG • CHRISTOPHER A. HARVEL • CHAD M. HAWES • KENNETH R. HAYDEN • EMILY K. HEBELER • CHARLES R. HECKART JR. • CHINMAY L. HEGDE • PETER C. HEIMBERG • ROBERT E. HELLAUER III • RONALD E. HELMICK • SHARYN HERMAN • JOHN E. HICKS • CHARLES E. HIGGS JR. • PATRICIA K. HIGGS • MARI J. HILL
• TABATHA M. HILL • TONY L. HILLIARD • KEITH O. HINDER JR. • ROBERT C. HITE • EDWARD L. HODGES JR. • RENEE C. HOGUE • KELLY A. HOLDEN • ALAN L. HOLMES • OCK Y. HONG • AMANDA HORIKE • LARISSA N. HUDSON • JENNIFER L. HUERGO • AZMAT HUSAIN • JODY R. IBANEZ • HENRY H. IHM • JANICE M. JACKSON • ZUGELL L. JAMISON • WILLIAM JAUREGUI • TAMMARA M. JEAN PAUL • VICTOR JENG •
DANIEL D. JOHNSON • JOHN W. JOHNSTON • ANN M. JOLLY • EVETTE M. JONES • ALIMELU S. JONNAGADLA • ELIEZER G. KAHN • DANIEL R. KATZ • KURT H. KELLER • PATRICK D. KILDUFF • BYONG J. KIM • GARY H. KIM • DOUGLAS G. KINNEY • KAREN W. KIRBY • RAISSA V. KIRK • LINDA K. KRESS-MCDONALD • HEDI A. KRICHENE • DEBORAH A. KUHNS • RYAN M. KURTZ • JOSHUA F. KUSNICK • HEESUNG KWON •
ERIN D. LABARRE • GREGG A. LAFAVE • JOHN J. LAH • PAUL J. LASKOWSKI • MEGAN R. LEAHY-HOPPA • PATRICK J. LEDUC • PAUL A. LEDUC • CRAIG B. LEESE • JONATHAN LEVY • CHRISTOPHER S. LEWIS • JENNIFER LI • ANDY C. LIANG • DAVID M. LISHEGO • MARK S. LITTLETON • TERESA M. LOPEZ • MICHAEL R. LOPRESTI • RALPH D. LORENZ • MICHAEL S. LOTITO • JEFFREY B. LUTZ • CHRISTOPHER M. LYNCH •
HARVEY L. MACY • JARED R. MALES • KELLY ANN MANION • COIRE J. MARANZANO • BELINDA G. MARCHAND • RAY H. MARINER JR. • AMEN RA MASHARIKI • THOMAS R. MASON • SONY MATHEW • ROBERT C. MATTESON III • JOHN E. MATTSON • JOSHUA R. MAXIMOFF • LEWIS J. MCARTHUR • EILEEN M. MCCARTHY • DAVID K. MCDONNELL • BRENDAN D. MCELRONE • BETHANY M. MCGEE • TIMOTHY G. MCGEE
• LAURA D. MCINTYRE • BRIAN J. MECHLER • YARILIS MENDEZ • THOMAS A. MILAM JR. • MARGO S. MILDVAN • MATTHEW D. MITCHELL • ZARUHI R. MNATSAKANYAN • BRENDA J. MOFFETT • ADAM I. MOHAMED • ROBERT W. MOHR • ELAINE C. MORGAN • MICHELLE C. MURRAY • PATRICK B. MYLES • MICHAEL S. MYRICK • MARCUM N. NANCE III • ALDO NASCIMENTO • JOHN P. NELSON • KENNETH E. NEWSOME JR.
• ROBERT T. NEWSOME • CHRISTINA P. NGUYEN • VI H. NGUYEN • TIMOTHY V. NICHOLSON • STANLEY L. NOLEN • MICHAEL E. NORD • AMY E. OAKS LOPRESTI • MICHAEL J. O'DRISCOLL • BRIAN J. OLSON • CHRISTOPHER C. OLSON • MIRANDA D. OLTMAN • PETER A. OLUFEMI • JARED D. OSBORN • JEFFREY G. OSBORN • FENG OUYANG • HUDA B. OWEIS • JAMES R. PARSONS JR. • CHANCELLOR T. PASCALE •
JULIA B. PATRONE • RAMON PENA JR. • RICHARD A. PERFIDIO II • RICHARD M. PEROUTKA • WILLIAM K. PETER • ROY J. PFEIFFER • TRUDY L. PHILIP • ROBERT S. PILATO • RICHARD A. PIMENTAL JR. • PATRICK J. POON • HARRY J. PORTER JR. • DAVID A. PORTNOY • KANIKA T. POWELL • DAVID R. PRICE JR. • MICHAEL J. PRUSZ • TERRY L. PURKABLE • YATTA T. QUIRE • ALEXANDER S. RATTNER • JAMES D. REEVES JR.
• ALAN C. REINER • STEPHEN R. RIESE • GEORGE R. RITMILLER III • TIMOTHY A. ROACH • RAQUEL Y. ROBINSON • AARON Q. ROGERS • NATHAN W. ROLANDER • WAYNE K. ROSS JR. • MARK S. ROUNTREE • STEVEN E. ROUTH • JOHN F. ROYCROFT JR. • LUKE K. RUMBAUGH • DENNIS P. RUTTEN • SUZANNE L. RZEPKOWSKI • NICOLAS SALCICCIOLI • LINDA F. SAMUELS • SARAH A. SASLOW • REBECCA Z. SCHMIDT
• LESLIE A. SCHROEDER • KATHERINE A. SCHULTE • MARIA A. SCHWARTZ • KIMBERLY D. SEELOS • TIMOTHY G. SEIPP • CHRISTINA M. SELBY • DEBORAH A. SHACKELFORD • ARJUN A. SHAH • PAUL A. SHELTON • BRIAN J. SHERMAN • THOMAS R. SHERMAN • ALI-REZA J. SHISHINEH • CHRISTOPHER G. SIGGINS • JOSHUA M. SILBERMANN • CHARLES H. SIMPSON • MELANA J. SINGLETARY • ALLEN H. SIU •
ERIC G. SMITH • ERIN R. SMITH • KEVIN Z. SNOW • THOMAS M. SOKOL • JAY H. SONG • ERIK D. SONTHEIMER • STEPHEN L. SORLEY • KENNETH A. SOWERS • ANDREA D. ST. CLAIR • CHRISTOPHER R. STEEN • DANIELLE STEPHENSON • MENAHEM D. STERN • PAMELA L. STEWART • BRADLEY G. STICKLES • DONALD W. STREETT • TERESA C. STRITCH • JASON H. SU • SUMA B. SUBBARAO • THOMAS G. SUDBRINK
• ELIZABETH A. SULLINS • ANGALENE SUTTON • RONDA J. SYRING • FARID S. TAWASHA • ARTHUR L. TAYLOR • BRIAN T. TAYLOR • KEVIN P. TAYLOR • LEROY T. TEAGLE • DANIEL J. TEBBEN • CATHEY E. THELLEN • RONALD E. THELLEN • STEVEN P. THIBAULT • MICHAEL C. THRESHER • EVAN R. TIBBETTS • MICHAEL P. TIERNEY • DANNETTE M. TINNIN • NATALIE T. TRANCUCCI • BRUCE R. TRETHEWEY JR. •
JONATHAN T. TROSTLE • ELIZABETH P. TURTLE • EARLEEN D. UPTON • KELLY N. UPTON • MARIA E. VACHINO • JENNIFER M. VALENCIA • CAROL L. VAN DYKE • BRIAN D. VENTRE • LINDA L. VENTURELLA • AIDA L. VERA-LOPEZ • RUTH A. VOGEL • MORRIS L. WADE • JOHN M. WALTERS • MEGHAN E. WARNER • DEVIN L. WARREN • MONICA M. WATERS • LAUREN A. WATKINS • BRIAN C. WATTS • CLAYTON N. WAUNEKA
• ANGELA L. WHALEN • EDWARD G. WHITMAN • CARLETHA S. WIGGINS • VANESSA L. WILKAT • DANA-MARIE WILLIAMS • IAN D. WING • KERRY N. WOOD • LAGUNA A. WOODWARD • STEPHEN E. WRIGHT • JOHN A. YAHIRO • JULIE Y. YEE • CHARLES C. YOUNG • JOHN C. YOX JR. • PHILIP J. YUENGLING • WARREN E. ZANDER • CHRISTOPHER L. ZANSKI • BRUCE F. ZINK • GREGORY B. ZISKIND • **2007** • CHRISTOPHER L. ABBOTT
• MICHAEL S. ADAMS • ERIN D. ADEDIRAN • UTHMAN K. ADEDIRAN • CAROLYN P. ADEZIO • DANIEL ADUSEI-POKU JR. • AISHA AHMAD • BRIAN E. AHR • JOHN J. AIELLO • RYAN A. ALLEN • HENRY J. ALME • RANDI K. ALSTON • JULIA ANDERSEN • TARA E. ANDERSON • WILLIAM A. ARDANUY • ASHLEY M. ARNOLD • PERRY M. ATKINSON • DEBRA I. AUERBACH • ERIC J. AUPPERLEE • ANNA K. AUSTIN • ANTONY M. BACA
• KATHERINE F. BACKOF • LYNN M. BAILEY • KATHLEEN P. BAKER • BRIAN M. BANOS • LANCE C. BARLEY • JEFFREY P. BARNES • FRANCES C. BASHFORD • STEVEN E. BATIS • BRIAN P. BATTAGLIA • SCOTT L. BATTOCCHI • AMANDA K. BAUMAN • WILLIAM G. BEAVERS • KRISTOPHER A. BELL • JASON J. BENKOSKI • BARBARA J. BENNETT • LUCY L. BERGLING • TERRY G. BICE • RACHEL E. BINFIELD • MICHAEL A. BLACKWELL
• DAVID T. BLEWETT • ROBERT E. BOGGIO II • AUSTIN C. BOGUS • MATTHEW F. BOKULIC • SHAUN T. BOLTZ • JOSEPH L. BONDI • VERONICA G. BOWERS • LEROY BOWLES • LINDA L. BOWLES • WESTON R. BOYD • LAYNE H. BRADLEY • ZACHARY C. BRANDENBURG • ROBERT M. BRAUNGER • VALERIE B. BROCKMAN • EMILY B. BRODERICK • TED W. BROOKS • CHRISTOPHER Y. BROWN • MATTHEW D. BROZOWSKI •
MATTHEW L. BRUBAKER • THOMAS J. BUCKLEY • RONALD J. BUIKEMA • JEFFREY M. BURDICK • KEVIN A. BURKE • ERIK D. BURNETT • CRAIG M. BURRIS • ALAN F. BUSBEY • WESLEY S. BUXTON • CHRISTINA M. CAIN • JOSEPH F. CALLIER • RICHARD B. CAMPBELL • PATRICK E. CARR • DAVID J. CARRELLI • THOMAS P. CASCIANI • HANNAH H. CHAE • MURTY S. CHALLA • DAVID C. CHAMBERLIN-LONG • ERIC C. CHANG
• WILLIAM C. CHEEZUM JR. • ANDREW CHEN • PETER B. CHUI • MICHAEL J. CIOTTI • JAMES H. CLARK • DAVID E. COHEN • JAMEY B. COHEN • THOMAS M. COMBERIATE • JOSEPH P. COMER • ELIZABETH A. CONGDON • ANTHONY E. COOK • DEREK J. COOK • ROBERT G. COOPER • SCOTT A. COOPER • DAVID J. COPELAND • MARY L. CORDER • LAURA E. COTTON • RONALD N. COUCH • TIMOTHY A. COULTER •
KIMBERLY A. CRANFORD • JOHN H. CREWS • MATTHEW J. CROWNE • ALICIA M. CURRAN • BENJAMIN H. CUSHWA • KATHERINE M. DARAGO • JANET L. DARRAH • CHARLIE DAVIS III • CLEON E. DAVIS • RICHARD M. DAY • RYAN M. DEACON • DAVID M. DEGLAU • ELLVERA A. DELASKO • DAVID A. DEMAY • DAVID DESROCHER • JOHN P. DEVALE • JENNY L. DICKERSON • JONATHAN E. DIERKSEN • RYAN P. DINELLO-FASS
• DESYREE A. DIXON • LAWRENCE M. DOBBS JR. • BRUCE W. DORSEY • SHARON D. DOTSON • JOHN V. DRAPER • KEVIN L. DRURY • WALTER R. DYER • REBECCA E. EAGER • CHRISTIAN A. EBLE • TARA K. ECHLIN • DAVID J. EDELL • YEVGENIY ELBERT • TERRON H. ELLERBE • GREGORY A. ELLERS • CHRISTOPHER L. ERDMAN • HADI A. ESIELY-BARRERA • MELISSA D. ESTES • TARA C. EYLER • CHARLES A. FANCHER
• JOHN S. FEGER • EUGENE C. FELTON • JARROD J. FENSTERMACHER • STEVEN F. FERRARO • ROBERT J. FEUERBACH • STEVEN J. FILO • CHERYL M. FINN • HARRY L. FISHER IV • RICHARD J. FITZGERALD • JOEL M. FRANKWICK • DONALD M. FRECH • JENNIFER R. FRY • ANDREW B. FULLER • JOSHUA R. FULLERTON • JESSICA K. FUNK • MARK B. GABRIELE • LIBET GARBER • ANTONIO GARCIA • AUSTIN T. GARDNER
• JEFFREY S. GARRETSON • STANLEY E. GAUMER • SHAYNE B. GERBER • ERIC R. GERDES • JOSLYN D. GIBSON • RONALD J. GICKA • JACOB A. GILBERT • REGINA S. GLOWNIA • DEVON C. GOFORTH • CHARLES E. GOLDBLUM • LISA GONZALEZ • ALLISON A. GOODMAN • CHARRON L. GORDON • MARY GORDON • SARAH L. GRADY • ALAN G. GRAHAM • BARBARA L. GRANT • WILLIAM R. GRAY RONCAL • JONATHAN F. GREEN
• GREGORY J. GRESETH • WINSTON A. GREY • REBECCA F. GRIFFITHS • JOHN P. GUNSIOROWSKI • NATALIE E. HAGAN • GERALD D. HAHN • CHRISTINA M. HAMMOCK • MATTHEW P. HANEY • ASHLEY L. HANKINSON • JERAMY A. HANSEN • LAWRENCE O. HARNISH • DEREK S. HARSHBARGER • MATTHEW S. HART • CORWYN C. HAVERMANS • AMANDA L. HAWKINS • KALMAN HAZINS • SEAN D. HEALY •
GREGG R. HECKERT • LELAND B. HEIN • JOHN B. HELDER • DONALD S. HENDERSON • LEE A. HENDRIX • MATTHEW H. HENRY • BRYAN E. HERDLICK • JASMINE N. HILL • DANIEL P. HIPSLEY • MICHAEL D. HITESHEW • MINHTRI T. HO • CHARLES J. HODANICS • JOAN A. HOFFMANN • TERRY L. HOLLEY • STEVEN A. HOLT • SHARJEEL M. HOODA • RICHARD L. HOOKS • KAZUO R. HOSOKAWA • TERRY R. HUBER •
NATHANIEL J. HUNDLEY • LANG M. HUNG • TERESA A. HUNT • ANDY S. IM • WILLIAM A. IRIZARRY-CRUZ • DARCIA P. JACKSON • JOSHUA D. JACOBS • VIOLET J. JAMES • ERIC D. JANSING • NANCY J. JARVIS • ANDREA M. JENSENIUS • XIAOSONG JIANG • SULEYMAN JOHNS • TOMMY O. JOHNSON • MICHAEL C. JONES • JOEL M. JORGENSEN • LYDIA B. JOYCE • KAPIL D. KATYAL • BLAKE K. KAWAMOTO • SUSAN M. KELLEY
• LISA A. KELLY • JENNY L. KHUON • TIMOTHY S. KHUON • JACLYN A. KILHEFFER • SEAN M. KINAHAN • RICHARD D. KINDER • ALBERT C. KINNEY • PETER L. KIRBY • LISA M. KIRK BROWN • ADAM J. KIRK • KATARINA E. KNUTSEN • HEBA KOCH • BRIAN C. KOHAN • PHILLIP T. KOSHUTE • RADHA G. KOWTHA • PETER S. KRUUS • PAUL R. KUCHER IV • BRIAN J. KWONG • MICHAEL B. LABARRE • ALAN L. LANE •
PATRICK T. LANGLEY • NAM H. LE • JEFFREY K. LEE • MAY L. LEE • YUN H. LEE • ALLYSON E. LEFEVERE • DANIEL C. LEGGETT • JOHN T. LEIZEAR • MICHAEL W. LEONARD • SAMUEL D. LIEBER • ANGELINE G. LIM • MELANIE B. LINEWEAVER • GE G. LING • DAVID W. LISKA • EDWINA P. LIU • THOMAS A. LONGSTAFF • MARK J. LORENZ • EDWIN J. LORENZO • ANNA LOSKIEWICZ-BUCZAK • DALE J. LUCAS • CESAR A. LUGO
• JONATHAN R. LUMAN • GORDON L. MAAHS • JASON R. MADSEN • DEANNA M. MAHANAND • ADAM J. MAISANO • DEETI K. MAJMUNDAR • ALISON E. MAJORS • DAVID E. MANION • KYLE C. MANNING • JEFFREY P. MARANCHI • ANDREW F. MASON • SHENEKA G. MASON • BRIAN J. MATT • JORDAN M. MATTHEWS • CHERIE L. MAUCK • BROOKE A. MAYS • JASON A. MAYS • CORMAC D. MCCARTY • JENNIFER M. MCCORMICK
• KENNETH R. MCKEEVER • ADAM W. MCKIBBEN • PAUL MCKINNEY SR. • RYAN W. MCVEY • JULIA A. MEHOKE • KAVITA G. MESTER • MICHAEL B. MIDGLEY-BIGGS • JAMES M. MILLER • MICHAEL J. MILLER • THERESA M. MILLS • SHARON C. MILLS-YOUNG • ROBERT M. MINCH • RAY W. MINIHAN • TIMOTHY MIRALLES • AIDA MIRANDA • CHRISTINE M. MIRANDA • LINDA J. MONIZ • CHARLES B. MOORE JR. •
CHARLES R. MOORE • CHRISTOPHER R. MOORE • GREGORY T. MOORMANN • MICHAEL S. MORENO • KIMBERLY S. MORGAN • TERESA L. MORGAN • ERICA M. MORTON • PAUL D. MULHARE • GALEN E. MULLINS • RACHEL L. MURPHY • ROBERT J. MURPHY • CHRISTINA L. MURPHY-CLARK • A. H. NAIR • AMIR C. NAJMI • GEORGE P. NANOS JR. • KAREN A. NAPOLITANO • CASSANDRA L. NEVELEFF • MICHAEL A. NEWKIRK
• THONG N. NGO • RICHARD L. NICHOLS • BRUCK NIGUSSE • MAEGEN L. NIX • GARY G. NIXON • WILLIAM A. NOONAN • DANIEL C. NOWICKI JR. • COLLEEN M. NOWICKI • DEBORAH L. NOYES • SEAN R. O'CONNOR • GBOLABO OGUNMAKIN • ROBERT L. OLBERS • PETER C. OLSEN • KENNETH R. OLSON • HANEEF E. ORIDEDI • DAVID M. ORR • BERNARD V. OTTLEY JR. • SCOTT PAPSON • STEVE PARR • ANDREW T. PARRISH
• CHINMAYI N. PATEL • JODY C. PATILLA • ANDREW M. PATTERSON • GERALD W. PATTERSON • ALEXANDER J. PEARSE • KAREN M. PEARSON • STEVEN J. PEREIRA • RONALD E. PERISON • DANIEL R. PHIFER • RAJEEV U. PILLAI • KEMAL O. PISKIN • KATHRYN F. POHLMEYER • SCOTT T. POLLOCK • SARAH H. POPKIN • MARTHA S. POST • JONATHAN H. PRIETZ • JASON L. PRINCE • ALEX J. PROESCHER •
CHRISTOPHER A. RAGLAND • SHANNA A. RATNESAR-SHUMATE • KYLE P. REESE • LYNN M. REGGIA • JONATHAN I. REINFELD • WILLIAM F. REISKE • RICKY O. REX JR. • GERALD F. RICCIARDI • HOLLY A. RICE • CHANCE R. RICHARDSON • JENNIFER E. RICHARDSON • ANDREW N. RIEL • JAMES L. RIGGINS II • SARAH RIGSBEE • SIGITAS J. RIMKUS • JULIE M. ROBERTS • JASON S. RODGERS • CHARLES K. ROGERS JR.
• STERLING S. ROOKE • HOLLIS L. ROSS JR. • JULIE M. RUBI • LAURA B. RUPPALT • TERRY L. RUSHING • DAVID M. SABOL • TREVOR M. SAFKO • TONI J. SALTER • JOHN J. SAMSOCK IV • PHILLIP A. SANDBORN • JOSHUA L. SANTARPIA • KENNETH L. SAUNDERS • ROSE F. SCHMITT • BRUCE W. SCHNEIDER • JEREMY S. SCHUHMANN • BRUCE E. SCOTT • HELMUT SEIFERT • DREW P. SEKER • BRANDY M. SELBY •
LINDA M. SEMMEL • JOSHUA H. SHRADER • NATHAN W. SIBLEY • SUSAN B. SICKINGER • LEIGH P. SIEGEL • BRENDAN J. SIEVERS • STANLEY R. SILBERMAN • MIKHAIL I. SITNOV • ISHWAR K. SIVAKUMAR • CHAD D. SLICK • COREY T. SLICK • EMILY E. SMITH • HOWARD T. SMITH • LYNN Y. SMITH • RONALD D. SMITH • STEPHEN P. SMITH • WALTER A. SMITH • EILEEN M. SORENSEN • THOMAS M. SOUTHALL •
MICHAEL K. SOUTHWORTH • ELISE M. SPEDDEN • JASON A. SPITALETTA • WILLIAM C. STARR • LORETTA J. STEVENS • RYAN T. STEVENS • JOHAN D. STEWART • ROBERT A. STOLL • SUZANNE STRICKLER • JEFFREY C. STUCKMAN • ANTHONY C. STUMP • ROBERT A. SUMMERS • STEVEN E. SUMNER • JENNIFER M. SUPPA • ROMAN A. SVOYSKY • THOMAS W. SWINDELL • JAMEY R. SZALAY • EMILY M. TAI •
JULIE A. TARR • ERIN M. TAYLOR • KELLY D. TAYLOR • STEVEN R. TAYLOR • TRENT M. TAYLOR • YVETTE G. THEIS • MARK A. THOBER • KATHERINE L. THOMAS • KEENA D. THOMAS • TAMYSHA M. THOMAS • ANGELA D. THOMPSON • JOSEPH W. THORNBERRY • RICHARD J. TOM • WILLIAM E. TORRUELLAS • DANIEL J. TOSH • KATHLEEN TOWNSEND • GRACE M. TRAN • EDWARD W. TUNSTEL JR. • KENNETH R. TURNER
• EDELE D. TURNEY • BRENT D. UNDERWOOD • PAUL G. VELEZ • SAMIAIYA VENKATESH • DAVID VESPOINT • JENNIFER A. VINCENT • META M. VOELKER • RACHEL J. VOGELSTEIN • DOAN-TRANG T. VU • CHRISTOPHER J. WACLAWSKI • BRIAN J. WADSLEY • JANSEN A. WASHINGTON • RAYMOND P. WASKY • ADAM S. WATKINS • GABRIELLE V. WATKINS • MICHAEL E. WATKINS • CHRISTOPHER B. WATSON •
STEPHEN M. WAUGH • BEVERLY L. WEBER • JAMES E. WEBER • ANTONIO A. WEEDON SR. • JOSEPH D. WELTER • GEOFFREY G. WERTMAN • CHADRICK L. WHALEY • MELVIN J. WHITE II • HARRIET E. WHITE • ELIZABETH A. WHYMS • KEITH O. WICHMANN • VANESSA J. WICHMANN • BENJAMIN R. WILHELM • ANN T. WILLIAMS • JEFFERSON A. WILLIAMS • LAVERN F. WILLIAMS • MICHAEL P. WILLIAMS •
KEVIN A. WINNER • WESLEY E. WITHROW • LAWRENCE S. WOLFARTH • JOSHUA T. WOLFE • KRISTIN A. WORTMAN • DAVID O. WRIGHTSON • YIYI WU • CHRISTOPHER D. YOUNG • ADAM W. YOZWIAK • PATRICK T. YU • DAISY L. ZHANG • QINQING ZHANG • CHARLES A. ZOGBY • **2008** DERONLEI ABLE SR. • ELENA Y. ADAMS • NORMAN H. ADAMS • FARID AHMED • PATRICK D. ALLEN • LISA G. ALPER •
MARSHALL H. ALWORTH III • CHINMAY H. AMIN • BRIAN E. AMISS • ALAN E. ASHLEY • DEREK M. AUCOIN • JOSHUA D. AUSTIN • KIMBERLY A. BAHR • CHUN-HUEI BAIR • DAVID N. BATCHELDER • CORINA C. BATTISTA • CHRIS W. BAUMGART • DONALD J. BEAVER • MELANIE L. BELL • NEILL B. BELTRAN • WALTER R. BENDER • BRUCE P. BENJAMIN • DEBRA S. BENNING • JOSE A. BERMEJO-FERRER • CHARLES S. BERRY
• FREDERICK E. BERTHIAUME • MICHAEL H. BIGGINS • JUSTIN M. BILIK • WILLIAM T. BISHOP • ANDREA M. BLANDER • CAROLINE E. BOGDAN • DAVID V. BONNER • MAURA A. BOOKTER • RICHARD W. BOWEN JR. • CLYDE C. BOYLLS JR. • LAUREN C. BRADEL • NICHOLAS G. BREZZELL • CORINNE J. BRINNIER • ROBERT D. BROMWELL • DAVID M. BROWN • LAWRENCE E. BROWN • DANIEL W. BRYDEN • BRIAN M. BUBNASH
• SARAH E. BUCIOR • BRENT A. BUMFORD • DEVON E. BURDICK • JASON T. BURKHOUSE • JEFFREY J. BURTCH • SHANNON C. BYRNES • DEAN E. CALCAGNI • PATRICK T. CALLAHAN • LINDA J. CECCHINI • NARAYAN CHAKRAPANI • KIMBERLY A. CHAMBERLAIN • RICHARD K. CHANG • ARLENE J. CHEN • SANG H. CHIN • CONSTANTINE K. CHRISTAKOS • RONALD A. CIANO • JOSEPH L. CLARY • DANIEL E. CLEMENS •
KYLE M. CLIFFORD • FELICIA A. CLOPEIN • BRANDON C. CLUTTS • LAKEESA D. COATES • ALENE C. COCHRAN • JOI-ANA COLLINS • EDWIN J. COLWELL • CHRISTOPHER M. COOK • JENNIFER L. COOPER • ADAM J. COX • MATTHEW W. COX • LESLIE G. CRAIG • MARIA D. CREEL • JANE M. CREWS • AARON T. CRISS • RODNEY J. CROMER SR. • PATRICK R. CULVER • ADAM W. CUSHMAN • CAITLIN A. DALRYMPLE •
AARON M. DALTON • ANGELA B. DALTON • JOHN G. DASKAL • KATHRYN T. DECAMPO • AUSTIN N. DEHART • MOHAMMAD M. DEHGHANI • ALFONSO E. DEL VALLE • DAVID A. DELGADO • DANIEL F. DEMENTHON • STEFANI R. DENNER • MARIANNE C. DEVARONA • JONATHAN DIAZ • MATTHEW D. DINMORE • AUSTIN G. DIORIO • ELSPETH M. DODGE • CHRISTOPHER P. DONG • MARTHA A. DONNELLY • BRENTON J. DUFFY
• REEMA DUNN • JARED M. ENGLISH • ELIZABETH E. ERDMAN • CAROLYN M. ERNST • TARL C. ESCUDERO • EDDIE V. EUBANKS • LAVERN O. EVANS • JASON E. FABRITZ • MARIA T. FARQUHAR • VIBHA FAUVER • ROBERT M. FELL • KIMBALL E. FERGUSON • MARCIA J. FERGUSON • MICHAEL R. FEVANG • MARGARET Y. FIELD • DEAN R. FISHER JR. • BRIAN P. FLAHERTY • SARAH H. FLANIGAN • TIFFANY F. FLANNIGAN
• JONATHAN A. FOSDAL • ALYCIA A. FRANKLIN • GARY S. FREDERICK • BARRY E. FRIDLING • MICHAEL B. GAILEY • DANIEL T. GALLAGHER • ANTONIO X. GARCIA • MEGAN D. GARDNER • MICHAEL W. GARDNER • JEFFREY F. GARSTECKI • OSCAR D. GATEWOOD • THOMAS S. GIAMPAOLO II • ANDREW D. GIBSON • JEROME U. GILBERRY • CARRIE N. GINGRAS • JOHN M. GOMES • PAUL K. GONG • GABRIEL N. GORELICK-
FELDMAN • MEAGHAN R. GOUGH • JOSEPH C. GREEN • TAYLOR A. GREEN • TODD M. GUSTAFSON • KEVIN B. GWYNN • ROBERT W. GWYNN • JENNIFER E. HALLYBURTON • STEPHANIE L. HAMILTON • STEVEN A. HANDY • THOMAS R. HANLEY • MARK D. HAPPEL • JASON R. HARPER • RICKY J. HARRIS II • RAYMOND HARRIS • MARK D. HART • ROBERT G. HARTLING • CURTIS G. HAWTHORNE • JULIE C. HEDGECOCK
• STEVEN N. HEMSTREET • MARY A. HENDRICKSON • RAYMOND M. HENSON • BENJAMIN E. HENTY • BRENDA G. HESS • WENDY S. HESS • MATTHEW J. HILLYARD • MARK A. HINTON • ANNA M. HOFFACKER • ERIK M. HOHLFELD • KENNETH R. HONECKER JR. • BOR ZEN HONG • MARY L. HOPKINS • RAMSEY S. HOURANI • DEBRA A. HOWE • JUI-HUANG W. HSU • JAMES W. HUBAND • DAVID M. HUBERDEAU •
ANDREA C. HUGHES • ROBERT L. HULSLANDER • SHAMEEKA L. HUNT • JASON H. HUNTER • DANA M. HURLEY • VINCENT T. IPPOLITO • ALEXANDER S. IWASKIW • FLORA IZZO • BRENT C. JACKSON • SHEKEAB JAUHARI • MATTHEW S. JOHANNES • BERNARD J. JOHNG • OLLIE J. JOHNSON III • BRYAN A. JOHNSON • CHARLES E. JOHNSON • DONALD W. JOHNSON • LANIECE A. JOHNSON • THOMAS R. JONES JR. •
DANIEL G. JONES • ANNE A. JORSTAD • ARJUN D. KALRA • MARSHALL H. KAPLAN • RACHEL M. KARRAS • DANIEL J. KATZ • LORAYNE G. KAUFFMAN • JOHN C. KELLEY • KATHRYN M. KELLY • LIAM P. KELLY • MICHAEL B. KELLY • ROBERT J. KENNEDY • LAUREN R. KENNELL • SAMUEL KEREM • DARLENE C. KESTERSON • GEORGE H. KLAUS III • JENNIFER R. KLEINBERGER • JAY A. KOMSA • JONATHON J. KOPECKY •
REBECCA L. KOSLOVER • KEITH D. KOWALSKI • NICHOLAS M. KRATZMEIER • EDWARD J. KREINAR • MICHAEL E. KRUSKAL • ALOIS A. KUDLACH • JILL C. LA FAVORS • NGUYEN K. LA • DAVID B. LANE • REID B. LARSON • GEORGE B. LAWRENCE III • DAVID J. LAWRENCE • GEORGE M. LAYNE • SAUL R. LAZO-GUZMAN JR. • MICHAEL G. LEATHERMAN • ANNA R. LEE • MAUREEN A. LEE • GREGORY P. LEGER •
JASON P. LEGGETT • BRIAN R. LEGINUS • GREG T. LEON GUERRERO • TODD J. LEVY • MITCHELL J. LEWIS • JENNIFER L. LEYDIG • YAN LI • KURT L. LINDSTROM • RONALD N. LINTON JR. • SHAWN P. LOVERIC • QUANG T. LUONG • GREGORY A. MACK • COLIN D. MAGEE • LAUREN E. MAGEE • THOMAS J. MAGNER • JESSICA K. MAKOWSKI • JAWAD A. MALIK • SHERRILL D. MARCH • CARL A. MARRESE • DANIELLE M. MARSH
• JEFFREY P. MASON • TODD M. MASSE • THURMAN MASSENBURG JR. • JASON G. MATHENY • LEOPOLDO M. MAYORAL • DOUGLAS R. MCCAW • ELIZABETH A. MCCUBBIN • LINDA D. MCDANIEL • WILLIAM R. MCDANIEL • JEROMY W. MCDERMENT • MICHAEL N. MCINTYRE • LEAH C. MCLAREN • ALYSIA M. MCMELLER • RONALD W. MCNEIL • LAWRENCE S. MCQUAY • RICHARD H. MEIDENBAUER • ERIC D. MELIN •
DANIEL R. MENDAT • JEFFREY T. METCALFE • JEFFREY J. MIKIONIS • PATRICIA L. MILLER • RODNETTE A. MILLER • ZARNA S. MISTRY • MICHAEL H. MISUMI • EDMOND S. MITCHELL • ANTON J. MOBLEY • DAWN P. MOESSNER • ANDREW H. MONICA • SCOTT B. MOONEY • VANESSA MORALES • COURTNEYLEIGH W. MORAN • RICHARD A. MORGAN • TONI L. MORGAN • KEVIN B. MORLEY • KATHERINE L. MORSE •
BRUCE P. MOSIER • JOSEPH J. MULLEN JR. • LINDSEY D. MURPHY • SHIRLEY A. MUSGROVE • PAMELA J. NAPOLILLO • OBIBOBI K. NDU • EUGENE C. NEIGHOFF JR. • LISA R. NEWCOMB • KEITH B. NEWLANDER • JONATHAN A. NICOLAIDES • PATRICK J. NORTON • MARLENE R. NOURBAKHSH • NNAKE I. NWEKE • JOEL G. OGREN • ELISABETH J. OLSON • KIMBERLY J. ORD • JOHN J. ORNDORFF SR. • MARCOS OSORNO •
RONALD J. OSTRENGA • ASHLEY L. OURSLER • MATTHEW J. OUSBORNE • DEMETRIUS S. OWENS • BRIAN C. PAGE • RICHARD PAPPALARDO • JAMES A. PARKER • NATHANIEL J. PATTISON • JEFFREY M. PAULSON • MICHAEL D. PAVLICK • CHRISTOPHER J. PAXTON • LINDA M. PELETSKI • MICHAEL E. PELLEN • NORA E. PENCOLA • JOHN J. PERANIO JR. • BRYAN T. PEROZZI • RICHARD J. PFISTERER • TUAN A. PHAMDO
• JOHN P. PHELAN • ANNA P. POBLETTS • CHRISTINE A. POLLOCK • HEATHER E. PONTIUS • MARIE A. PORTA • KIRK L. PORTER • TRACY G. POSNER • KELLY S. POULTON • JOHN D. PRETEL • JOSEPH L. PROCTOR IV • JODY B. PROESCHER • DEREK M. PRYOR • STANLEY D. PUCHALLA • ANN M. RAGER • VIGNESH R. RAMACHANDRAN • PAMELA L. RANDOLPH • NOUREDDINE RAOUAFI • ERIN H. RAUTH •
GREGORY R. RECKENWALD • NAOMI P. REDMORE • SCOTT M. REED • TOBY E. REED • ANGEL S. REESE • CHRISTOPHER T. REGAN • ELIZABETH P. REILLY • IRWIN O. REYES • CRAIG M. REYNOLDS • LISA A. REYNOLDS • ANDREW F. RHINE • JAMES H. ROBERTS • RICARDO A. ROCA • BENJAMIN M. RODRIGUEZ II • AXEL RODRIGUEZ • GLENDA P. RODRIGUEZ • CAROLINE A. ROGERS • RICHARD B. ROGERS • JESSE E. ROHWER
• DAVID L. ROMERO • CHRISTOPHER M. ROSE • PAUL E. ROSENDALL • ELIZABETH A. ROYCROFT • KATHERINE M. RUBEN • KELLIE A. RUEBENS • BRADLEY C. RUSH • SHAVESHA L. RUTLEDGE • AMBER R. RYAN • ROBERT J. SAGMILLER • JEAN M. SAMUELS • FIDEL E. SANCHEZ • KIMBERLY R. SANDERS • JOHN W. SARNESE • KARLA J. SAUR • JOEL J. SCARIA • GILBERT V. SCHAEFFER II • RANDY P. SCHLOTTERBECK
• ERIK M. SCHMIDT • WHITNEY A. SCHOLZ • EMMA K. SCHROEDER • MATTHEW O. SCHROEDER • RICHARD J. SEAGRAVES II • RYAN E. SELBY • CHRISTOPHER M. SEMON • CHRISTOPHER G. SEXTON • PARVEEZA M. SHAIKH • ANDREI L. SHAMKOVICH • PAULA H. SHELTON • RALPH W. SHELTON • CHRISTOPH D. SHIPLEY • KARA R. SHIPLEY • ABIODUN B. SHONAIYA • MICHAEL R. SHOOP • FAZLE E. SIDDIQUE •
KAREN M. SIEGRIST • ADAM J. SIERAKOWSKI • JEFFREY S. SIMPSON • DAVID W. SIZEMORE • NICOLE M. SLACK • ELAINE D. SLUJTNER • CHRISTINE A. SMITH • ELLEN P. SMITH • JOSHUA A. SMITH • JOSHUA D. SMITH • JUSTIN R. SMITH • WILLIAM E. SMITH • EDWIN K. SMOCK JR. • JASON E. SOHLKE • CHRISTOPHER M. SPIVEY • RONALD R. SPRINGER • SEAN P. SPROUSE • SCOTT A. STANCHFIELD • RICHARD A. STARTT
• JAMIE M. STEADMAN • DAVID M. STOPP • RUSSELL J. STRICKLAND • SHADRIAN B. STRONG • ALBERT S. SUN • SCOTT A. SWETZ • RACHEL B. SZCZESIUL • RAMEEN TAEB • SARA E. TANKARD • GARRICK TAYLOR • FRANCESCO V. TENORE • TRACY J. TERRY • FRITZ A. THELUSMA • ALEXANDRE S. THIBAU • AARON T. THOMAS • JUSTIN R. THOMAS • BRYAN L. THOMPSON • BRADLEY J. THOMSON • JENNIFER A. THORNE
• DAVEY S. THORNTON • EVAN P. THRUSH • JOHN D. TINSLEY • ALAN D. TIPTON • MICHAEL A. TOMASSI • JOSEPH E. TOUCHTON • JACOB P. TREADWAY • MORGANA M. TREXLER • TIMOTHY TRUONG • JAY W. TURNER • JOHN M. USCILOWICZ • MICHAEL E. VALMONTE • WILLIAM L. VAN BESIEN • JAMES D. VARGO • ANGEL L. VEGA JR. • RADHA A. VENKAT • CRISTINA T. VIGIL LOPEZ • PAMELA C. VIOLETTE •
MARY L. VIRTUE • VIVEK VISWANATHAN • SHELBY A. WALLNER • DAVID A. WALTON • ROBERT E. WALTON • ANNA H. WANG • BRAD M. WARD • WILLIAM J. WARE • GEORGE T. WATKINS • ANTHONY M. WEBBER • KYLE T. WEBER • CHAD N. WEILER • MICHAEL J. WEISMAN • CHRISTOPHER C. WELLONS • VERNIE E. WELLS JR. • MICHAEL E. WELLS • LASHAWNA S. WHITE • LOUIS A. WHITE • ALEXIS C. WICKWIRE
• GREGORY S. WILLIAMS • MICHELLE M. WILLIAMS • TYRA L. WILLIAMS • TONYA M. WILLIS • MARC N. WILSON • JAMES P. WISSMAN • ROBERT C. WOJCIK • BERNARD P. WONG • KENAZ S. WONG • JAUNICKI C. WOOSLEY • ALVINIA S. WRIGHT • FELIX M. WYATT • ANDRINA YANKAH • STEPHEN K. YEH • DANIEL L. YERKEY • MICHAEL J. ZEHER • JUDY ZHU • DARRELL A. ZINN • DENISE H. ZONFRILLI • RUIXIA ZU •
2009 • ELISABETH D. ABEL • ANDREW T. ADKINS • FARID A. AHMED • ALISON C. ALBIN • MATTHEW S. ALDRICH • BENJAMIN B. ALVAREZ • LYNNE M. AMBUEL DONALDSON • KEVIN J. AMES • THERESE M. ATTICKS • JON K. AYSCUE • JANICE A. BADESHA • ZACHARY S. BAILEY • DUSTIN R. BALISE • JASON R. BALMUTH • CHRISTOPHER K. BARKER • GLENN A. BARKER • NATALIE B. BARRETT • RYAN A. BAXTER •
ELAINE K. BEACHAM • JEFFREY S. BECK • JOSEF C. BEHLING • EDWARD D. BEKSINSKI JR. • IVERSON C. BELL III • DAVID S. BENNETT • ROBERT A. BERARDINO • BRENDAN M. BERMAN • ANGELINA H. BOAMPONG • ALEXANDER B. BRACE • GORDON D. BREIGHNER JR. • DAVID B. BRENMAN • KRISTINE BRENNEMAN • NATHAN T. BRIDGES • MARC A. BRIERE • LINDSAY B. BRINDLEY • ERIK R. BRINKMAN •
BRETT W. BRODERICK • ANDREA M. BROWN • MARTIN K. BROWN • RYAN P. BROWN • WILLIAM M. BUCHTA • MATTHEW J. BURGER • JESSE C. BURGOON • MELISSA L. BURIAN • KENNETH A. BURLEY SR. • MARK E. BURTNER • BRYCE A. BUSCHMAN • ARTURO I. CABREJO • ROBERT W. CAMPBELL • TIMOTHY C. CAMPBELL • STEVEN T. CAPERNA • JOEL L. CAPLE • STEPHANIE J. CAPORALETTI • JUDITH A. CARACOFE
• CATHERINE M. CARNEAL • MARVIN D. CARR • LUCY M. CARRUTH • MICHAEL L. CASCIO • WENDY J. CASKER • NOEL P. CERVINO • DAVID C. CHALLENER • LUANNE B. CHAMBERLAIN • KATHERINE S. CHANG • THOMAS W. CHAPMAN • ABBY L. CHARFAUROS • ZAHRA CHAUDHRY • SRIDHAR CHEBROLU • SKY C. CHEUNG • SUNGSHAN CHIANG • DENISE R. CHILCOTT • SHAWNA E. CHISHOLM • CHRISTOPHER J. CHO
• SHEA CHYOU • ANTHONY A. CIRIO • JOHN M. CLEMENS • JOHNNY F. COBERLY JR. • AARON S. COHEN • TIMOTHY J. COLE • CHRISTOPHER G. COLLINS • ECATERINA I. COMAN • JOHN M. CONTESTABILE • JEREMIAH J. COOK • KIRK T. COOK • KEVIN M. COOKE • HOLLY A. COOLEY • CHERITA L. CORBETT • GAVIN C. CORNWELL • RAIZA L. CORTES HERNANDEZ • TRISTAN K. COSSIO • ALLISON K. COTILLA • TIARA COTTAM
• AUSTIN B. COX • BRIAN J. CRAWFORD • ANNA M. CRISPIN • JOSEPH L. CROSSETT • ALEX W. CRUZ • FELICIA CRUZ • JACLYN B. CUA • ELIZABETH J. CUSTODIO • STEVEN M. D'AMBROSIO • DENISE M. D'ANGELO • BHAWNA DARYANI • ARNAB DAS • DRUSO DAUBON • DEEPU E. DAVID • SAMANTHA E. DEIGHAN • THOMAS A. DIBARTOLOMEO • DAVID H. DO • SUSAN N. DONAHUE • MARC D. DONOHUE • ROBERT R. DOVERSPIKE
• DAVID L. DRAKE • GREGORY S. DRENNING • DAVID G. DREWRY III • RICHARD A. DUDLEY • MICHAEL A. DUMESH • GREGORY J. DUNN • LARS P. DYRUD • BRENDAN L. EBERS • ERIK H. EISENMAN • ROY N. EMANUEL • EMILY P. ENGLISH • STEVEN M. ENGLISH • TREFOR G. EVANS • JARED S. EVERETT • CHUKWUEMEKA U. EZEKWE • ADAM R. FAGAN • TIMOTHY E. FAIR • JEFFREY J. FARRELL • STEPHEN A. FARRIS •
AUNGELA M. FEAZELL • WILLIAM A. FENDT JR. • NICHOLAS S. FEZIE • MARJORIE E. FIORAVANTE • MATTHEW E. FIORAVANTE • KRISTIAN H. FISCHER • BRIAN M. FISHER • ERIN B. FITZHENRY • BLAIR D. FLEET • ROBERT C. FLEMING • TIMOTHY M. FLOTT • WILLIAM T. FONG • BETTE L. FONTAN • ANNETTE L. FORMBLY • RYAN J. FORREST • REBECCA C. FOUST • PAUL D. FOWLE • NICHOLAS J. FRANKOSKI •
JAMES M. FRYE JR. • BENEDICT W. FULLER • DANNY L. FURCHES • EDWARD M. GADDY • MORGAN F. GAITHER • EDWARD J. GALLIGAN • KEISHA L. GARRETT • ALAN T. GAUMER • DAVID W. GEORGE • BRYAN T. GERVAIS • HEATHER W. GILBERRY • MARK W. GILSON • KIMBERLY A. GLASGOW • BENJAMIN I. GOLDBERG • MATTHEW C. GOMBOLAY • DOMINIC GOMES • SARA J. GOONASEKERAM • JONAH R. GOTTLIEB •
JENNA L. GRAHAM • HANNAH M. GRAMLING • RACHAEL S. GRANICO • DELEATRICE Y. GRATE-CURTIS • PATRICK C. GREGG • PHARES J. GREY • KIMBERLY M. GRIFFIN • SIMONE M. GRIFFIN • BRIAN J. GROOMAN • MOLLY R. GROSSMAN • THOMAS M. GRUBB • ROGER D. GRUNEISEN • CLARE K. GUDENIUS • DONALD S. GUMAS • EMRE GUNDUZHAN • MATTHEW C. GURKOVICH • RYAN T. HACALA • SEAN I. HAGAMAN
• ERIN N. HAHN • JUSTIN D. HAHN • KELLEY A. HALL-GIBSON • JOHN G. HAMBRIGHT • STEPHEN T. HAMER • YISU HAN • PAUL W. HARBISON • ELAISSA L. HARDY • THOMAS R. HARLEY • NICOLE M. HAROLD • TIMOTHY P. HARRIGAN • JAMES W. HARRIS JR. • CLARENCE L. HART JR. • EHAB S. HASSAN • PAUL R. HEATH • STEVEN A. HECHTMAN • JENNIFER L. HEDLUND • NYLES N. HEISE • BRYAN T. HENDERSON •
RASHAWN L. HENRY • PETER D. HEPPLEWHITE • CHI W. HICKEY • GREGORY P. HICKS • SOPHIA G. HILL • JACK D. HILLIS • JOHN A. HITCH • PAUL M. HOBBS • GUY F. HOLBROOK • MICHELE L. HOLLIFIELD • TAEHO HONG • WILLIAM W. HONG • VALERIE A. HORKY • BILLY J. HORN III • KATHRYN E. HOUSE • ANTHONY J. HRYNYSHEN • CORY W. HUYSSOON • KARLA V. ISCHIU • STEPHEN J. IZON • DARRYL E. JACOBY •
ROBERT E. JAMES • DAVID M. JANUARY • CLARENCE D. JOHNSON • JOSHUA E. JOHNSON • SHAWN F. JOHNSON • SUNDEEP K. JOLLY • MATTHEW E. JONES • MELISSA R. JONES • SHARON D. JONES • SHAYLYN JOY • ANDREW D. JURIK • MATIWOS H. KAFEL • JEFFREY M. KALTER • WILBUR W. KAN • CASEY F. KANE • HONG KYU KANG • NIKHIL P. KARNIK • DANIEL S. KASSAYE • ANN E. KEDIA • TARA KEDIA • CYNTHIA L. KEE
• LAKE A. KEE • ERIC J. KEIL • KATE R. KERBEL • ANNE E. KING • JOHN E. KING • MICHAEL R. KING • MIKLOS Z. KISS • DAVID C. KNIPFER • MARK C. KOCHTE • HENRY D. KOENIG • KALLE R. KONTSON • ZACHARY H. KOTERBA • ANDREW F. KOVACH • MICHAEL F. KRASON • JOSEPH D. KRIMM • GAIL A. KROEDEL • DANIEL P. KURIKESU • RALPH S. LABARGE • DONALD P. LAGATOR JR. • JOHN K. LAI • KRISTOPHER N. LAMONT
• NORI R. LASLO • MARK A. LAWSON • TIMOTHY T. LEACH • FREDERICK W. LEBLANC • CHONG C. LEE • SUNG J. LEE-SECK • ALEXANDER B. LEISHMAN • CHARLES F. LEPPLE • DAVID H. LESSER • SHAWN X. LIANG • LISA J. LIU • ROCHELE A. LLANSO • SHAUGHN M. LONDON • ALFRED W. LOOKINGLAND III • RICARDO LUNA • KATHRYN E. MACKEY • KATRINA A. MAGALOTTI • HEATHER A. MAGUIRE • HANS U. MAIR
• NADIA MALIK • ALEXANDER T. MALONE • ALLISON J. MANKIN • JEFFREY S. MANNING • SCOTT A. MANNING • ANNE M. MARCOTTE • SHANA R. MARSHALL • GINA M. MARSHALL-JOHNSON • SCOTT C. MARTUCCI • SCOTT K. MAYNARD • ROBERT M. MAYO • DOLORES L. MAZELIS • ANNE E. MCGOVERN • SARAH A. MCKEE • DANIEL R. MCKINNEY • MATTHEW B. MCKNIGHT • RYAN T. MCMICHAEL • MARK D. MCMILLEN
• JON M. MEASE • NELSON M. MENDEZ-GOMEZ • JORGE MERCED • MARK A. MERCREADY • KAREN A. METZ • KELLY Q. MIDKIFF • ETHAN S. MILLER • JEFFREY A. MILLER • MARK A. MILLISON • SANAZ S. MIRZAEI • CARLY J. MITCHELL • KATHERINE E. MITCHELL • BRIAN C. MONTGOMERY • MARGARET M. MOORE • TAMMERA A. MORRISSETT • JOHN R. MORROW • BRANDON G. MORTON • RYAN N. MUKHERJEE •
JOHN S. MUNDELL • ETHAN Y. MYERS • DENNIS C. NAGLE • DEEPA J. NAMBIAR • JEFFREY A. NANZER • CATHERINE D. NEISH • DANIEL C. NELSON • RUSTIE L. NEWBERN • SUMMER D. NEWTON • THUYTHAO M. NGUYEN • VINA H. NGUYEN • JOHN R. NICHOLS • DAVID A. NILES • BORGE H. NODLAND • ALEXANDER A. NOLLEY • KEVIN T. NOONAN • MARK A. NORRIS • JOHN F. NORTON • MARK D. NOTEWARE •
REBECCA L. NUSBAUM • KATHLEEN O'CONNELL • JACK E. O'DONNEL JR. • AKHILOMEN O. ONIHA • JAVIER F. ORTIZ • JOHN E. ORTIZ • KYLE A. OTT • CHARLES PAO • EUGENE T. PAPPAS • MARCIA W. PATCHAN • HITESH V. PATEL • SHRADDHA V. PATEL • AJAY M. PATRIKAR • CRAIG M. PAYNE • CONNOR M. PENCEK • AMY E. PHILLIPS • SHAWN A. PHILLIPS • MARK L. PLETT • ADJOA M. POKU • DEVAMANOHAR PONNUSAMY
• ROY R. PORRAS • CHRISTA N. PORTER • CHAD A. POTOCKY • KATHRYN E. POWELL • JOSHUA C. PROTEAU • MONIKA A. PUNJABI • JUSTIN L. RAABE • DANIELLE M. RAGER • JOHN F. RAISH • ARAVIND RAMACHANDRAN • SEAN R. RANTA • NIGEL G. RAY • MICHAEL H. REILLY • RACHEL E. REIS • YO-RHIN RHIM • DOYLE W. RHYNARD • WILLIAM C. RIGGS • ZACHARY B. RILEY • SARAH E. ROBERTS • JAMES M. ROBINSON